Langues des Métiers

⟷

Métiers des Langues

Collection dirigée par Daniel Gouadec

La Maison du Dictionnaire
98, Bd du Montparnasse – 75014 PARIS
Tél : 33 1 43 22 12 93 – Fax : 33 1 43 22 01 77

Dépôt légal : 2ème Trimestre 2001
ISBN : 2-85608-165-7
Code livre : 3.55.24.103
Imprimé en France

Aspects of specialised translation

Edited by

Lucile Desblache

University of North London

With the support of :

University of North London
Institut Libre Marie Haps of Brussels

FOREWORD

Over recent years, interest in specialised translation has increased markedly. The need for skilled communicators who can deal with complex technical material and master electronic tools efficiently is growing.

This volume of essays will be a useful source for both trainers and translators working in this area. It addresses teaching and training as well as topic and language specific issues.

Arabic, Chinese, English, French, German, Greek, Italian, Russian and Spanish are considered in turn, in relation to a wide range of fields: medicine, technology, law, politics, media, philosophy. From subtitling to place name transfers, it also covers different categories of specialised translation and examines pedagogical, technical, terminological and cultural aspects of communication.

Prefaced by Professor Newmark and designed with the support of the University of North London and the Institut Libre Marie Haps of Brussels, this book will be of value to any translator and translation teacher.

Contents

Acknowledgments

I would like to express my sincere thanks to the numerous individuals who have supported me with the editing of this book: Dr John Kidman for his practical assistance and encouragement, Professor Peter Newmark for his enthousiasm and for agreeing to write the opening pages, Professor Mona Baker for her advice, Hugo Marquant and Daniel Gouadec for making contact with the *Maison du dictionnaire*, Chris Oreilly for his help with graphics my colleagues teaching on the MA Applied Translation Studies at the University of North London, particularly Dr Karen Seago for her help with technical problems and all the contributors for their time and patience. I am grateful for the unfailing support which I have received and without which this book could not have been published.

Lucile Desblache

Peter Newmark, University of Surrey
Introduction

The University of North London's timely conference on Specialised Translation raised several important questions:

1. To what extent is the ex-technical specialised and indeed the non-literary translator in general responsible for securing the factual and the moral truth of her translation, as opposed to the (old-fashioned?) view that she is only responsible for ensuring the accuracy of her translation vis a vis the original?
2. To what extent must the translator be an expert in his particular text topic?
3. Should the non-literary translator be trained as a generalist or as an expert?

I don't think there are any yes/no answers to these questions, since they have to be qualified and properly illustrated in each instance. What is important is that they should be discussed as they were here, and that some tentative, at least majority agreements should be reached, and that employers, translators, examiners and exam students should be made aware of them.

This volume is largely the result of this colloquium, although some relevant contributions from writers who did not attend it are also included here. The conference was opened by the distinguished conference interpreter, the late Robin Scott, who gave a delightfully discursive talk about his career. He brought out several important points: the essential (basically monosyllabic) simplicity of English, the successor as world language, in point of time, of Greek, Latin and French, in spite of its vast vocabulary and varied syntax and sound system; the sheer humour of the 'worst' howlers, even made by masters of language such as Churchill; the effectiveness of obsolete words, in the midst of the modern language, like feal (fealty, fidelity) in a great speech by de Gaulle (cf. Hamlet's 'mobled' queen); the resemblance between the connotative nuances of great translation and great music, not always cultural; the world emergence of Spanish in the United States, and then Chinese; the continuous replacement of words in language (raft, airbrush); the new importance of translated surtitles in international opera and drama and of new uses for punctuation in translation; the translator's responsibility for style, truth, and contribution to peace; this was a lovely talk.

Marcel Thelen argues the case for specialisation in translating texts in a particular field of knowledge; here translators should have training in the subject and its terminology, be members of professional bodies, and be experts in their specialisms and their localisation. Paul Wijnands discusses the philosophy and the abstractions behind specialised knowledge and language. Janet Fraser discusses the changing status of non-literary translators, who used to be in-house staffers, but are now mainly self-employed and work at home. Recent statistics indicate that there are now 115,000 translators in Europe, only one third of them full-time; 6000 in UK, 15,000 in France, 27,000 in Germany; only a tiny number are in professional organizations. Janet emphasises the need to involve the translator at every stage of the job, in particular the context and the purpose of the text and the requiremenrt of the client.
Joelle Commeau-Fanghanel prefers a generalist approach, and indeed disdains, like many of the contributors to offer any translation examples. I suspect her outline of an enormous programme would leave no time for any practical translation, which should occupy 80% plus of the time. Nadia Rahab contributes a useful paper on the importance of theory in training

translators. Genevieve Parkes discusses the marketing and publicity for translation courses. Begoña Rodriguez de Cèspedes and Caterina Jeffcote highlight various difficulties in technical and economic texts, unfortunately without analysing foreign language equivalents.

I would say that Eve-Marie Aldridge is, after Robin Scott, the first contributor who not only knows the literature but can discuss in a fruitful way the practical difficulties of translating political speeches, in this instance, those of Tony Blair. Sue Lilley in her discussion of legal terminology suffers by producing principles rather than examples, and she appears to be unaware of Martin Weston's indispensable comparative guide to the French and English legal systems. The upside of Nicole Berry's paper on cultural language in political translation is that it informatively discusses the ample literature; the downside is that it introduces some unnecessary neologisms (Nord's para-, dia-, idio-culture, which are dire indeed); the discussion of translations is productive if too brief. Graham Ketteringham contributes a superb discussion of political, social and legal terms and their various translations, and includes a para on Nida's preference for the term 'functional' rather than 'dynamic' equivalence, which isn't easily accessible. The paper on translating Spanish medical texts by Lola la Torre is thorough, whilst Pieta Monks on post-Soviet business transactions with Russia has an enormous sweep and concludes with practical translation notes. Both Dora Blagova and Hugo Marquant will mainly interest theoretical linguists. Kang Zhihomg proposes an interesting curio, since he prefers semantic translation of proper names to their phonetic transcription, and ignores their naturalisation as transonyms (e.g. Venezia > Venice, Wien > Vienna, Moskva > Moscow). Jamal Giaber's learned treatise on the varieties of the suffix -eme will fascinate the linguist but may horrify the translation theorist, who might prefer to abolish the 90% of these words which are fossilizing.

The collection ends with Dennis O'Keeffe's brilliant and witty excursus on the understanding of Benjamin Constant, Karen Seago's learned excursus on the XIXth century translations of the fairy tales of the Brothers Grimm, and Jorge Diaz-Cintas's widely-referenced and joke-filled excursus on the semiotics of subtitled humour.

I often wonder how many institutions and how few individuals subscribe to voluminous conference transactions like these. However, in this case, those who actually read them will be richly rewarded.

Teaching and training related matters

Present issues in teaching specialised translation: a practice-oriented MA programme

Marcel Thelen, Hogeschool Maastricht

Abstract

This paper will argue that a particular type of specialisation and a subsequent change in the field of activity of the translator may ultimately contribute to the prestige of the profession, and translation quality in general. The type of specialisation that is meant here is specialisation in Subject-field-Specific Language and/or languages. The type of concomitant translation may be called 'SSL-oriented translation'. In SSL-oriented translation, the translator - in other words, the SSL-oriented translator - is not merely and only a translator who has specialised in the translation of a particular subject field and has thus built up a sound knowledge of the subject field in question; he is also and above all a translator who is a specialist in the language of communication of and between subject fields. In other words, an SSL-oriented translator combines the particular translation competence that is required of a 'traditional' translator (viz. knowledge of translation techniques and procedures, knowledge of language(s), knowledge of the structure of the subject field of translation) with communication expertise and considerable knowledge of the mechanisms and structure of the subject field language of translation.

In this paper, the notion of SSL-oriented translation will be further elaborated upon in the context of the MA programme in Applied Translation Studies. The latter is an international MA programme in translation under the auspices of the University of North London and is jointly operated by the University of North London, the Maastricht School of Translation and Interpreting and Institut Libre Marie Haps (Brussels).

Introduction

In this paper I will discuss, against the background of the status of the translator (the list of aspects discussed is not exhaustive), a particular type of specialisation of translators, viz. specialisation in Subject-field-Specific Language or SSL specialisation, and the concomitant type of translation - SSL-oriented translation. I will argue that this type of specialisation may be a good option for contributing to the status of the translator. I will also give an outline of their role in an international MA programme in London, Maastricht and Brussels, i.e. the MA in Applied Translation Studies.

The status of the translator

In 1999, the social and legal position of translators still leaves much to be desired. This is the opinion not only of practising translators, but also of leading translation scholars and of translation institutions. This situation is not new. Already in 1992 Snell-Hornby wrote:

> The translator seems to occupy a position similar to that of the local barber in bygone centuries, who not only trimmed hair and shaped beards but also performed functions now entrusted only to professional dentists and surgeons. The translator in Europe today frequently works free-lance and part-time, usually under extreme time pressure, for meagre pay and without a legally protected professional status, and indeed often accepts such conditions as an inevitable fact of life. Other translators are employed with varying security and esteem in industry or in public organizations. Much translation is carried out as mere secretarial work, and it is unfortunately not unusual for important translation assignments to be handed over unthinkingly to the odd foreign language student or the chance native speaker who happens to be available. In the world of today, however, where international dialogue and interlingual communication have become so complex and so vitally important, it is essential that the amateurish image of the present-day Figaro should disappear at least into the wings of history. (Snell-Hornby 1992: 9-10)

In 1995, Samuelsson-Brown (1995: 1) described the situation as follows:

> People usually become translators in one of two ways. Either by design or by circumstance. There are no formal academic qualifications required to work as a translator. However,

advertisements for translators in the press and professional journals tend to ask for graduates with professional qualifications and three years' experience.

Since then, not much seems to have changed.

Ways to improve the status of translators

In what follows I will discuss a number of ways that might improve the status of translators, which is apparently still far from satisfactory. At this moment, there do not seem to be any institutionalised attempts at improving it; if these exist at all, they do not seem to have much success.

Legal protection

Of course, the first and best way to give translation the status that it deserves is to protect the profession by law and stipulate formal requirements for entering the field. However, in this time of privatisation and deregulation this seems unlikely. In the absence of any legal protection of the profession as such, other means are perhaps more promising.

Tailoring training to practice

The need for drastic change of the status of the profession is felt equally strongly by translators and translator training institutions. As a result, the two groups are co-operating more and more and there seems to be a growing awareness that such a co-operation will be mutually beneficial in the long run: in this way, theory, training and eventual practice may be brought into line, thus strengthening the image of the translator and translating. Snell-Hornby (1992) does not seem to go as far as this; in her course proposal she only takes heed of comments and points of criticism from the professional field. Tailoring the training of translators to the practice of translating and to the needs of the market and society is only one option, an option that, in my opinion, should be applied very carefully; neither party would benefit if the training of translators is directed completely and only towards practice, thus eliminating an independent and fresh input from outside actual practice.

And as far as theory in training is concerned, Adab (1995: 281-282) rightfully states that:

> For those involved in the teaching of translation all theory has to be related to practice, to empirical observation of what has been done and consideration of what can be done in a given context and for a given communicative intent. […]
> The translator trainer should […] refuse to adopt one particular theory, but seek instead to develop his own eclectic approach, based on a carefully considered set of criteria and according to the aims and objectives of the course he is teaching.

One of the greatest weakening factors of attempts at tailoring training to practice is the absence of consensus among the parties involved as to what should be included in the training, and what the actual practice of translating is about. It is not uncommon that, when trainers and practising translators meet, there are as many opinions on what is important for translation as there are participants in the discussion.

Clearly, other and more direct options are called for. What is important, though, is that training institutions should try and recruit more students by making their programmes more attractive. This could be done by including current issues, like for example localisation (see paragraph below 'Specialisation in a particular kind of translation'). The more students graduate from training institutions, the more common it may become that translators are qualified for their jobs, thus strengthening their position.

Professionalisation
Professionalisation is another instrument. Since the translator, either as a self-employed worker or as an employee with a translation company or agency, is dealing with business, he should adjust to current modes of business behaviour. It is common for professional translation organisations to have a so-called code of professional conduct for translators, which is intended to hold for any translator who is a member; think for example of the code of conduct as formulated by:

* ITI, the Institute of Translation and Interpreting, in the U.K.
* NGV, Nederlands Genootschap voor Vertalers, in the Netherlands
* ATA, American Translators Association, in the USA
* FIT, Fédération Internationale des Traducteurs, etc.

Also attitude and conduct should, of course, be explicitly trained in translator training programmes. The option of tailoring the training of translators to the actual practice of the profession, and the option of professionalisation of attitude and conduct are, however, 'superficial' only, even if they are implemented together.

Specialisation
A fourth and perhaps most important, and certainly most complex, option that pertains to what translators actually do and what translation is about is the option of specialisation. Generally, specialisation is an efficient and well-tried economic instrument to secure one's position and consequently build up a good reputation and status in business. It entails that the person who specialises becomes an expert in the field of his specialisation.

Snell-Hornby (1992:10) describes the ideal translator as someone "… who should have the knowledge, the competence, and the recognised status of an expert".

Clearly, the translator should be such an expert that he is granted this recognised status, and be an expert in such a field that is deemed important enough to give this recognition. The translator's expertise should make it impossible for Figaros and untrained translators by circumstance to do this expert work. The most important question here is, of course, what type of expert the translator should be, or rather in what field he should be an expert. There are various answers to this question.

Specialisation as an expert in languages and cultures
In Snell-Hornby's opinion,

> […] translation is primarily a sociocultural activity which presupposes not only language competence but also extensive factual and encyclopaedic knowledge as well as familiarity with the norms and conventions of both source and target culture. (1992:11)

Consequently, the translator should be a multilingual and (multi-)cultural expert. From the description of the course that she proposes for her Vienna institute, it becomes clear that she has in mind a translator who has a profound grounding in the languages 'under translation', coupled with excellent translation competence and good knowledge of the cultures of the translation pair at hand. In her opinion, a translator is:

> […] an expert, who, as a specialist in the fields of language, culture and communication, can work as a generalist in a great many areas where translation is required. (1992: 22)

Communication is not explained any further, but from the rest of her article it becomes clear that communication is to be understood in a rather general way as the process of mediating between source text and target text, and thus between source and target languages and cultures.

Specialisation as a subject field expert
Closely related to the former type of specialisation is the specialisation as a subject field expert. This kind of specialisation may refer to two types of translator (cf. O'Neill 1998):

* a translator who has had a training in one or more languages, Linguistics or Translation Studies and who has developed into a subject field expert through long experience in translating in one and the same subject area;
* a translator who has had a training in a particular subject field and who has turned to translating in this subject field.

The first type of translator would be a "medically knowledgeable linguist" in O'Neill's terms (she discusses medical translation) - or a subject field knowledgeable linguist in more neutral terms -, and the second type a "linguistically knowledgeable medical professional" - or linguistically knowledgeable subject field expert. Who would produce better translations is a long-debated issue among translation scholars and translators, and who would be more eligible for a job as a translator seems to be dependent on employer preferences rather than on statistically measurable differences in competence. Who of the two, finally, would know more about a given subject field and could be called the expert *par excellence* is a question that I will discuss later on. The question is, of course, how much a subject field knowledgeable linguist should know so as to be able to translate properly. Gile (1995:131-2) argues that

> […] the Knowledge Base of interpreters and translators of non-literary texts seldom contains all the information necessary for them to perform their work, so that Knowledge Acquisition is a regular and important part of their Translation operations.

Specialisation as language broker and information broker
Another type of specialisation is mentioned by Obenaus (1995: 250) who describes the role of the translator in legal translation:

> Translators act as intermediaries between a source text and a target text. Information brokers act as intermediaries between information sources and people who need information. In order to be a good language broker, the translator also has to be a good information broker, especially in a field such as legal translation. Information brokers are not necessarily experts in a certain field. They are trained to find the right information quickly. The amount of information available today on a topic, place, or person is mind-boggling. The fact that it is available, however, does not necessarily mean it is easy to find. It takes skill and expertise to retrieve and to manage it, and the development of such skills should be a major part of any translator training program.

Specialisation in a particular kind of translation
Some 15 years ago a new kind of translation emerged, and that is localisation, more specifically software localisation. Since it so relatively young, there are variations in definitions of the key terms. Dohler (1997: 2-3) describes localisation as

> [...] the process of adapting a product, in our context a software program, to a specific locale, i.e. to its language, standards and cultural norms as well as to the needs and expectations of a specific target market. A properly localized product also meets all the legal requirements in force in the user's region.
> Users can interact with a successfully localized product in their own language and in a setting that feels natural to them. This means, for instance, that they can input names, addresses, dates, and other data in the same way they would write them down on paper, that they can freely use their standard keyboard characters wherever an entry can be made, and that any error messages are comprehensible to them rather than representing American geekspeak. [...]
> Typically, localization is undertaken from English into other languages, as most software continues to be developed in the U.S., and even some of the software developed elsewhere is originally developed in English.

A similar description is given in http://www.intlconsultg.com/localiza.html, and by Esselink (1998: 2), who defines localisation as:

> The process of adapting and translating a software application into another language in order to make it linguistically and culturally appropriate for a particular local market.

What is important is how the role of the translator is described. Dohler (1997: 3) says:

> Plenty of books on localization ... have been written that are addressed to software engineers, web site designers, and others. Unfortunately, the role of the translator in the localization process has, to my knowledge, not been given any specific attention.

He does not give any further information himself. Esselink (1998: 6) is a bit more specific:

> Localization specialists review the work that translators do and manage terminology. [...] Translated software, help, and documentation files are proofread by a dedicated proofreader or editor.

Formulated in this way, the translator seems to do his 'traditional' work, i.e. function as a specialist in languages and cultures, and as a specialist in a particular subject field, in this case software.

Specialisation in a sub-discipline of translation
This is a rather old type of specialisation. It mainly involves terminology and terminography (I will not go into subtitling or dubbing). I need not say much about these here. It does not make any difference, in my opinion, whether terminology is 'traditional terminology' or 'socio-cognitive terminology' which is based on a cognitive and prototypical approach to language (Temmerman 1998).

Degrees of success of the various ways to improve the status of translators
Of all the options mentioned before, specialisation seems to be the most obvious and successful when it comes down to improving the status of the translator. When one looks, however, at what is going on in reality, one cannot but conclude that the types of specialisation mentioned are apparently not always good enough: the translator's prestige is

still much the same as before despite of the fact that many, if not all, good and successful translators combine types of specialisation in their work. Clearly, other types of specialisation have to be developed. In what follows, I will outline the type of specialisation that I have in mind.

Let me conclude this section by saying that since localisation is an extremely fast-growing kind of translation, it would be a missed chance if translators did not try and establish a form of expert position in this field. Even for this kind of translation the particular type of specialisation that I will describe presently would be extremely relevant.

Specialisation as an expert in Subject-field-Specific Language (SSL specialisation)

By specialisation in Subject-field-Specific Language (henceforth SSL specialisation) I understand that type of specialisation in which not knowledge of a particular specialist subject field is important but knowledge of the language of a subject field. SSL specialisation requires a particular type of, or rather attitude towards translation, viz. SSL-oriented translation. SSL-oriented translation does not only focus on the language characteristics of a particular specialist subject field as they manifest themselves in written or spoken texts, it also tries to acquire an insight into the ways in which the specialists use their language and package their thoughts in language, in other words, into the way in which specialists organise their own specialist subject field by means of the language that is specific for their field. In addition to this, SSL-oriented translation focuses on the communication between people with the same or different degrees of specialisation in a given (sub-)field (i.e. on one and the same level of communication or between different levels of communication), and all this in a given communication situation (i.e. a particular written or spoken text on a particular topic of this (sub-)field); it also focuses, of course, on the transition of a particular level of communication to another level within one and the same language or the transition of this level of communication from one language into another.

By 'level of communication' I refer to the so-called 'communication pyramid' that was assumed for SSL-oriented translation and that displays the various levels of specialisation ranging from the topmost level with communication between participants belonging to the same sub-domain of a field of specialisation and using highly specialised language to the bottom level with communication between participants using general language. It does not have any similarity to the communication pyramid used in mass communication (see e.g. McQuail 1999: 7), except for the shape. McQuail's pyramid distinguishes the following levels of the communication process from bottom to top: 'intrapersonal' (e.g. processing information), 'interpersonal' (e.g. dyad, couple), 'intragroup' (e.g. family), 'intergroup or association' (e.g. local community), 'institutional/organizational' (e.g. political system or business firm), 'society-wide' (e.g. mass communication).

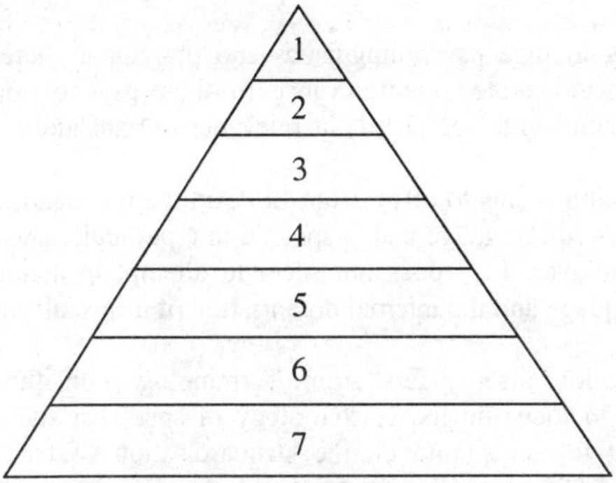

Fig. 1 : communication pyramid

The communication pyramid we use has the following levels (from top to bottom):

Level 1: specialist in a sub-domain of a science ⇔ specialist in same sub-domain of this science
Level 2: specialist in a sub-domain of a science ⇔ specialist in a domain of this science
Level 3: specialist in a domain of a science ⇔ generalist or all-round specialist in this science
Level 4: generalist in one science ⇔ generalist in a number of sciences
Level 5: generalist in a number of sciences ⇔ educated, interested layman (vulgarisation)
Level 6: educated layman ⇔ general public (popularisation)
Level 7: standard language (ordinary people to ordinary people)

One could think of the following examples:

Level 1: a medical specialist involved in implanting pacemakers vs. a medical specialist involved in implanting pacemakers
Level 2: a medical specialist involved in implanting pacemakers vs. a cardiologist
Level 3: a cardiologist vs. a doctor of medicine
Level 4: a doctor of medicine vs. science journalist
Level 5: a science journalist vs. an educated, interested layman
Level 6: an educated, interested layman vs. the general public
Level 7: the general public vs. the general public

Summarising, the characteristics of SSL-oriented translation are that SSL-oriented translation:

1. focuses on the Subject-specific Language of specialist subject fields;
2. attempts to acquire an insight into the ways in which specialists use their language and package their thoughts in language, in other words, into the way in which specialists organise their own specialist subject field by means of the language that is specific for their field;
3. focuses on (levels of) communication, where psycholinguistic, sociolinguistic and pragmatic factors play an important role;
4. focuses on the transfer between levels of communication within one and the same language or between languages.

I also and explicitly include psycholinguistics and pragmatics here. Sperber and Wilson (1986/1996) have demonstrated the relevance of their psychologically-based Relevance Theory to communication and Gutt (1991) its relevance to translation.

SSL-oriented translation seems to differ from LSP, on the one hand, in that LSP focuses on the acquisition and use of language that is specific to a particular specialist subject field and not on transfer. Moreover, LSP does not seem to attempt to acquire an insight into the relation between language and the internal organisation of a specialist subject field.

SSL-oriented translation also differs from Terminology, on the other hand, in that Terminology seems to focus on the epistemology of specialist subject fields and the way concepts are related to terms, and on the standardisation of terms; Terminology does, however, not seem to focus on how terms function in communication. Here there is no difference whether Terminology is 'traditional' or 'socio-cognitive'. In both cases, terms are treated in isolation, and not from the perspective of communication.

The SSL-oriented translator goes further than the LSP specialist or the terminologist. In fact, the SSL-oriented translator could well use the data and knowledge of both the LSP specialist and the terminologist; he will deal with these data in relation to the social communicative context of the text to be translated. The SSL-oriented translator could well be the discussion partner of specialists in a certain field, simply because he knows the language of this field even better than the specialists; therefore he may give them an even better insight into the structure of their own field. The specialist contributes to this insight into his own field by means of the subject specific knowledge he has, the SSL-oriented translator by means of his knowledge of the language characteristics of the field. It is a fact that language mirrors conventions, traditions and consensus as regards all sorts of subject specific aspects. It is also a fact that specialists seldom know why they use the language they use and what part language plays in their understanding of their own field. And this is very important when, for example, it comes to the vulgarisation and popularisation of science in general; with the help of an SSL-oriented translator the specialist may get to know in what way he can reach the public at large and how he can formulate ideas in a way that they will understand. The SSL-oriented translator, in his turn, will be able to acquire more in-depth subject specific knowledge because of his focus on the language of a field.

Hatim and Mason (1990: 223) rightfully state that translators, next to mediating between languages, also mediate between cultures:

> Translators mediate between cultures (including ideologies, moral systems and socio-political structures), seeking to overcome those incompatibilities which stand in the way of transfer of meaning.

The SSL-oriented translator may go even further: he may use his language-based intercultural SSL knowledge to give advice in a capacity of communication specialist in a particular specialist subject field to companies, for example. This may be important in the case of a multinational that has bought up another company and now wants to streamline the internal organisation and communication. This is only one of a number of career options for an SSL-oriented translator. For more examples I refer to the section below concerning the MA Applied Translation Studies.

The term 'SSL-oriented translation' is a newly coined term, but the underlying concept of this kind of translation has its roots in actual practice, though the explicit formulation of this concept in terms of SSL-oriented translation itself encompasses more (see below). There is a growing tendency among translation companies to not only do the traditional translation work, but also to include technical documentation in their portfolio. And it is this technical documentation, or technical writing, which "cross-fertilises" translation in such companies (e.g. http://www.eclipse.translation.co.uk). Technical documentation focuses on the communication between manufacturer and user of a product and 'translates' the language of the particular subject field from one level of specialisation to another. This development, among other things, led the formulation of SSL-oriented translation. The company mentioned even seconds staff to the factories that produce the product for which technical documentation has to be written or for which translations have to be made.

It may now be clear that SSL specialisation will have great chances: not only will it enable translators to create a niche in the market that only translators have access to: the SSL-oriented translator will be an autonomous person between the subject field specialist and the language specialist who may act as a discussion partner for both. SSL-specialisation is also in line with the spirit of these times to break barriers between disciplines and be multi-employable. As such this type of specialisation would be a good way to improve the status of translators.

The MA Applied Translation Studies

SSL specialisation and SSL-oriented translation form the basis of the programme of the MA Applied Translation Studies. This MA course was developed between 1995 and 1997 and was first delivered in 1997. It has a strong vocational basis and orientation. It is operated jointly by the University of North London, the Maastricht School of Translation and Interpreting and Institut Libre Marie Haps (Brussels); the actual course locations, however, are London and Maastricht. For both places the programme is identical, though there are small individual differences. The UNL programme includes, for example, subtitling, whereas Maastricht has plans to introduce localisation. For both goes, however, that they are SSL-oriented. It is a one-year course in full-time mode and a two-year course in part-time mode.

The MA programme consists of 8 modules, viz.:

Core Module 1:	Translation: theoretical issues and recent developments
Core Module 2:	Characteristics of non-literary specialist translation
Core Module 3:	Translation tools and the translator
Specialist Module 1:	The translation of non-literary specialist texts
Specialist Module 2:	The translation of non-literary specialist texts
Project Module 1:	Annotated translation project
Placement Module:	Placement or skills lab
Project Module 2:	Research paper on project and placement

Because of this modular structure, students may change locations easily. The programme is practice-oriented in that it has a placement module and 3 modules where students produce translations of an increasing level of specialisation (Specialist Modules 1 & 2: 2000 words; Project Module 1: 3000 words). In addition, there is Core Module 3, in which students are acquainted with modern aides for the translator, e.g. word processing, the Translator's Workbench, MultiTerm, the Internet and HTML, etc. During the course, students are further prepared for the actual practice by means of assignments on the Code of Practice for translators, translation bureau management and documentation and (re)searching techniques. The whole course has a cyclic pattern in that it starts out with theory (Core Modules 1 and 2), then proceeds to practice and comes back to theory again in Project Module 2, where students write a theoretical paper on the practical modules. The course deals with 6 specialist subject fields, viz. Law / Politics, Business / Economics, Medicine / Biology, Science / Technology / IT (Information Technology), Tourism, and Media and the Arts. Students make a selection of these fields for their translations.

The basis of MAATS is SSL-oriented translation. Core Module 2 is devoted completely to the communication pyramid, the language characteristics of the various specialist subject fields, the culture-bound character of these language characteristics, cross-cultural differences, and implications for translation. We do not go into the subject matter of these specialist subject fields, but into their language; one could say that subject matter and language are taught in an integrated way with the prime focus on language. Part of all assignments that student have to do is devoted to an SSL analysis of the text in question, as well as a discussion of anticipated problems and their implications for the translation.

The course is intended not only for students who have graduated in Translation Studies, Linguistics, a language or one of the specialist subject fields, but also for working translators with good translating experience. Because of the SSL orientation and because of the variety of student backgrounds, we have been able to formulate a number of career perspectives:

Translator
Software translator, Software localiser
Terminologist
Subject field specialist (specifically for graduates in one of the specialist subject fields)
SSL specialist
Reviser, Post-editor
Technical writer
Communication specialist
Scientific journalist, Scientific information official
SSL-communication trainer.

Not all of these positions do already exist and some may still have to be negotiated. Graduates can be employed, or self-employed, work full-time or part-time, and the positions could be with companies or government departments operating on a local, national or international level.

Epilogue

In this paper I discussed SSL-oriented translation, its importance for the status of the translator and its role in teaching specialised translation. What has become clear, I hope, is that SSL-oriented translation deserves a place of its own and has more perspectives than the 'traditional' kinds of translation. It has proved very successful in the MA Applied Translation Studies.

I have tried to distinguish SSL-oriented translation from LSP and Terminology. From my description of SSL-oriented translation it may have become clear that it has a different focus. I hope that it will contribute to Translation Studies and will get the attention it deserves.

References

Adab, Beverley. 1995. "Training students to see how the pieces of the jigsaw fit together". In Thelen, Marcel and Lewandowska-Tomaszczyk, B. (eds.) *Translation and Meaning, Part 3*. Maastricht: Hogeschool Maastricht, School of Translation and Interpreting: 281-292.

Dohler, Per. 1997. "Facets of Software Localization. A Translator's View". In: *Translation Journal* vol 1 (1) July 1997._http://www.accurapid.com/journal/softloc.htm

Esselink, Bert. 1998. *A Practical Guide to Software Localization*. Amsterdam/Philadelphia: John Benjamins Publishing Company.

Gile, Daniel. 1995. *Basic Concepts and Methods for Interpreter and Translator Training*. Amsterdam/Philadelphia: John Benjamins Publishing Company.

Gutt, Ernst-August. 1991. *Translation and Relevance. Cognition and Context*. Oxford: Basil Blackwell Ltd.

Hatim, Basil and Mason, Ian. 1990. *Discourse and the Translator*. London/New York: Longman Group Limited.

http://www.eclipse.translation.co.uk

http://www.intlconsultg.com/localiza.html., "Localization 101".

McQuail, Denis. 1999. *Mass Communication Theory. An Introduction*. Third edition, fifth reprint. London: SAGE Publications.

Obenaus, G. 1995. "The Legal Translator as Information Broker". In: Morris, Marshall (ed.) *Translation and the Law*. American Translators Association Scholarly Monograph SeriesVolume VIII 1995. Amsterdam/Philadelphia: John Benjamins Publishing Company: 247-259.

O'Neill, M. 1998. "Who makes a better Medical Translator: the Medically Knowledgeable Linguistor the Linguistically Knowledgeable Medical Professional? A Physician's Perspective". In: Fischbach, Henry (ed.) (1998), *Translation and Medicine*. American Translators Association Scholarly Monograph Series, Volume X 1998, Amsterdam/Philadelphia: JohnBenjamins Publishing Company: 69-80.

Samuelsson-Brown, Geoffrey. 1998. *A Practical Guide for Translators*. Third edition. Clevedon/Philadelphia/Adelaide: Multilingual Matters Ltd.

Snell-Hornby, Mary. (1992), "The Professional Translator of Tomorrow: Language Specialist orAll-round Expert?". In Dollerup, Cay and Loddegaard, Denmark (eds.) 1994. *Teaching Translation and Interpreting. Training, Talent and Experience*. Amsterdam/Philadelphia: John Benjamins Publishing Company: 9-22.

Sperber, Dan. and Wilson, Deirdre. 1986/1996. *Relevance. Communication and Cognition*. Oxford: Blackwell Publishers Ltd.

Temmerman, R. 1998, *Terminology beyond Standardisation. Language and Categorisation in the Life Sciences*. Ph.D. thesis. Catholic University of Leuven, Department of Linguistics.

Subject field knowledge via specialised language
Paul Wijnands, Hogeschool Maastricht

Abstract
This paper will argue that the acquisition of specialised (or better, specialist) knowledge, in this case subject field knowledge, is very well possible by analysing and mastering the specific language pertaining to that field. The definition and naming of a concept is a problem of diagnosis. Moreover, scientific and technical practice reveal a never ending reformulation of utterances and a permanent updating of a continuum of texts, both resulting from the inevitable adaptation to changing audiences. That scientific discourse has a clear and unique structuring is not a myth. Discourse analysis and terminology are not, as specialists tend to believe and text theoreticians want to present it, enemies for ever, but are, on the contrary, complementary approaches by which emphasis is put on traditional significations of empirical meaning. The semantic, syntactic, collocational and pragmatic characteristics of the language of specific subject fields result in a very natural way from perceptive actions of scientists and technicians. Rationality and reality are linked by means of taxonomies. Since a technique is not an object on its own but an object in a technical context, it seeks other connections with standardisation as science does. A growing number of domain experts study the interrelation between subject field knowledge and the language of specific subject fields and conclude that if this interaction is not always well-structured, it certainly is characterised by a close partnership between knowledge and language.
Proposals will be made aiming at structuring the interaction between specialist knowledge and subject field language in such a way that this interaction can be integrated in an adequate and workable didactic model. This interaction and its proposed structuring are, of course, very appropriate for an SSL-oriented translation training as offered by the MA Applied Translation Studies.

There is a growing trend in translation towards specialised translation. Translators are no longer striving for an universal, unattainable subject field knowledge. Instead, they are specialising in a specific subject field. "Qui trop embrasse, mal étreint". The trend towards specialised translation is due to the increasing influence of technology and science on society. The arrival of specialised translation, however, has not solved the problem of attempting to produce a faithful translation with an optimal equivalent functionality in the target language. Those who are willing to face the reality are forced to conclude that a specialised translator first perceives the subject field world linguistically, and then from a world of external and non-internal involvement. Even an expert is unable to keep pace with these developments. Permanent updating of expert knowledge is therefore an exceptionally beautiful illusion which a translator, like it or not, cherishes. Specialised translation can be compared to a vehicle which is continuously attempting to overtake a vehicle in front of it (the 'carrier' of subject knowledge), without much success. Overtaking is a manoeuvre that must be carried out as quickly as possible in order to avoid hindering traffic approaching from behind. A specialised translator is a troublesome road user and will always be a nuisance. Subject field specialists have always regarded translation as a tedious activity which we have no choice but to accept.

An analysis on the driving behaviour of a specialised translator will reveal that although this road user has managed to adjust to the driving behaviour of other road users (subject field specialists), he will be always be singled out due to several strange traffic manoeuvres. Paradoxically, a translator is unprepared for the technical and scientific discourse of a subject field specialist. Anyone studying this discourse can no longer approach the knowledge field using components of the subject field. It must instead be particularly approached, and even occasionally, solely from linguistic dimensions. I will now elaborate on this approach without the use of the metaphor in my introduction. We can approach the linguistic dimension by allowing the concept of technique to merge with the concept of technology. This enables us to approach the phenomenon of linguistic dimension using several questions relating to the characteristics and statutes of science.

The question 'What is science?' is the first requirement for this linguistic approach. It is therefore also necessary to discuss the history and ideology of scientific thought. During this presentation, however, we will have to make do with a reference to theology, philosophy (the science of all sciences), positivism, naturalism, scientism, logicism, structuralism and epistemology. The concept of science also requires us to make a statuary distinction between natural sciences and social sciences. Scientific character refers to operations /activities/ thought patterns according to certain rules. In addition, an analysis of the foundations of science (which brings us back to philosophy) enables us to identify types of sciences. This is important as, if we accept on the basis of our professional activity that language determines thinking, if not entirely but to a large extent, then this is the first area of discourse activity of the subject field specialist.

Generally, we differentiate between three types of sciences, namely formal science, empirical formal science and hermeneutic science. Formal science uses axioms and deductions while validation occurs on the basis of proof and plausibility. Empirical formal science, like physics, uses two types of language, namely theoretical and experimental language (formal refers to the internal statute of the object and empirical to the external statute of the object). Theoretical language contains logical, mathematical and descriptive terms for semantic interpretation while experimental language contains observational and non-observational terms for interpreting experiments. Hermeneutic science uses action and behaviour to denote/interpret meaning. The use of words from empirical and hermeneutic science is described as being classificational and/or topical/thematic. Grouping classificational vocabulary is a fundamental and conceptual problem. A concept is far more a diagnostic problem, i.e. a characteristic concept related to empirical indicators by statistical probability features, than a complex of features and characteristics. An object laid down by a definition therefore does not carry only that semantic information required in the text. After all, as a semantic entity, a term is the sum of all the characteristics it acquires, depending on the propositions produced. As a result, attributes play an important role as dimensions of ordened aspects. Practitioners of a science and mutatis mutandi translators may form a collective authorship, but they are definitely not an organised collective. The two laws involved here are the law of composition and the law of change and evolution. Technical language is therefore the formulation of meaning by means of concepts that denote processes and structures. Despite categorisation and the use of taxonomies, the signifying practice is dialectical and not classificational. This is because text is production, productivity, and not a product. It is a multiple open field with an infinite number of languages. Moreover, text is a 'tree' - the rudimentary nature of our organs is responsible for this temporary designation (Roland Barthes). Neopositivism has tried in vain to reduce the meaning of theoretical terms to one consisting of pure observational terms. In a reputable training for specialised translators, the comments pertaining to the question 'What is science?' could serve to trace the stages in the development of subject field language and its components via the history of science and technique (technology).

In view of the linguistic approach I have in mind, I cannot ignore the question 'What exactly is technique?' since I resolutely classified technique (technology) under the sciences. Technique is the application of knowledge and know-how, but is non-technical by nature. The exploration and devirtualisation which is typical of the rationality of reality, naturally has all sorts of linguistic consequences. Technique is the application of science, an extension thereof, which, due to its neutrality, attains its sole value, means and goal in a value-free manner: efficiency. That is why specialists are keen on deepening their knowledge, developing specific methods, supporting a social paradigm and becoming the masters and rulers of nature. Critics refer to these desires as a programmed 'phantasm', which is of course an irrational formulation in the midst of the rational discourse of technique. In order to understand the language used by specialists and their way of thinking, it is worthwhile examining how the concepts of art and technique, which became identical hundreds of years ago, gradually drifted apart. Technology is the science of technique. Its objectives are to research, describe, codify, explain, combine and discover. However, the nomenclature, which will never reach completion, displays sociocultural structures which create and support a terminology typical of the group. In this context, the term 'group' must encompass subject field external, transdisciplinary and subject field internal groups of communicators. Scientific/technological texts do not only contain signifiers from nomenclatures and taxonomies, but also reveal a subject-differentiated syntax and a subject-differentiated word formulation procedure. Far too many methods used to introduce the phenomenon of subject field specific language are restricted to presenting either only wordlists or discussing the numerous deficiencies which are recorded in the language of a particular subject field by an attentive observer.

I have not included the phenomenon of subject differentiated syntax in the following proposals for developing instruments which can enable a translator to fathom scientific and technical ways of thinking. Instead, I will concentrate on conceptology and onomasiology, which play a key role in scientific and technical thinking. Every researcher has the urge to be innovative. I will therefore be blatantly iconoclastic when I present semasiology - a generator of concepts - as a discipline which plays a third key role. 'Discourse' receives the place it deserves in pragmatics, which studies the relationship between proposition, context and co-text, and retains the difference between utterance and expression as an instrumental basic distinction. Although I do not wish to maximise the pragmatic concepts of act, context and performance, I inevitably have to turn to hermeneutics to deal with subject field specific problems, irrespective of whether they are onomasiological or semasiological. Semantics endeavours to discover interpretative routes, but it is up to hermeneutics (the philological in particular, not the philosophical) to describe the problems which occur along the way and to place these results in a hierarchy using plausibility levels. There is a general assumption that the ideal of formulating a single exact meaning for a word/term, for the so-called natural languages, is unattainable. However, that ideal should, in theory, be attainable for a specialised vocabulary as it would lose its technical/scientific structure without the objective of explicit polysemy. Time and time again, the principle of polysemy appears unwilling to give way to the recent achievements in pragmatics or dynamic 'comprehension' of the inevitable polysemy (subject field languages included). The recent pioneering work of several linguists will hopefully offer a dynamic perspective on statistical interpretation of the subject field related concepts of terminology and taxonomy. A specialised vocabulary is not only dynamic in social sciences, which examines events and actions, but also in empirical formal science. The 'Praxiling' research team at Université Paul Valéry in Montpellier, France, has done pioneering work on polysemy and dynamic semasiology. Praxematics served as the basis for their research work. Paul Siblot, in particular, is using the model of the praxeme to study the dynamic understanding of polysemy in language and discursive regulation. Praxematic linguistics is a reaction to the objectifying, abstracting, reifying, semic and lexicographical analysis. Praxematicists argue that our relation to objects is of a practical nature since it is the practical importance of the object to us and not the object itself which arouses our interest. Names are therefore based on that dialectic relation with the real world.

Thus a name and the meaning construals it carries with it is only possible in terms of the dynamics of a dialectical relation with language and reality. In any case, praxematicists regard the praxeme as an operational concept which can be used to describe the signifying productivity in the denomination. The praxeme comprises two polysemous structures. Firstly, the diversity of praxis (practical activities) with reality and subsequently the large variety of viewpoints with respect to how objects and life forms must be considered and named. Secondly, the diversity of linguistical praxis (the existing discourses) which naturally supports multiple relations with the manipulative, technical and social praxis. Two analyses can be used to conduct an in-depth examination of polysemous problems, which are virtually always present. Firstly, an analysis of the concept of practical relations which exist with reality and which identify constitutive semantics of polysemy. Secondly, an analysis of the discursive actualisations and how signification is introduced into the discourse. In the first analysis, perceptology, cognitive psychology and ergonomics play a more important role than semantics.

The dynamic approach of subject field specific vocabulary defies terminology where the latter originated in the cognitive domain of mechanical engineering and looks down on the vocabulary of social sciences. Dynamic semantics is non-discriminatory and therefore covers all subject fields. Moreover, the value of semantics is immeasurable and its diachronic, contextual and cotextual dimension leads linguists to thought patterns and linguistic usages that dominate a given science and a given field of knowledge. This is an invitation which a specialised translator will definitely not turn down, especially because he is confronted with an entire field which needs to be analysed urgently. The specialised translator or specialist translatologist is the most suitable person for this task, namely dynamic interlinguistic semantics.

I have already mentioned my desire to no longer support the contemporary belief in the hegemony of onomasiology in terminology by giving the area of activity of general language registrars, namely semasiology, a chance. Most subject field specific specialists shun semasiology since a concept would only originate from a real or fictitious world and not from language. Those unwilling to examine all discursive actualisations of the signifier must indeed conclude that concepts only originate from the signified, from a preceding combination of relevant features and characteristics of a designated referent. There are signifiers, however - particularly in social sciences of course- which generate extremely realistic concepts due to associative references and usually on the basis of playing with language, but also on the basis of associative extension of meaning derived from a common cultural fields such as literature. I wrote a detailed article on the study of the subject field of ethnicity, which appeared in the Université de Rouen publication “Cahiers de Linguistique no. 33”. It was entitled “Le rôle du signifiant dans les appellatifs de langues, peuples et territoires chez les francophones d’Amérique du Nord”. There are relatively many examples of signifiers, especially in all types of jargons used colloquially within a subject field, which, like true rebels, have produced concepts for empirical formal sciences and technical devices for general subject field use.

It has occurred to me that social sciences form a field which encourages a variety of semantic research. The results could be incorporated into current methodology, but more and more terminologists and lexicologists are choosing to boycott this approach. The terminological-lexicographical boycott of social sciences is all the more surprising, given the constant pleas from social-scientific circles for lexicological-terminological solutions to all types of conceptual problems. I will limit myself to the example of ethnology. Isac Chiva, director of studies at L'EHESS, *laboratoire d'anthropologie sociale* in Paris, stated that the *Dictionnaire international d'ethnologie et folklore régionaux européens* - published in 1960 with the support of UNESCO- was a failure and that it was about time that the reasons for this disaster were examined (Chiva 1996). He declares that the terminology of his discipline is not only characterised by a multitude of national, historical and epistemological variants, but also by the proliferation of concepts which are vague and far too broad. The essence of his argument, in my opinion, is his view on the problem involving the identification of fundamental differences between schools of thought and subsequently between scientific ideologies. In other words, his outlook on subject field specific language problems returns us to my starting point, namely language is an extremely suitable means for acquiring an insight into technical and scientific thinking. The multitude of new opportunities provided by computer technology, such as all kinds of research work based on electronically stored texts, means that we cannot ignore the urgent need for an in-depth analysis of the way of thinking of specialists in the language of specialist subject fields.

Translation: S. Horvath

References

Chiva, Isac. 1996. "Les ethnologies de l'Europe: traditions, politiques, perspectives" In Fabre, D. (ed.) *L'Europe entre cultures et nation*. Paris, Ed. de la Maison des Sciences de l'homme.

Sauer, C. 1990. *Vaktaalkennis*. Leiden: Alpha.

Siblot, Paul. (no date). "La polysémie en question: une question mal posée?" in: Fall, Lérd, J.M., Siblot, Paul. *Polysémie et construction du sens*. Montpellier, Praxiling Université Paul Valéry.

Siblot, Paul. 1997. "Nomination et production de sens". In: Siblot, Paul (ed.). *Langue, praxis et production de sens*. Languages, n°. 127.

Wijnands, Paul. 1999. "Le rôle du significant dans les appellatifs de langues, peuples et territoires chez les francophones d'Amérique du Nord". In: *Cahiers de Linguistique Sociale*, n°. 33, Université de Rouen.

'Rolls Royce quality at Lada prices': a survey of the working conditions and status of freelance translators.

Janet Fraser, University of Westminster

Abstract

The traditional 'apprenticeship' for languages graduates in the translation departments of major companies, where they learned the tools of their new trade under the supervision and guidance of experienced translators, has all but disappeared in the UK. Would-be translators now follow a languages degree with a postgraduate course in translation prior to launching themselves onto an unsupervised, and largely unrepresented, freelance labour market. While they arguably enjoy a better theoretical grounding than the translators of the past, the disappearance of staff posts means that they do not have the chance to learn the full range of skills associated with 'being a translator'. This paper reports on the findings of substantial empirical research among practising freelance translators and identifies some aspects not normally included in academic syllabuses.

This will be an unusual paper: there are very few references, and those there are relate in most cases not to academic works but to practitioner journals. The literature on translation in its many facets is wide and growing all the time. It is not merely theoretical but attempts to apply differing strands of theory to syllabus design. However, despite a strong vocational emphasis in postgraduate translator training courses, the everyday problems and working practices of professional translators have very little influence on curriculum design. In the past, this hardly mattered, as languages graduates served an in-house apprenticeship where they learned to be translators and not just linguists. As I set out in some detail below, however, the career paths of translators now take quite a different direction, necessitating a refocusing of the skills taught on postgraduate courses. This paper aims to highlight three aspects of the 'real lives' of freelance translators, identified by the translators themselves, that hold part of the key to learning to be a successful freelance in the changing translation labour market.

The changing translation scene

The last 10 to 15 years have seen a radical change in the labour market for translators. The traditional career path was a degree in modern languages followed by a job in an in-house translation department in a large organisation, under the guidance and supervision of older, experienced translators. Here, young translators could build on their language skills and acquire the 'tools of the trade' in a real-life setting. However, under the combined pressures of economic recession, changes in management theory, and globalisation of business activities, companies have increasingly disbanded their in-house translation facilities and out-sourced their translation work. For the companies themselves, the costs - loss of expertise in the company's history, work, and specialised terminology along with the high fees charged by many translation agencies or companies - are perceived to be outweighed by lower fixed costs and greater flexibility. For young translators, however, the balance sheet looks very different. Instead of being able to learn their trade in the relatively 'safe' atmosphere of a translation department, and having the experience and knowledge of senior translators to draw on, they are in a majority of cases pitched on to an unsupervised freelance market from the moment they complete their academic training; indeed, many of them work for agencies in what one disgruntled freelance translator has called the 'bottom end of the translation business'.

It is notoriously difficult to quantify the size of the translation labour force, but figures from Allied Business Intelligence (quoted in Lockwood 1999) suggest some 115,000 translators across Europe, with roughly twice as many part-time as full-time translators; ABI does not, however, break down the figures on a country-by-country basis. Recent statistics compiled by Bureau van Dijk Electronic Publishing for the European Commission on the basis of a survey of translation agencies, meanwhile (same source), suggest that there are some 6400 translators and interpreters in the United Kingdom out of some 100,000 across Western Europe. The corresponding figures for France and Germany, by way of comparison, are 15,500 and 27,000. The BvD figures are controversial (other estimates for France put the total number of translators at either 4000 or 8000, for example, while there may be as many as 48,000 translators and interpreters in Germany according to one source); they also include those working in a staff capacity, and do not distinguish between translators and interpreters. Nevertheless, they do at least give some indication of the size of the pool of freelance translators operating both in this country and more generally across Europe.

Against these estimates, the membership figures of most translators' professional bodies look very small. The UK-based Institute of Translation and Interpreting (ITI), for example, has 1400 qualified members, of whom around 1050 live in the UK, a 16% membership density on the basis of the estimates given above. By way of comparison, figures for its French counterpart, the SFT, are around 750 (91% of whom are based in France); this represents a membership density of 17% at best and 4.5% at worst, but in either case a low proportion of the putative pool of translators. In Germany, with membership of the main professional body BDÜ at around 5000, membership density is at best 19% and at worst 10%. Whatever the exact figures for the total number of translators active in any country, it is clear that in these three countries, at least, there is a large and broadly unrepresented pool of freelance translators providing translation services in a largely out-sourced market.

Parallel to this development has been the mushrooming of new postgraduate translator training courses: forced by successive governments to recast their mission in terms of competences and transferable and vocational skills, UK universities have rightly seen translation as a major opportunity, and the last four or five years have seen not only numerical growth but also increasing diversification of the courses on offer. They clearly have a sound academic training to offer, on which there is a wide and growing literature. Against the background of changes in the labour market, there is also, however, a case for academic institutions to equip their students with the broader skills needed to function in an unsupported translation environment. Questions such as how the translation process is perceived in the commercial world and the needs of freelance translators within that role, perceptions of translators' professional identity, and the effects on translators of the relationship between agency and client all impact on the skills our newly qualified postgraduate translators need. Yet the answers to these questions are at best patchy and anecdotal, even in the profession itself, and at worst are simply ignored on translation courses.

It was to provide a basis in fact for the anecdotal evidence that I conducted the research that forms the basis of this paper, and the findings I shall report here relate to selected aspects of our training of the future generation of freelance translators, specifically training in what I shall call 'attitudinal' skills rather than the core linguistic and textual skills.

The research

I shall be using three separate sources for this paper. First, I conducted two surveys of freelance translators – some 650 in all – in 1996 and 1998. 300 UK-based members of ITI (about one in five of its total membership) and all members living outside the UK (about 350 people) were sent the same questionnaire, asking questions about the flow of information and support between clients or translation agencies and companies and their freelance translators. A total of 296 translators completed the questionnaire (a 45% response rate), giving a base of more than 20% of ITI's total membership; to the best of my knowledge, such information has never before been obtained from such a large group of translators. The overseas responses came predominantly from Europe (especially France, Germany, Italy, the Netherlands, Spain, and Sweden) but also from the Middle and Far East and North and South America.

Second, a similar questionnaire was sent in 1996 to 150 UK-based translation agencies and companies, attracting 84 replies or a response rate of 56%. These responses served, thirdly, as the basis for selection of 12 translation companies, which I visited and interviewed in depth in spring 1999. More detailed accounts of the findings of the two questionnaire surveys can be found in Fraser (1997, 1999), and my conclusions about their relevance for the design of training courses are set out in Fraser (forthcoming). For the purposes of this paper, however, I shall focus on aspects of the findings that are of relevance to the broader aim of equipping students to function in a changing labour market: recognition of the translation process and translators' needs within it; perceptions of professional identity; and the effect on translators of the client/translation company relationship.

Recognising the translation process

I have written extensively (Fraser 1996, 1997, forthcoming) on the need for translators to be given a full 'briefing' for the translation they are about to do, including information such as the readership of both the source text and the translated text, how the translation is to be used (for information, as the basis for a decision, for purposes of record, for legislation or litigation, as publicity or as a speech to be read aloud, to list but a few possible uses), and full contextualisation, including background documentation and terminology support; indeed, I touch on these issues again below. While reinforcing those comments here, however, I would like to focus in this paper on the scheduling the of documentation process and on the need for translators to be involved at the earliest stage. They are the inter-cultural experts and their expertise needs to be brought in from the very outset of any documentation process. My findings show clearly, however, that translation still gets overlooked in many instances until a very late stage: "We are often the 'tail-end Charlies', but with a little more forethought and planning on [clients'] part, translators would be able to spend more time researching", commented one translator. Another added that "there are too many cases where the client is sitting on documents until he realises that the court case is tomorrow or that he has a plane to catch!", while several bemoaned the 'Friday afternoon deadline' syndrome, requiring a translator to rush to finish a job "when it is obvious that the translation will be lying on somebody's desk until the following week", as one respondent put it.

It is, however, not just a question of the late stage at which translators actually receive the documents they are required to translate. It is rare for translators to be involved in pre-translation or even pre-drafting discussions of documentation, yet the benefits not only to the translator but also to the client of involving the translation team at the earliest possible stage are clear. Where multilingual projects are concerned, the text may need not just translation but 'localisation' or even 'transcreation' (particularly where advertising material is concerned). This enables account to be taken of factors such as audience expectations in differing countries, religious, political or cultural sensitivities, or the appropriateness of a particular approach to (a section of) the target audience.

While, of course, local offices and staff will often have input into this process, the translator should feature large at the writing or pre-translation stage since, as a linguistic and cultural intermediary, he or she is, arguably, the person best qualified to advise on such matters. Some 50% of the UK translators and 60% of the non-UK translators surveyed said that they were so involved, either automatically or on request, better figures than might be expected. Nonetheless, up to half of all translators are not given any chance to influence the document they will have ultimately to translate. This was generally bemoaned by translators: "I can iron out the many 'non-problems' caused by sloppy thinking or poor formulation in the original", wrote one, while another said that early notification of texts while they were still at draft stage gave him the chance to begin research, whereas time pressures inevitably increased if he was given the text only when it was in its final version.

However, recognition of the translation process, and of translators' needs within it, is closely linked with both translators' own perceptions of their professional identity and their clients' perceptions of it.

Perceptions of professional identity

The title of this paper was inspired by a comment from a survey respondent living and working in Belgium and came in the context of his description of his 'ideal client'. Many translators agreed about the lack of realistic expectations in relation to fees, yet underlying these and other comments is a more wide-ranging issue of professional identity: the translators' own, and how their clients perceive it. "There are still too many occasional – and not so occasional – clients who think that translating is typing into another language", reported one translator, while another referred to himself as a "semi-mechanical adjunct to the documentation process".

Such comments give a discouraging picture of the professional identity of translators, and can perhaps be summed up by the respondent whose only demand was to be accepted as "a professional on a par with those who produce texts" – or as "part of the team", as another put it. Nor do translation agencies and companies that deal with clients report better understanding of what is involved in translation. One company said it had been asked to provide costings for "photocopying into French". Another, asked for its charges, queried how long the document for translation was: "Oh, about a centimetre thick", came the reply from the client. Virtually all the companies I interviewed said they had been asked to deliver translations in less time than it would take a skilled word-processor operator to copy-type the document in English. One had, moreover, offered its clients free sessions to help them get the best out of translation and save money, only to have to cancel the series because of lack of interest. The Association of Translation Companies had experienced similarly poor take-up for a series of seminars.

The picture is, of course, not universally gloomy, however, and there are translators who enjoy excellent and respectful relations with their clients. There are, however, two issues here for trainers. One concerns the controversial topic of 'client education', the other the even more controversial topic of 'translator personality'.

It can sometimes seem that clients for translation services are inexperienced purchasers. As we saw above, many clients simply do not have the skill to specify what it is they want from a translator, and even less to provide the type of background information and support that will enable the translator to do a first-class job for them. On the face of it, this seems extraordinary: nobody wanting to buy, say, a new computer system would tell the supplier merely that they wanted it "for office work", nor – in another sphere altogether – would anyone go to a doctor and say only that they "felt unwell" or "had a pain". Yet precisely that level of imprecision frequently applies to the purchase of translation services where clients will, at best, specify that the translation is "for publication" or "for information" and at worst leave it up to the translator to "make sense of the context", as one translator put it to me.

Of course, clients cannot be expected themselves to be translation experts, any more than computer buyers can be expected to know exactly what system they need or patients to diagnose their own illness. In those fields – indeed, in most fields where professionals are delivering services – we expect to be asked a series of questions by the sales staff, doctor or other professional, designed to elicit the exact information they need if they are to meet our requirements or, indeed, to help us understand our own requirements. The analogy appears to break down where translation is concerned, however. A substantial number of translators in my surveys referred to clients' inability to respond to such questions from translators. One respondent summed it up: "One thing irritates me immensely: when I ask for information and the client doesn't have an answer, they sometimes ask 'But can't you just translate?'".

We may speculate on why this is: the legendary inability of the British to learn foreign languages is one possible cause, and, as I explain above, poor organisation may be another, meaning that people commission translations very late on in the process when there is no time for discussion. A third factor may be that the person actually placing a translation job is often not the author or user of the document, but is someone to whom the task has been delegated and who simply cannot answer questions. Underlying all these possible explanations, however, is a lack of understanding of translation as a skilled professional activity.

Translators need to become much more assertive when it comes to educating clients in the best way to deal with them, and my own surveys show some evidence that this is, indeed, a fruitful venture. I calculated a numerical 'score' for each translator in the survey, based not on any qualitative criteria but on the extent to which their clients gave them the kind of briefing and support referred to above or on the translators' failure to ask for such information. On a range of –7 to +21, this produced an average 'score' for UK translators of 9.8 and for non-UK translators of 11.0. In analysis of the questionnaires, however, I isolated those responses from translators who commented on client education and calculated their 'scores' separately: although hardly scientific, this calculation produced a 'score' of 11.7 for UK 'educator' translators and one of 14.8 for non-UK 'educators'. Even on a non-significant sample, differences of 19% and 35% should give us pause for thought about the need to encourage trainee translators to take 'client education' seriously as a skill they will need in their professional lives.

This skill is, of course, one that some translators will find it easier to acquire than others will, and I suspect that that distinction may well be related to the even more controversial question of 'translator personality'. In his methodologically impeccable study of the personality profiles of both translators and interpreters, Henderson (1987) found that the generally accepted stereotypes of the perfectionist, introverted translator and the sensuous, extroverted interpreter were generally true, albeit more unevenly and less markedly than in popular opinion, but that there was a significant area of overlap between the two profiles. This paper is not the forum for a scholarly exploration of his findings, but two aspects strike me as being of particular relevance to the training of specialised translators.

First, if translators are, typically, perfectionist and concerned above all with accuracy and detail, they will have a very clear picture of exactly what they need from their clients:

translation is, after all, "associated with application and a painstaking approach" (1987: 49). Henderson found, though, that when his figures were weighted for experience, translators emerged as "significantly more reserved and apprehensive [than interpreters]" (1987: 97) and, moreover, "somewhat more affected by feelings". If they are relatively more introverted and shy, they may be insufficiently assertive to ensure that their clients understand their needs and give them the necessary support. Second, however, the findings point to translators being more self-sufficient than interpreters; given the problems I explore elsewhere in this paper with getting briefing support and feedback, this is clearly a very positive personality trait for the translator. While trainers cannot, clearly, change a student translator's underlying personality, we need to understand what in their psychological make-up is helpful to them in doing the job and to build on it in exercises and discussions.

Of course, the ability to 'educate' clients will arise primarily in the case of translators working solely or largely for direct clients. My findings showed that in the UK, about 60% of freelance translators work mainly or only for translation agencies or companies, as opposed to about 30% who work mainly or only for direct clients (the remaining 10% work equally for both). In such cases, the translator has at best only limited contact with the client or end-user of the translation and is often reliant on the agency or company to communicate their needs and wishes to the client. The new generation of translation companies often, however, fulfils a very different role from that of more traditional translation agencies, and this impacts substantially on the translator, particularly as regards the multiple relationships involved.

The client and agency/company relationship and its impact on translators

As I comment in the introduction, the translation scene has changed rapidly over the last few years; not only have in-house translation departments all but disappeared, but also the traditional providers of work to freelance translators – translation agencies – have been joined in the market by a newer breed of translation companies. These companies differ to varying extents from agencies, which also of course cover a spectrum of size, activity and quality. However, in general terms, a company is likely to distinguish itself from an agency in one or more of the following respects:

* It is more likely to employ its own staff, rather than out-source all its work to freelances. However, of the 12 companies I interviewed in detail, half out-sourced all their work and none handled more than about 30%-35% in-house.
* The staff employed are likely to combine any translating they do with the role of project manager or translation co-ordinator, taking responsibility for all aspects of management of large, often multilingual, translation or localisation projects, including liaison between client and translator(s).
* A company is more likely to be registered under a quality assurance scheme, ensuring among other things that all work is subjected to certain checking procedures before being passed on to the client, whereas agencies are less likely to do this or at least to have documented procedures in place for such checking. The overwhelming majority of agencies/companies in my postal survey were not registered under any such scheme, and only 12% were registered; however, of the companies I interviewed, six had such a registration while the others had their own internal quality assurance mechanisms in place.

This has several implications for freelance translators working for translation companies:

* Translators are likely to be part of a very large pool of freelances who can be called on when a job matching their profile arises. The pool for the companies I interviewed varied

from 20-50, for companies working in very specialised areas, to 1000 and over for companies with a more general profile, although the companies were mostly working with a relatively small number on a regular basis.

* Translators may nevertheless have the chance to build up expertise by being regularly allocated work from one particular client: all companies try to do this, to reduce familiarisation time with the client's work and queries, but it is by no means always the case.

* Translators are in most cases unlikely to have direct access to the client for any difficulties or questions, and queries are routed through the project manager or co-ordinator at the agency or company (about 40% of translators in my postal surveys were given direct access to the client, although many translators qualified this as being only occasional or under strict supervision). There are of course many good reasons for this, including confidentiality requirements and efficiency in routing all queries through one person, especially where multilingual projects are concerned; however, one acknowledged or unspoken reason in many cases is also the fear of 'poaching' of translators by clients or vice versa.

* Translators are therefore dependent on project managers for much of the information and support identified above. While many companies make every effort to provide background documentation, terminology resources, website addresses and contacts to assist the translator, some translators will be unable to have their queries answered and will be thrown back largely or even wholly on their own resources.

* The question of feedback becomes crucial when translators are reliant on the company to mediate between them and the client. Translators taking part in my questionnaire survey were asked about feedback (from direct clients, agencies or companies): 18% said they received it "automatically", 59% "on request", 21% "never", and 2% that they "did not want feedback". Even among the companies selected for interview because of their generally good profile in translator support, the responses on communication of feedback varied, from "there's no time for it with the turnover of work we have" to an admission from two companies that they would pass on criticisms but not comments about client satisfaction. To be fair to the companies concerned, four of them did comment that they would pass on feedback from the client "when it [was] forthcoming" but that many clients simply did not understand the value of feedback in ensuring a better job next time, let alone in helping the translator to develop professionally. An additional complication in multilingual projects was that finished translations are often delivered to the client but then passed on to local offices where further changes are made unknown to both the translation company and the translator.

The picture that emerges is of a freelance translator drawing largely on his or her own resources, even when working regularly for a large translation company. Time and time again, the companies interviewed responded to questions about briefing and support by saying that they would pass on briefing, background information, terminology and feedback if the client made them available, but that generally, this was not the case.

I discuss above the need for 'client education', which applies as much to companies and agencies as to individual translators, but another issue emerges here, that of the parallel and sometimes conflicting relationships involved in the translation industry: that between the translation company and its client, and that between the translation company and its 'supplier', the freelance translator. The structure can perhaps best be visualised as an incomplete triangle, with the translation company at the apex and the two sides leading down to the client and the supplier. The base of the triangle – the connection between client and supplier/translator – is, however, missing in this set-up. One freelance translator put it pithily:

> The most useful person for the translator to talk to is the customer. But agencies and companies think you [the translator] will lure the customer away, so they keep you apart. And this makes it hard to tap into the customer's expertise.

I believe training courses do not take sufficient account of this structure when training future translators for the freelance market. It is, however, crucial that newly qualified translators understand the implications for them of the 'two-sided triangle' model. One company was particularly candid, and the comments made to me by one of its directors are worth quoting at some length. "Our relationship is with our client, not with the translator", she argued, "and this link is the most important thing for the company. The translator is irrelevant to this relationship although, of course, they are crucial to the project as a whole." (Indeed, this model interprets the translation company as being the translator's client, not the end-user of the translation.) She admitted that the passing on of comments arising out of quality control was "not as good as it should be" in her company and that "We don't ask clients if they're happy, as it raises doubt in their minds." She acknowledged, though, that this meant that translators were not given any opportunity to improve: if a client came back with justified criticism, it meant that the company's system had failed and the issue was tackled at that level rather than involving the translator.

In these comments, she echoed the view of another company, which had taken part in the postal survey: "Some translators do not seem to grasp that they are part of a supply chain", it wrote. "We have the legal and financial responsibility for managing a project that is frequently multilingual. If all the translators were to speak to our clients, then (a) the clients would be annoyed by repeated queries for a number of languages and (b) we would not have control and therefore could not be held responsible for situations that were unknown to us" (original emphasis).

The clear message is that the translator has to accept that he or she is a service provider in this equation, rather than the 'hub' of a professional operation. The agency or company may be unwilling or unable both to provide the resources and feedback that the translator wants and needs and to 'educate' its own clients into better ways. One company director told me, "If we can't get the information we need, it's not the client's fault"; the thrust of his comment was that the translation company should be able to elicit the information it needs, but another interpretation is that if the information cannot be obtained, the translator will have to muddle through with his or her own resources rather than the client being told clearly that lack of information will result in a poorer, and potentially more expensive, end product.

It would, however, be wrong to infer from this that companies generally take little account of the needs of their freelance translators. One held twice-yearly forums at which freelances could raise issues of concern, another held a Christmas social to which all freelances were invited, and a third – a model in this respect – provided feedback on every job, offered an annual bonus to regular translators in the form of a contribution towards the cost of upgraded equipment, long-term loan of a piece of equipment or similar, and tried to meet translators socially as much as possible (however, its base of regular translators was much smaller than that of other companies interviewed).

At the same time, companies sometimes criticised their translators who, for example, relied on the checking process to resolve difficulties they should have resolved themselves or who failed to comply with basic quality checks such as running their target text through a spell-checker before submitting it. It is a moot point how much influence the 'two-sided triangle' has on translators' perceptions of their own role in the overall process of producing documentation. What is clear, however, is that freelance translators need to be much more self-reliant than was perhaps the case in the past: they need to ensure that their own quality control procedures are rigorous, that they build up excellent translation resources of their own (not only glossaries and electronic sources but also networks of experts, linguistic and otherwise, who can be consulted), and that they take every opportunity to publicise translation issues as widely as possible, so that users gradually become more aware of the needs of the translator. In the light of this, membership of professional associations – which, as I indicated earlier, is low in comparison with the estimates for the numbers of translators working – is crucial.

Conclusions

It is clear from these findings and these comments from practising translators that, given the new conditions in the translation industry, we need to review the content of postgraduate translation courses. Syllabuses need not only to take account of the latest developments in translation and linguistic theory, and the new technological aids, but also to ensure that our students reflect on the broader skills that they will need to compete successfully in the market. These include:

* understanding of the generally low priority translation has in many clients' minds coupled with the assertiveness to raise that profile;
* a strong sense of professional identity coupled with recognition of the ongoing need for 'client education';
* and the self-reliance and self-motivation to work successfully for translation companies or agencies in the new commercial realities.

In short, our postgraduate translators should be taught to deliver 'Rolls Royce quality', in the words of my respondent, but to educate their clients to give them Rolls Royce treatment in return.

References

Fraser, Janet. 1996. "Mapping the process of translation", Montréal: *Meta* 41 (4). 84-96.

Fraser, Janet. June 1997. "Briefing? What briefing? Findings of a survey on the flow of information between clients, translation agencies or companies and freelance translators". London: ITI Bulletin. 13-16.

Fraser, Janet. June1999. "Can't you just translate? Findings of a survey of freelance translators living outside the United Kingdom". London: ITI Bulletin. 12-15

Fraser, Janet (forthcoming). "The broader picture: how freelance translators define 'translation competence'" in book on translation competence to appear in John Benjamins Translation Library series.

Henderson, John. 1987. *Personality and the linguist: A comparison of the personality profiles of professional translators and conference interpreters*. Bradford: University of Bradford Press.

Lockwood, Rose. June1999. "Bigger than a breadbox?". Language International. 18-20.

Teaching specialised translation .... or not?

Joelle Commeau-Fanghanel, University of Luton

Abstract

This paper aims to highlight effective teaching and learning strategies to foster specialist knowledge acquisition in the context of teaching translation. It will then challenge the notion that there is an increasing need for the 'specialised communicator' and propose that a generalist approach might be more adapted to the needs of the aspiring translator.

Educational research shows that deep approaches to learning (Marton & Säljö 1976 and subsequent research) foster active and long-term learning that warrants student autonomy. In the context of specialist knowledge acquisition, it seems to me that unless deep learning is fostered, the exercise of terminology acquisition could be compared to that of a trophy hunter accumulating booty made up of disparate - if valuable - items. For a collection of items to become useful, connections between the items and relation a larger whole must be made evident.

I will review the most common approaches and suggest more effective strategies in the light of the concept of 'situated learning' (Lave & Wenger 1991), a rough equivalent of learning *in situ* or 'learning by doing'. The conclusion will challenge the view that it is the role of universities to generate 'specialist communicators'. Indeed, as Roger Bell suggests (International Islamic University 'MA Course Proposal'), specialisation might not need be embedded in a translation course. The 'GP approach', based on the medical - or legal - model, might be more relevant in view of market demands (multi-skills, multi-disciplinarity). In the context of student employability, should universities therefore aim to produce the 'GP communicator'?

Introduction

The issue of specialist knowledge acquisition within the context of translation teaching is often disregarded or seen as a mere side-issue. Generally embedded within the more highly regarded questions of theory and translation practice, specialism is at best mentioned as an area where students are often left to their own devices. In this paper, I will examine teaching methods commonly used by teachers of translation in respect of specialist knowledge acquisition, an area that is often left uncharted in the syllabus. I will consider ways of developing effective teaching and learning strategies for this aspect of translation where, to a large extent, individual needs differ and autonomy must be fostered for the long-term benefit of the student. Taking into account educational views on knowledge acquisition and relating these to my own experience of teaching translation at undergraduate and postgraduate levels, I will suggest that a course provider's main priority ought to be to generate a learning environment that contributes to the empowering of students. I will consider in this paper the extent to which the concept of 'situated learning' might be useful to those in charge of teaching translation. In my conclusion I will however challenge the notion that there is an increasing need for the 'specialised communicator' and conversely propose that a generalist approach might be more appropriate to the needs of aspiring translators and more beneficial to the profession as a whole.

One of the first aims of a vocationally-oriented course ought to be to encourage student autonomy. This rather hackneyed term conceals a number of definitions and it is perhaps useful to make the distinction between what educationalists refer to as "the development of autonomous individuals" (Candy: 1988), that is the making of self-reliant graduates, the achievement of "autonomy as a goal for education" (Boud: 1988), and the narrower sense of developing students "who accept more and more responsibility for their own learning, for setting goals and objectives, for finding resources, and for evaluating the outcomes of their learning activities" (Candy: 1988): that is, in Boud's terms, "autonomy as an approach to education". A third definition proposed by Philip Candy is one that refers to the fostering within students of a thirst for knowledge that will inhabit the individual for a life time. All three definitions have, in effect, a common denominator in that they shift the emphasis from the solely didactic approach to a more student-centred or group-centred approach.

Common approaches: specialist knowledge embedded in course provision

In many institutions where specialised or semi-specialised translation is taught at undergraduate or postgraduate levels, some or all of the following strategies are recommended: perusing of specialist dictionaries; use of encyclopaedias and reviews/journals in both source and target languages; attendance at seminars or lectures on specialist subjects; visits to Internet sites and access to on-line terminology databases; visits to companies and plants; contacts with friends and subject experts (journalists, PR departments of major industries, technicians, etc.).

The obvious advantage of the latter two is that they allow students to engage in a dialogue about the topic they are interested in: they must ask and answer questions that will contribute to a more thorough understanding of the subject than if they were just reading in a journal or listening to a lecture. These strategies involve the student in 'deep learning'[1],where students concentrate on concepts and meaning rather than try to memorise terms for replication.

In the context of specialist knowledge for translation purposes, it seems to me that unless deep learning is fostered through the acquiring of the founding principles of a specialist area, the exercise of terminology acquisition and management could be compared to that of a trophy-hunter accumulating booty made up of disparate - if valuable - items. The links between the items are not always apparent and the whole is not necessarily coherent. This is an essential point as it relates to the divide between aggregate vs. holistic knowledge; for a collection of items to become useful, connections between the items and relations to a larger whole must be made evident. The acquisition of specialist knowledge can thus be seen as the mapping of a territory in which the learner becomes the land owner. If the student translator is only taught to surf through databases or compile glossaries, accumulating data and subject-specific language out of context, the knowledge acquired will be of little use.

Acquisition of a specialism is essential for translators and it is part of the role of teachers of translation to seek to instil this urge for systematic inquiry within a specific field. In order to foster the type of holistic approach mentioned above, I would like to consider how the concept of 'situated learning' might be of use to the teacher of translation.

Contextualist approaches to learning

Situated learning introduces the notion of contextualised learning. It is a rough equivalent of learning *in situ*, 'learning in practice'. In the context of situated cognition, "thinking is an interaction between an individual and a physical and social situation" (Greeno 1989).

This sociocultural theory was developed in the late 80s early 90s by cognitive psychologists out of frustration with cognitive science which confined itself to developing a theoretical paradigm for acquiring and processing knowledge, without being able to relate it to everyday experience (Hirst & Manier 1995). The exponents of situated learning, alongside activity theorists, critical psychologists, and a whole school of educationalists interested in a contextualist approach, "want to direct cognitive psychology's attention away from the

---

[1] Details of the seminal work on the disctinction between 'surface' and 'deep' learning, by Marton and his colleagues at Gothenburg, can found in Marton, F. & Säljö, R. 1976. "On qualitative differences in learning: I - Outcome and Process", *British Journal of Educational Psychology*, 46, 4-11.

characterisation of cognitive 'machinery' in the abstract and toward the uses people make of this machinery" (Hirst & Manier 1995).

These psychologists emphasise in particular the fact that the way people learn and memorise depends on many factors, including developmental and cultural ones. In a simple but convincing manner, activity theorists show for example how memory is embedded in various activities people perform. Istomania's examination (Istomania 1977[1], quoted in Hirst & Manier 1995) of memory within two groups of children is referred to by Hirst & Manier as an example of how 'involuntary memory' (in which the task of remembering is embedded in a related activity) surpasses 'voluntary memory' where the subject - here, a group of children - is simply asked to memorise facts such a list of grocery items. Two groups of children are asked to memorise and then recall a list of grocery items; one group does this by way of rote memorisation while the other is sent to the grocer's shop to get the items to provide lunch. Istomania's experiment demonstrates that children in the involuntary memory exercise performed better than those in the voluntary memory condition. Although Istomina's conclusions have been subsequently revisited, Hirst & Manier confirm that "this study and others like it effectively demonstrate that children's use of memory skills depends on their goals, the enveloping activity, and the broader context" (Hirst & Manier 1995).

This emphasis on activity and context is also at the root of situated learning. Situated psychologists argue that cognitive acts cannot be dissociated from the context in which they occur. Lave & Wenger for example base their analysis on the observation of various learning groups and make explicit the way group dynamics and immersion in the community of practice dictate how learning occurs. Their research considers examples drawn from the apprenticeships of Yucatec midwives, Vai and Gola tailors, American naval quartermasters, meat cutters and non-drinking alcoholics, and the authors define their approach in the following terms:

> The notion of situated learning now appears to be a transitory concept, a bridge, between a view according to which cognitive processes (and thus learning) are primary and a view according to which social practice is the primary, generative phenomenon, and learning is one of its characteristics. There is a significant contrast between a theory of learning in which practice (in a narrow, replicative sense) is subsumed within processes of learning and one in which learning is taken to be an integral aspect of practice (in a historical, generative sense). In our view, learning is not merely situated in practice - as if it were some independently reifiable process that just happened to be located somewhere; learning is an integral part of generative social practice in the lived-in world.
> (Lave & Wenger 1991)

In the cases studied, Lave & Wenger show how the learner is gradually introduced to a learning environment which allows his/her gradual incorporation into activities, discussions, decisions, etc.. Lave & Wenger call this approach "Legitimate Peripheral Participation":

> [...] learners inevitably participate in communities of practitioners and [...] the mastery of knowledge and skill requires newcomers to move toward full participation in the sociocultural practices of a community. Legitimate Peripheral Participation [...] concerns the process by which newcomers become part of a community of practice. (Lave & Wenger 1991)

---

[1]Istomania, Z.M. (1975). 'The development of voluntary memory in preschool-age children', *Soviet Psychology, 13*, 5-64.

This model of learning through gradual engagement and increasing task complexity is developed from ethnographic studies of various forms of apprenticeships, the conditions of which vary tremendously: in some cases the learner is closely related to the teacher (as is the case for Yucatec midwives for example), in some cases not (Vai and Gola Liberian master-tailors are separate from the learner's household); some learners are paid, some not; some forms of apprenticeship are crafts, others not. In these contexts, learning is seen as an 'increasing participation in communities of practice' (Lave & Wenger, 1991). Lave & Wenger show that learning is not simply a matter of internalisation of skills but rather results from acquiring an overall grasp of the concepts and structures of the community of practice. I must stress that my reference to this model is not meant to reopen the old debate about translation as an art or as a science; it is introduced here to show how a shift occurs in respect of the process and locus of learning that lays the emphasis on to a dynamic that is self-generated by the very 'bringing together' of the agents. So although mainly derived from the observation of craftsmen, it only obliquely relates to the art-science debate. Furthermore, although, for the purpose of the approach I advocate here, I have highlighted the apprenticeship paradigm within the concept of situated learning, this is no way intended to be seen as the only learning procedure legitimised by situated learning theorists.

Implications of a situated perspective for the teacher of translation

I would like to consider at this stage the ways in which this approach may be relevant to the teacher of translation? First and foremost, 'situated learning' questions the content of and interplay within the teacher-learner entity. In most of the cases observed by Lave, Wenger and their team, not much teaching goes on, learning takes place through observation of masters, of peers or near-peers, discussions and so on. The master is not an authoritative pedagogue and learning is a shared process.

In this set-up, the learner performs several roles. S/he is not always in the position of novice. S/he can be a subordinate, a learning practitioner, also, in some tasks, the only person in charge, etc. The learner is part of a learning group and develops relationships with masters and with other learners. The dynamic of newcomers vs. experienced practitioners is essential to enable this participation at multiple levels. In this environment, practice evolves by the exchange of experience and knowledge. Newcomers input their own experience and ideas and contribute to the making of the community's practice. This approach infers that learning is taking place in a dynamic manner. The flux of knowledge and experience circulates amongst learners and teachers in an interactive, mutually beneficial way.

Furthermore, it must be noted that in the cases studied, Lave & Wenger highlight the fact that the learning environment is very different from any conventional educational space. Learning is not divorced from everyday activities. The Maya girl for example, learning to become a midwife, acquires knowledge from her mother from an early age. She hears stories of difficult births and accumulates indirect knowledge as she is gradually allowed to participate in the process, to run errands, administer prenatal massages and so on. In the cases described, "learning is an integral and inseparable aspect of social practice" (Lave & Wenger 1991)

Towards new educational practices and environments

I would like to consider at this point how this concept of learning may cast a fresh light on the educational practices teachers of translation are accustomed to and contribute to the development of more effective teaching and learning strategies.

Although Lave & Wenger deliberately chose in their study not to consider the issue of schooling as they wanted to build a fresh view of learning, separate from the accepted premises of conventional teaching environments, it is interesting to see how their analysis might affect current educational practices. Situated learning raises, amongst others, questions about the sociocultural organisation of learning environments. It broaches the issues of the circulation of knowledge and the distribution of power within teaching institutions and would of course suggest an open structure where teaching is not confined to the *ex-cathedra* approach and where authoritarian control by the teacher is relinquished. Lave & Wenger indeed suggest that learning is not an individual act but belongs in a collective framework and is, in fact, dependent on this participatory dynamic. Learning is a collective process which generates a dynamic that, in turn, feeds back into the practice. The most radical proposal in this approach is the related suggestion that the locus of learning is not the individual's mind but the collective setting. Thus, there is clearly a shift from focusing on the product to focusing on the process that creates the product.

The 'situated' paradigm is also a source of inspiration in respect of the teaching and learning strategies. In this perspective, it becomes clear that effective learning is not directly attributable to teaching. Rather, effective learning derives from dynamic factors contained in the environment and more is achieved through direct interaction than through the pure mediation of cognitive representation. An essential component of this dynamic is willingness by the learner to engage in problems that present a challenge, and the desire to explore new grounds. Student goals are primary. It must be emphasised that learning can in fact take place where there is no teaching (and vice versa, as all teachers know, teaching can take place without actuating any learning!). Because of their engagement in practice, learners define their own goals of what there is to be learnt and thus set up the learning curriculum. The product of this learning is a social as well as an individual construction.

Consequently, learner and tutor roles and positions are not fixed or pre-determined. Teaching is no longer a central cascading of knowledge, and the respective positions of the learners and teachers become flexible and mobile. Learners do not just learn from their tutor but also from interactions with peers, involvement in practice and discussion. Deep learning is fostered; skills acquired are seen as part of a whole, the structure of which is evident (therefore accessible) to the learner. Living learning takes place; learners' input influences, refines, and further structures the framework of practice. A dynamic is created; skills and practice are being transformed by this input.

Practical ways of applying these principles to the acquisition of specialist knowledge for translation purposes

It is clear that a 'replicative' approach to the acquisition of specialist knowledge is not helpful. In order to ensure that deep and living learning is actuated, teachers of translation may want to consider introducing some of the following methods into the learning environment:

* Reciprocal teaching between students which provides learners with the means of evaluating their own understanding of what they have 'learnt'. A learning dialogue based on reflection is thus instigated.

* Self and peer-assessment, through which students can monitor and evaluate their own performance or that of others, may be introduced.

* Learning from talk. Knowledge is assimilated through discussions of problems, answering questions, listening to accounts of difficulties etc. This can be achieved by bringing experts into teaching institutions or by providing discussion forums for students and might further encourage them to comment on each other's interpretations and explanations. Multiple perspectives are thus constructed.

* Effective reading strategies.
Where reading is recommended, the focus should be on fostering creative reading skills which will stimulate reflective learning[1].

* Immersion in a learning environment which goes beyond acquiring the technical skills of a practice: institutions may offer corporate 'stages' or work placements that enable students to become acquainted with professional practices and thus make informed decisions about their own choices for the future. It is also possible to establish closer links with industry that ought to be reciprocal. Ideally these ought to be seen as an exchange dynamic in which partners mutually benefit.

* Virtual learning environments may be considered; students can engage in an interactive dialogue with the system, be challenged, check their understanding and receive and give meaningful feedback.

* Involvement of students in real translation projects (within a framework that warrants 'legitimate peripheral participation', i.e. with peers, post-graduate students, experienced translators, etc...). This is already carried out in some institutions where Translation Services exist, but one might need to reconsider student input, support and feedback rather than concentrate on the purely financial aspect of such ventures.

* Networking with other students and subject experts so as to gradually map and expand specialist knowledge. This may remind one of the former ITI's Guardian Angel scheme, but more of a two-way approach could be envisaged in which the newcomer is allowed to observe, discuss, participate and influence his/her mentor’s practice.

These strategies offer alternative routes to learning that enable learners to reflect on their respective relevance and choose those that are the most suitable for their own learning styles. They also constitute a reciprocal flux of input, away from the one-way stream of knowledge circulation generally present in our teaching institutions.

The need for a generalist approach
The assumption that students of translation should undergo increasingly specialised training needs *in fine* to be challenged alongside the view that translation courses providers need to generate 'specialist communicators'.

According to a survey carried out in my own institution on past and current students, as to whether they think postgraduate translation courses should aim to develop a specialised provision, students often answer yes *and* no! Although this survey only concerned a small number of students (15 student replies to a questionnaire), their responses epitomise the

---

[1] Some useful advice can be found in Weinstein, C & Mayer, R. 1986. “The teaching of learning strategies” in Wittrock, Merlin (ed). *Handbook of Research on Teaching*. New York: Macmillan, 315-327.

paradoxical situation a student of translation - and later, newcomers to the profession – find themselves in. Tradition, professional bodies and professional ethos require that one should become a specialist in one field. Consequently, students acknowledge in their answers the need for a specialised course provision. At the same time, they express a wish to confine their studies to generalist texts for the following reasons:

* it provides a better foundation from which to build a career
* it gives you a extensive exposure to a variety of fields/text types
* it opens vistas on areas one might not know at all
* the translator must be flexible/adaptable, it is no good just being able to translate one subject.

In all cases, students seem to think that specialisation is a very personal choice and should be left to the individual. They are also aware that the acquisition of a specialism is a long-term process that cannot be accomplished overnight. It is less clear whether they expect a translation course to provide them with that specialisation by the end of their studies.

I would like to suggest that the idea of specialisation being embedded in a translation course is perhaps inapt and further, that the concept of a 'specialist' translator is perhaps 'fraudulent'. Although it may well be true that, as Roger Bell puts it, 'To comprehend a physics text, one must think like a physicist' (Bell 1991), the notion that one becomes a specialist in a field as a result of carrying out some research as part of a postgraduate course in translation is erroneous and may impair the credibility of translators as professionals.

Bell is the one who first suggested that the 'GP approach', based on the medical - or legal - model whereby the competent multi-skilled linguist would only gradually develop a specialisation as part of his/her professional development, a process which could continue throughout the translator's life, is more apt to meet the requirements of the profession.

I can see many reasons to support this view. There is an increasing need for multi-lingual and multi-skilled linguists, in particular with the development of new technologies. Furthermore, the nature of freelance work, where those who commission the work do not necessarily recognise the distinction between the different ranges of skills - translation and interpreting for example, or the need to translate only into one's mother tongue -, lends itself to a generalist approach. The freelancer needs indeed to be responsive to market demand and entirely self-reliant. Finally, the nature of a discipline that is deceivingly specialised also calls for versatile, non-unique competence. Translation tends to demand overlapping skills and knowledge: technical specifications may include the translation of a legal contract, tourist brochures may include references to educational matters, and so on.

I would therefore suggest that a course which aims at developing a competent multi-skilled linguist might be more relevant than a course which advocates specialisation as a virtue. Such a course might include translation and interpreting skills (including sign interpreting), media skills such as voice-over, subtitling, interviewing, telephone interpreting, post-translation skills (revising, editing, abstracting skills), aftercare skills (bookkeeping, professional ethics) and transferable skills, including self-assessment. Such a provision would produce individuals who have become autonomous in the third sense highlighted by Candy and whose self-reliance and self-confidence would in due course feed back into the community of practice, thus informing the way the role of the translator is perceived by service users and society as a whole.

Acknowledgement
I am indebted to Prof. Roger Bell for sharing with me his views on the 'GP Approach' and casting an eye on an earlier version of this paper and to my colleagues, Dr Russell Barnes and Dr Tony Cline, for their support and helpful comments.

References

Bell, Roger. 1991. *Translation and Translating: Theory and Practice*, London & New York: Longman.

Boud, David. 1988. "Moving Towards Autonomy" in Boud, David. (ed), *Developing Student Autonomy in Learning*, London: Kogan Page, Second Edition.

Candy, Ph. 1988. "On the Attainment of Subject-matter Autonomy", in Boud, David. (ed), *Developing Student Autonomy in Learning*, London: Kogan Page,Second Edition.

Greeno, James, G. 1989. "A perspective on thinking". *The American Psychologist*, *44*, 134-141.

Hirst, W. & Manier, D. 1995. "Opening vistas for cognitive psychology". In Martin, Laura (ed.). *Sociocultural psychology: theory and practice of doing and knowing*, Cambridge: Cambridge University Press.

Lave, Jean & Wenger, Etienne. 1991. *Situated learning: Legitimate Peripheral Participation*, Cambridge: Cambridge University Press.

The role of translation theory in training the specialist translator

Nadia Rahab, University of North London

Abstract

There is a belief among professional translators, translation theorists and even those involved in teaching translation that translation theory is of little use, if any at all, in the training of specialised translators. Such beliefs are usually based on the assumption that teaching the craft to aspiring specialised translators should be restricted to such aspects as the study of specialised language characteristics in general as well as in relation to areas of specialism, the study of terminology and the translation of specialised texts.

The present paper strongly disagrees with such views and will attempt to explain the reasons by (a) proving the crucial role played by translation theory in training specialised translators and explaining why and (b) showing at what stage and how such knowledge becomes necessary in the training of specialised translators.

The conclusions reached by the paper will be mainly based on the writer's own experience in teaching translation to specialised translators.

Introduction

The aim of the present paper is to demonstrate that translation theory, contrary to the belief held by some, should play a crucial part in the training of the specialised translator. To do so, the paper will first review the arguments presented for and against the inclusion of a theoretical component in the training of specialised translators. Next, it will attempt to explain why theoretical knowledge should be part and parcel of any translator's training program and then will determine the source of such knowledge. Finally, the paper will look at the type of knowledge acquired from the inclusion of translation theory in the training program and its advantages.

The controversy over translation theory in training the specialised translator

The training of the translator has always been a much debated issue in Translation Studies. Eugene Nida, Paul Newmark, Daniel Gile, Mona Baker, Ian Masson, Déjean, Michel Ballard, Janet Fraser, Penelope Swell, Mildred Larson, Peter Fawcet, Paul Kussmaul, Cay Dollerup, Annett Lindergaad to mention only a few have all contributed with their views to the issue of translators training and what should or should not be included in it.

If asked what should be included in a syllabus set up for training specialised translators, a large number of translation teachers are likely to answer that priority should be given to introducing the student to different specialist subject fields, terminology, the characteristics of specialised texts, and the strategies specific to the translation of such texts. Few will include translation theory as an essential component in such a training. In fact, the list established by Critchley, Hartley and Salkie in a collective paper (1996) would be typical of what is commonly thought should come first in such a curriculum:

- a good command of the languages used
- the ability to target the text to translate
- he ability to apply a coherent typology of texts in formulating a translation strategy for the specific text
- to know enough about the relevant specialised field to understand the information in the text
- to be familiar with the special terminology used in the field
- to be able to write in the target- language of the appropriate kind for that particular text
- to provide a finished product of a professional standard.

Indeed, there seems to be a widespread opinion among translation teachers and mainly among translation practitioners that translation theory is of little use to the translator and should therefore have little or no part to play in his/her training .

The view that translation theory is of little help in the training of the specialist translator is usually based on the belief that translating is an intuitive skill, a 'gift' one may or may not have and which distinguishes a good translator from a mediocre one. This intuitive ability to translate can, of course, be further developed and perfected with practical experience. Eugene Nida describes the importance of this 'gift' in the following terms:

> "[…] without some inborn capacity for understanding and transmitting messages, a person's potential as a translator will certainly be limited."
> (Nida 1981: 402)

This emphasis on the intuitive nature of translating stresses the idea that translators are born and not made as conveyed in Nida's title of the article mentioned above. These gifted translators are thought to be born with what Nida describes as "a creative imagination" which, as he explains plays a crucial part in understanding a message in one's mother tongue, and involves a "capacity to spot problems in the source-language text" and " a capacity to sense ways of communicating meaningfully in a particular language" (Nida 1981: 404).

The present paper does not dispute the fact that some translators seem to have, indeed, a sort of sixth sense which enables them to produce exceptionally good translations. However, they are very few and very lucky. The rest of those working as translators seem to have reached the professional status through a great deal of practical experience.

At the other end of the argument, are those teaching translation who believe that the training of future translators can neither be complete nor satisfactory without translation theory taught to students as a crucial component in their curriculum. The main reason put forward to justify these views is that translation theory will give the trainee translator an insight into the translation process that can be provided neither by intuition nor by practical experience. Such an insight, it is claimed, will give the aspiring translator a better understanding of his future profession and consequently, will equip him in the best possible way to carry it in as a professional.

While acknowledging the part played by intuition and the undeniable benefits of practical experience, those who believe in the importance of theory in teaching translation maintain that intuition alone is neither enough nor reliable, for as Paul Kussmaul (1995) explains that one "cannot really hope to rely on arguments of the type, "This is better because I feel it is better."(Kussmaul 1995: 3). He maintains that "What our students need are rational arguments which, as far as possible, are based on objective principles. […] It is the rational approach which distinguishes the expert from the non-expert." (Kussmaul 1995: 4). These views are echoed by Mona Baker (1990) who affirms that "A trainee translator needs to understand why certain choices are more appropriate than others in certain contexts." (Baker 1990: 168). She further explains that "A trainee translator does not just need to be told that a particular choice is unacceptable or inappropriate in a given context, s/he also needs to identify the reason for its inappropriateness." (Baker 1990: 169).

Similarly, while recognised as being crucial and invaluable in learning the trade, practical experience is also seen as time consuming. Lanna Castellano, (1998: 33) quoted by Mona

Baker affirms that “Our profession is based on knowledge and experience. It has the longest apprenticeship of any profession. Not until thirty do you start to be useful as a translator, not until fifty do you start to be in your prime.”
(Baker 1992: 3)

Similarly, Mona Baker questions the feasibility of such a path for aspiring translators and observes that “one obvious problem with this career path is that it takes so long to acquire the necessary skills you need as a translator that your career is almost over before it begins.”
(Baker 1992: 3)

Why is translation theory necessary in the training of the specialised translator?
In full agreement with Mona Baker and Paul Kussmaul the general view put forward in the present paper is that while intuition is a great advantage to have if one is lucky enough and practical experience is necessary to achieve a professional status, to benefit from a well rounded and comprehensive training, it is crucial that the future translator acquires a specific type of knowledge which draws on translation theory.

In the next part of the paper we shall attempt to explain the reasons why the trainee translator needs to be exposed to such a theoretical knowledge. To do so let us first examine the profile of the students who enroll on a course designed to train specialist translators. The profile will by no means be exhaustive. It will look at types of students who are most likely to attend such a program.

The first type of students who may join such a course are graduates with a first degree or equivalent undergraduate qualification in translation and who want to specialise in the field. Such students will form only a small proportion of the overall numbers, unless the institution has its own undergraduate program in translation which means that a number of the students graduating from this program may decide to choose to read for a postgraduate course in the same field. This type of students should already be acquainted with translation as a process and should have a fair knowledge of translation theory.

The second cohort of students likely to join the course would be those with a first degree or equivalent undergraduate qualification in the field s/he wants to specialise in as a translator, such as law, economics, politics etc. Here again the numbers are likely to be small. And although the students will have a good knowledge of the subject field in question and its terminology, they are not expected to have much knowledge in translation.

The third type of students who may be interested in a formal training as specialist translators are professional translators or practitioners with practical experience in a specific field of specialism and working as freelance or as in-house translators in translation agency. The students in this case may have joined the course to 'formalise' their practical experience with a recognised degree. Such a decision is usually prompted by the fact that it is the policy for most translation agencies, nowadays, to require a postgraduate degree in translation from anyone applying for a translating post. The other reason could be that the translators want to improve their knowledge in the field of specialised translation or specialise after having worked for sometime as non-specialist translators.

This cohort of students are usually well acquainted with translation as an activity as well as with their areas of specialism. Their knowledge of translation theory will however vary depending on the importance given by each of them to the acquisition of such a knowledge through reading.

Finally the last group, which in this case constitutes the majority of the students on the course, will be graduates, with a first degree or equivalent undergraduate qualification in modern languages, usually combining two or three languages one of which is the mother language. These students are likely to have varying degrees of competence and linguistic knowledge of both their mother language and other languages. They may have attended a unit on translation in the final year of their undergraduate program and may therefore have some basic knowledge in translation and, depending on the syllabus, some notions on translation theory.

Looking back at the profile of the four types of students most likely to join a course training specialist translators, we may safely assume that apart from the students with a first degree in translation and some translation practitioners, the rest will have little or no knowledge of translation theory. This means that when they first join the course, most of the students will be unaware of notions on translation as basic as:

- what the translation process involves,
- the crucial notion of equivalence,
- the different translation types or methods,
- the types of problems likely to arise in the translation process,
- the translation strategies available to solve those translation problems,
- the metalanguage used to discuss translation issues or to explain or justify a choice or a decision made while translating,
- the different translation models.

The questions to ask ourselves at this point are (1) whether filling these gaps in the knowledge of the future translators is important, (2) whether such knowledge can be provided by intuition or/and practical experience and (3) if not, where to get it from and (4) what are the implications of acquiring such a knowledge?

The above mentioned notions are fundamental and elementary concepts every translator should acquire during her/his training whether specialising or not. Indeed, the student translator training to specialise should, like any other translator, be familiar with these basic notions before engaging in a more specific training. The future specialist translator should know what the translation process involves, how faithful can one be to the source text, what options and restrictions exist in translating, how to solve translation problems etc, applied to translating general texts first, before learning how to recognise the characteristics of specialised texts, how to deal with them in transfer, and what procedures and methods are applied to translate such texts. In other words, a basic theoretical training for translators should always precede any attempt to further specialise.

Intuition by its very nature will simply give the trainee translator a mere "feeling" that a decision or a choice is right or wrong. It will be of no help in providing the trainee translator with this theoretical knowledge. The practical training, on the other hand, may teach the future translator, if guided, how to draw his/her conclusions on the translation process through reflecting on the work done after each translation. This may be time consuming but the ability to do so will build up as the translator gathers experience. However, there is no guarantee, that the translator will be able to cover, through reflecting on the translations done alone, all the necessary knowledge needed even after a lifetime experience in translating. The translator without a theoretical training, if aware of its importance, will have to make a special effort through reading to keep abreast of new trends and approaches in translation.

Fundamental theoretical notions on translation can be and have been included, under different names in the curriculum of several programs training specialist translators. The aspiring translators are required to attend a compulsory theoretical module/unit at the beginning of their training alongside practical translation classes and before other more specialised modules. This module/unit should include the following components:

- an introduction to what translation is,
- an insight into what the translation process involves,
- a detailed description of the stages in the translation process (source-text analysis, transfer, revision, etc),
- the different translation types and methods and an analysis of their advantages and disadvantages / their suitability or unsuitability,
- a clear idea of translation at different levels of the text (word, above-word, sentence and text) and a review of the potential problems which may arise, the reasons for their occurrence and the possible solutions that could be applied.

This theoretical component, like its practical counterpart in the course cannot turn instantly novices into professional translators nor can it change a mediocre translator into a good one. It will, however, fill the gaps in the trainee's knowledge by allowing a better understanding of the translation process and will, as Robert Larose explains, teach the trainee the principles which will guide his choices during the translation process (Larose *Meta* 30 (4): 406).

Let us now be more specific and find what sort of knowledge can this theoretical component provides:

Awareness is the key word when it comes to the role played by the theoretical component in training the translator. It is an appropriate word because it presupposes the existence, as it seems to be the case with the trainee translator, of a latent knowledge, of which the trainee may be unaware and which may have been acquired from the trainee's work with languages and translation in his/her undergraduate years or practical experience as a translator. Awareness in this case comes as a result of a reasoned effort of reflection triggered by the newly acquired theoretical knowledge.

Alison Beeby (1996) describes this awareness as an awareness "of text types, strategies for approaching a SLT and for reformulating a TLT, awareness of the priorities and restrictions of every translation situation which will justify one set of strategies or another." (Beeby 1996: 305). Mona Baker (1990) uses 'understanding' to describe this awareness. She seems to fully agree with Beeby when she affirms that "what the trainee translators need is an understanding of the complexity of the process they undertake when they translate, the options available to them in the real world for dealing with common translation problems, the strategies they can make use of, and the implications of using certain strategies in certain contexts." (Baker 1990: 168).

The theoretical knowledge should enable the student to acquire an understanding of the nature of translation, what the translation process involves, its complexity, and its stages. It should also give the trainee translator an insight into the crucial notion of equivalence and its relativity and that of loss, its inevitability and its consequences.

Awareness of what source text analysis is about should be another type of knowledge the future translator will acquire. The knowledge that processing the SLT is not only to understand its meaning but to prepare the text for transfer as well. The theoretical component in the training should make the translator aware of the existing strategies set up for maximum understanding of the source text.

The trainee translator should, as he accumulates such knowledge, become acquainted with the different translation types and methods (word-for-word, literal, free, semantic, communicative, pragmatic). S/he should be made to understand the characteristics of each and recognise their suitability/unsuitability to certain text-types and contexts.

The future translator is to be made to see that equivalence is to be established at all levels of the text i.e., equivalence at word and sentential level as well as textual and pragmatic level. The translator should also learn that while the search for equivalence is under way, an eye should always be kept on the intention of the source-text producer, the text register, the text-type, the context, the target-text readership, and last but not least the target language rules and norms.

The trainee translator can, thanks to theoretical knowledge, become aware of the translation problems likely to arise in both source text analysis and transfer. S/he is also to be made aware of the reasons for their occurrence and should become able to recognise the strategies available to tackle them and thus to achieve equivalence.

Finally, theoretical knowledge can teach the translator how to talk about translation, describe translation phenomena, explain and justify the decisions and choices made, using appropriate meta-language.

It is crucial to add at this point that acquiring this theoretical knowledge essential as it is will not be of much use to the trainee translator if the student is not given the opportunity to test it and apply it in practical classes.

With the student's profiles before they embarked on the course in mind, let us now look at what the inclusion of the theoretical component in the curriculum will achieve. "Awareness breeds self-confidence" maintains Paul Kussmaul (1995: 32). Indeed, the knowledge mentioned above once acquired not only fills the loopholes existing in the trainee profile but develops his/her self-confidence as a result of such an acquisition.

Confidence in his/her ability to understand the source text intention and to convey it in the target text through a successful transfer. Confidence in his/her decisions and choices which will gradually rely less on intuition and more on concrete and well established knowledge, confidence to reflect on their experience after each translation and draw conclusion that can be used as future reference and, finally, confidence to produce, in time, translations that meet professional criteria.

To answer the question asked earlier as to whether this theoretical knowledge is necessary, we can, after the review of the loopholes in the trainee, safely affirm that such a knowledge is indeed crucial to the future translator. Its acquisition is not only advantageous but should be compulsory as well, as it lies at the basis of any training for translators. The translator should never go without it in his/her training whether or not s/he plans to specialise and no matter what his/her area of specialism will be. And given the importance, now obvious, of the theoretical component in translator training one should also stress the undeniable wide gape created in the training of the translator and caused by the unfortunate decision to overlook translation theory in the curriculum adopted by a large number of programs training translators.

Let us finish by saying that a good translator may be born with an intuitive ability to choose the 'right' equivalent. S/he may be capable to develop such a gift and fine tuning it with practice. It remains, however, that without the input of a theoretical component, the translator will be deprived of a source of reference which is both crucial and invaluable.

References

Baker, Mona. 1992. *In Other Words*. London: Routledge.

Dollerup, Cay & Loddegaard, Anne. (eds.) 1992. *Teaching Translation and Interpreting: Training, Talent and Experience*. Amsterdam/Philadelphia: John Benjamins Publishing Company.

Gile, Daniel. 1995. *Basic Concepts and Models for Interpreters and Translators Training*. Amsterdam/Philadelphia: John Benjamins Publishing Company.

Kusmaull, Paul. 1995. *Training The Translator*. Amsterdam/Philadelphia: John Benjamins Publishing Company.

Nida, Eugene. 1981. "Translators Are Born and Not Made" *The Bible Translator* 32 (4): 401-405.

Robinson, Douglas. 1997. *Becoming A Translator*. London: Routledge.

Wilss, Wolfram. 1996. *Language and Skill in Translator Behavior*. Amsterdam/Philadelphia: John Benjamins Publishing Company.

La 'compréhension' du texte technique

Hugo Marquant, Institut Libre Marie Haps, Bruxelles

Abstract

The 'understanding' of a technical text

Answering the question 'How can a linguistic translator understand a specialised technical text?' (using the principle that you have to understand in order to translate) requires two considerations which are objective (a set of contents) and structural (articulated) before eventually leading to a series of terminologico-textual elements such as reading, documentation, notions, specialised discourse, equivalences and other components of the 'translator's technical culture'. Moreover, the problem of understanding is not only a problem of definition, but may especially be a problem of training. How to train a translator capable of understanding a highly specialized and professional technical text? Is specific training or general training needed? Is a specialised translator or a translating specialist required? Finally, understanding a technical text falls within the perimetres of studying specialised languages (technolects). What are the links between the text and its field? How can we incorporate technical writing? In conclusion, the specialised translator is above all an unconscious technician, a 'virtual' (passive?) specialist, a terminologist heedful of the complete adequacy of his discourse to the realities they represent.

En partant du double principe qu'il faut comprendre pour traduire et que toute compréhension suppose une connaissance ou une information préalable, l'on peut se poser raisonnablement la question de savoir si le traducteur technique (= le traducteur de textes ou de produits techniques) doit être avant tout un spécialiste objectif ayant des connaissances linguistiques de haut niveau ou plutôt un linguiste de formation, spécialisé dans l'un ou l'autre domaine ou sous-domaine du savoir technique.

La réponse passe nécessairement par le concept de la compréhension du texte ou du produit à traduire. En d'autres mots, comment définir quantitativement et qualitativement la 'compréhension'? Quels sont les paramètres objectifs et structurels de sa définition? Quel est le lien entre ses composantes et les (sous)-activités de l'action traductive? Et surtout, comment la situer par rapport à un modèle cognitif (et pédagogique) de référence (et d'inspiration)?

Textualisation et technicité

Un premier élément de réponse se trouve dans la dynamique objective de toute hiérarchie abstractive. D'une part, nous avons un ensemble de procédures et de méthodes de textualisation progressive (notion - notion-terme - terme - phraséologie - texte) où, par exemple, l'élément notion-terme constitue une entité purement méthodologique et où la phraséologie peut se définir aussi bien en termes très stricts (comme terme composé) qu'en termes d'extension discursive (le discours technique). D'autre part, nous avons un deuxième axe qui est celui de la technicité et qui repose, en fait, sur un ensemble de données de plus en plus spécialisées. Le schéma obtenu (figure 1) constitue ainsi un véritable prototype qui, par rapport au domaine cognitif (objectif) en général, remplit la même fonction que pour le texte et son contenu : celui d'interface de hiérarchisation.

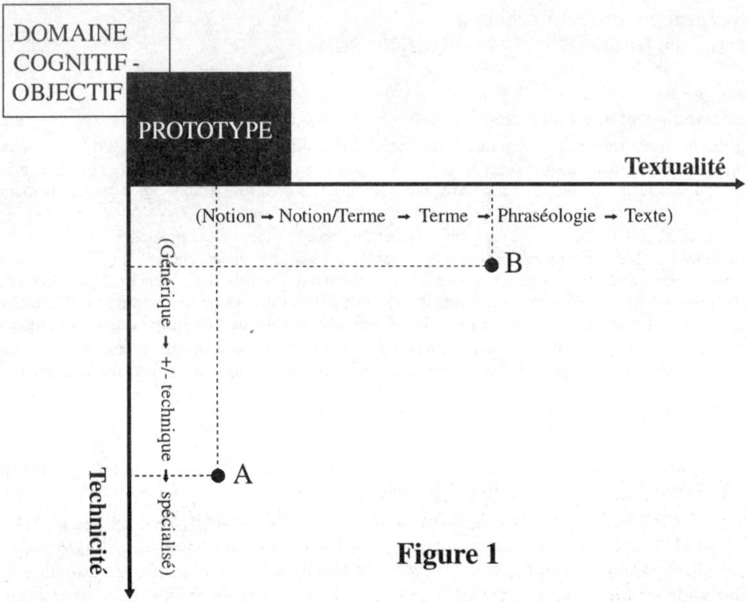

Figure 1

Prototypage et compréhension

Le prototypage implique l'identité fondamentale (définitoire) de la compréhension spécialisée et de la connaissance générale et se prête parfaitement à toute description incrémentale où les connaissances spécifiques sont obtenues par raffinement progressif de connaissances génériques. La banalisation et la vulgarisation techniques ne sont en quelque sorte que les aspects extérieurs d'une dynamique de connaissances par défaut et d'un ensemble d'informations incomplètes. Il s'agit également de la part objective implicite qui sous-tend toute compréhension textuelle.

Sur le plan des contenus, le contact avec le prototype ne résout pas nécessairement tous les problèmes de la compréhension (= identification). Le degré de ressemblance entre un individu et son prototype est parfois difficile à estimer. Il faut donc d'abord examiner la description de l'individu puis celle du prototype.

En revanche, le prototypage rend parfaitement le concept de technicité en tant que dynamique de spécialisation progressive basée sur des critères d'explicitation (par exemple, abréviation vs terme complet; références, virtualité), de proximité (par exemple, une nouveauté par rapport à son prédécesseur) et de complétude (les 'exceptions'), organisés selon le principe mathématique de l'inclusion.

Contextualité et spécialisation

Le schéma proposé met également en évidence l'importance de la notion de contextualité (contenus + texte). A l'intersection fonctionnelle et à différents degrés de deux axes de notre figure de référence (figure 1) se retrouvent des points de repère (A, B) qui constituent la véritable contextualité d'une valeur textuelle et technique donnée. La mesure quantitative de ces points de repère demanderait une étude exhaustive de tous les paramètres tant textuels que techniques qui interviennent dans la double progression méthodologique. Pour l'instant, nous ne disposons que d'études partielles et d'applications approximatives.

Terminologie et processus de traduction

La bivalence du modèle théorique se retrouve également au niveau des différentes activités constitutives de l'action traductive. Que ce soit en sa qualité de documentaliste, de rédacteur, de terminologue, d'expert objectif ou linguiste, le traducteur est constamment confronté à cette double articulation qui est celle, déjà mentionnée, de signifiant et signifié, de méthode et de donnée, de domaine et de discours, de fonctionnalité pragmatique et linguistique. En ce sens, la terminologie constitue peut-être un des accès (outil, méthode) et éléments (contenu) les plus caractéristiques de la compréhension technique: elle réunit, tout comme la traduction, notion et dénomination; son articulation est celle du domaine qu'elle incarne; en fait, elle symbolise la synthèse et l'intersection de la traduction technique en tant que spécialité objective et activité discursive (figure 2).

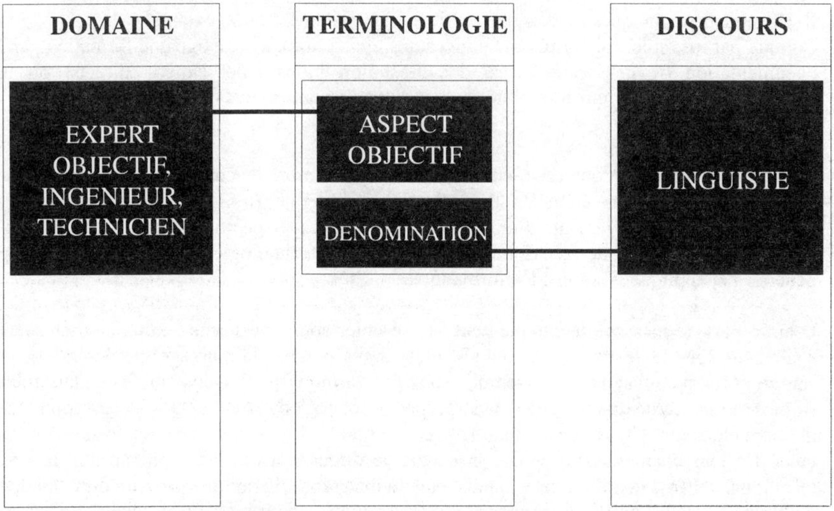

Figure 2

L'ingénieur utilise la terminologie pour documenter ses équivalents linguistiques tandis que le linguiste a besoin de la terminologie pour comprendre la dimension pragmatique de sa traduction. De là aussi la valeur pédagogique exemplaire de la terminologie. La rédaction du schéma notionnel constitue un exercice traductologique particulièrement riche. En même temps définitoire et formelle, sa structure (et l'effort de structuration sous-jacent) est une excellente entrée en matière pour la compréhension et la formalisation des ensembles terminologiques.

D'autre part, il est intéressant de remarquer que la traduction se situe à l'intersection des deux actes objectif et textuel. Ceci permet d'apporter un deuxième élément à notre question de départ. Par rapport au binôme expert linguistique / expert objectif, la traduction technique constitue une activité tout à fait spécifique caractérisée tant par le volet contenus que par le volet discours technique. Du point de vue de la traduction, la question de base devrait ainsi se compléter par un deuxième volet parallèle: comment un linguiste / expert objectif peut-il comprendre / traduire en langue le message dans sa formulation originale? En d'autres mots, comment le traducteur technique peut-il faire son travail ?

Traducteurs spécialisés ou experts linguistes?

Comme il s'agit d'une activité spécifique, il faut prévoir également une (auto)-formation spécifique. En réalité, nous pourrions même aller jusqu'à dire qu'il s'agit bel et bien d'un problème de formation avant tout. Et dans le cas du non expert objectif, d'une formation à la connaissance (dans le cas du non expert linguiste, il s'agit plutôt d'une formation LSP) axée sur la technicité du message. Le concept de formation recouvre aussi bien la formation académique que l'(auto)-formation par la documentation (notamment sur le terrain ou la lecture du texte à traduire) et son but est précisément de permettre la compréhension de tous les éléments constitutifs du message technique.

Il y a cependant quelques aspects qui requièrent un traitement quasi exclusif.
Comme par exemple, l'apparition de nouveautés, qui, à notre avis, exige une formation par la documentation (revues spécialisées, documentation industrielle, experts directs) ou les technologies générales qui font plutôt l'objet d'une formation plus classique (surtout si on la veut à but actif).

Le message technique comprend, en effet, un certain nombre de composantes cognitives qui sont les suivantes: les éléments de technologie générale (mécanique, électrotechnique, hydraulique, ...), les éléments d'une technologie appliquée spécifique (la fabrication d'une carte-mère PC) et l'interface industrielle. Certaines technologies sont en même temps générales et appliquées comme l'informatique.

D'autre part, le message technique peut se présenter sous une forme textuelle stricte, mais également sous la forme de 'textualités' plus larges comme le message graphique, visuel, sonore et même physique (par exemple, sous une forme virtuelle). Il s'agit, en fait, d'autres formes de la contextualité citée dans le paragraphe <u>Contextualité et spécialisation</u>. Ces derniers éléments relèvent également de la connaissance des technolectes représentés.sur leur étude (et leur connaissance) repose la deuxième dimension de la compréhension du texte technique, celle de la notion devenue discours (à différence du premier axe, qui est celui de la notion en spécialisation). Et ici encore nous retrouvons la terminologie systématique comme outil définitoire, méthodologique, textuel et pédagogique. En effet, la terminologie permet :
- de définir les notions en termes de compréhension cognitive,
- de structurer les informations en connaissances,
- de construire et d'interpréter les (con)textualités,
- d'organiser toute démarche d'initiation, d'abstraction et de spécialisation.

Elle constitue ainsi la base de la compréhension du texte ou du produit technique.

Culture technique et traduction spécialisée

Le concept qui répond le mieux aux exigences méthodologiques et cognitives de la compréhension du message technique est celui de la culture technique. Celle-ci peut être générale dans la mesure où elle permet de résoudre toutes les 'virtualités' du message, mais elle est souvent très spécifique et orientée en fonction d'un intérêt ou d'une curiosité bien ciblée.

D'autre part, elle n'est pas nécessairement active. On pourrait définir en quelque sorte la compréhension (minimale et suffisante) du message technique comme une connaissance passive du domaine où l'intéressé comprend mais n'est pas capable de traduire cette compréhension en initiatives concrètes (par exemple, de réparation, d'entretien ou d'installation) sur le terrain. Bien sûr, il comprend le message dans son intégralité (éléments génériques et spécifiques, éléments explicites et virtuels et tous les messages du domaine), mais sa connaissance n'est ni une méta-connaissance (progression du savoir en tant que tel) ni une base opérationnelle. Très souvent assisté par une documentation adéquate aussi bien systématique que ponctuelle, le traducteur (puisque c'est de lui qu'il s'agit) n'a aucun problème à appliquer le principe 'qu'il faut comprendre pour traduire'. Au niveau de la culture technique on retrouve donc les technologies générales et l'interface industrielle, mais aussi la ou les technologies d'application (actualisées) concernées plus spécialement par la traduction. Il s'agit d'une véritable culture du domaine basée sur un savoir spécifique (de référence ou explicite) et un contact privilégié (de nature psychologique, documentaire ou intellectuel).

En conclusion, le traducteur technique est un technicien potentiel, un spécialiste qui s'ignore. Bien sûr, sur le plan de la textualité, il excelle plutôt naturellement (= par définition, par formation et par expérience). Sur le plan des contenus techniques, sa culture générale et ses efforts de documentation spécifique font de lui un véritable spécialiste de la compréhension du message technique sous toutes ses formes.

Postgraduate translation courses, a marketing approach

Geneviève Parkes, University of Portsmouth

Abstract

This paper examines the changing role and function of translation teaching in Britain. Disillusionment with the use of translation as a language teaching tool led to a reduction in its use, if not its abandonment. Now, however, translation is increasingly treated as a vocational discipline in its own right, taught predominantly by linguisticians and experienced commercial translators, rather than by generalists. Machine translation, use of IT and consultation with professional translators all form part of courses in a number of institutions. Nevertheless, the precise relationship between conceptual and linguistic knowledge often remains undefined. The core of this paper is a quantitative survey of translation teaching in British Universities and other such institutions, showing what is taught and where.

In a forum which gathers translators, translation teachers, and linguists, the main subject of interest is both obvious and elusive. Practitioners meet in order to share their ideas on what they consider best practice. Can translation be taught in a useful manner? Should it? Would it not be terrible to find out that we, teachers of translation, are employed in communicating a redundant skill?

Translation, like interpreting, is now taught in a different way than it used to be. In order to illustrate these changes, I intend to use examples from British universities with reference to France as a comparison. Because education, especially in Britain, where government subsidies have fallen in parallel with a growth in the number of students, is now seen as another product or service, where value for money is the key to survival, it is more important than ever to look at what we are 'selling'. How can we make sure that we offer the training that is needed? Who has the definitive answer as far as stating what this need is? Traditionally, the concept of marketing was seen as incompatible with the idea of education, double-glazing after all has little to do with development of the mind. Now all universities (hospitals, charities and many Churches too) have a marketing department. What it is or should be about is trying to match courses to needs. In the case of a translation course, it is important that we know who the end user is. In the case of a product or service called a translation course, the compound customer is the student, but also the parents, the subsidising official body or bodies, the translation professional employers such as agencies, and the global translation market, with its growing or changing needs.

Whilst the end user of our translation courses is not identified as the same by all who teach or train, the ambiguity is far more marked when one considers the product or service itself. Because global communication is calling for communicability, structuring of knowledge has taken place in many disciplines which were hitherto considered as art or at best as a set of techniques. Now, translation, or translation studies (more clearly so when you use the French term *traductologie*), like sports science, nursing or even cultural awareness for business all have their own well established theoretical foundations.

Looking at courses currently offered in Britain, I shall seek answers to the relevance of the local offer. Two of my colleagues, Begona Rodriguez and Caterina Jeffcote will then offer possible pathways in methodology for what we consider to be the 'missing link' between theory teaching and professional needs.

This is all about trying to reconcile paradoxes: when, as an aspiring professional translator, you need to offer experience to a prospective employer, you are also asked to produce formal qualifications. When, as is their role, colleges and universities are offering more abstract, theoretical and scientific courses, they also at the same time need to show evidence of vocational status. Lecturers by definition are not usually full-time translators - although many publish commercial translations. Translators do not often have didactic experience. Also, in order to give future translators some training in what they are likely to be faced with, we need to vary genres; but could this dilution be detrimental if we think 'transferable skills'? Or it could be that we are talking about eating our cake and keeping it too?

Translation as a p.c. or a non p.c. concept

Most of us have been taught our second language by translation from Lesson One. We are conditioned. Translation is a basic language teaching device without a name, translation with an ulterior motive. The first sentence I was made to utter in English was an in-class translation of "*Il y a une mouche sur le couteau*"; nothing to do with anti-hygienic propaganda or the wonder of parallel written surface structure between French and English. We were being introduced to the English phonetic system. I similarly had to translate from Russian that there was a cow on the road, but only to be able to marvel at the absence of the verb 'to be' in the SL. The Communicative Approach did not kill translation classes, but it drove them underground. They became part of a mix used in language teaching by generalist language teachers, sometimes tacitly disguised as grammar or comparative stylistics classes by stubborn believers in their benefits as a language-teaching tool. Looking at examination papers for O and A levels, *Brevet* and *Baccalauréat* in the 70s and 80s, there was little or no translation theory taught with it, but translation was often part of the language syllabus and assessment. Adequate resourcing in British universities until the early 90s allowed for innovation, oral competence based approaches (students were often taught in small groups), and translation surviving in the curriculum was more often than not a sign of tradition vs modernism. In France, because of 'mass education' policies, foreign language at university has to be taught in large groups, and in most if not all language departments, prose and translation still constitute the basic diet of language teaching. Specialist academic Translation Institutes were rare and trained relatively few high-calibre translators. In daily life, some businesses and organisations, including international ferry terminals, still consider the competent translation of official documents, manuals, or signs as an unnecessary source of spending. Non native students on placements, secretaries or anybody having spent a holiday in the country of the TL are apparently being asked to perform the tasks, to the hilarity of their foreign customers, if not their satisfaction.[1]

Now, the tide has turned. Translation in British universities is taught as a scientific subject, by linguisticians, theorists, and occasionally by practitioners. Translation is taught both as language and as a vocational skill. In France, there has been a progressive and subtle change, a widening of the range of aspects of translation taught (students now have practice in various genres - not just literature, but also press translation, or economic/financial translation). In Britain, however, there has been a more radical reversal of approach. Translation no longer has to be taught with the vague disapproval of progressive colleagues or External Examiners. It has come out of the closet. Professional translators make contributions as guest lecturers on translation courses. There is a fertile corpus of research in translation theory, but also more normative advice on teaching translation and training translators (El-Shiyab 1996). Views tend to spread between text-based approaches, usually describing abstract theories that must

[1] Recently, a large poster on display at the Portsmouth Ferry Terminal offered the following translation in large letters for 'Safe Sea Travel': '*Voyages en mer sûrs*' For further edification, inspect the written notices in French in the rest rooms.

be applied, and student-based approaches which prescribe intensive training without theory teaching (Maréschal 1989). Interestingly, since Erasmus student mobility has fostered awareness of other European models amongst language students in particular, comparison of translation teaching vs expectations has emerged concerning France and Britain. I conducted a open-question survey in June 1999, based on one group of contemporaries in their final year of undergraduate courses with French at the University of Portsmouth, which established the following[1]: French students on general Applied Languages (LEA) or traditional language degrees in French universities are better theoreticians than their British counterparts, they have all been taught translation for a considerable amount of hours (because translation teaching starts in year 1, because training for the *CAPES* and *Agrégation concours*, which is selection by capacity for abstraction, has included translation from the beginning, and theoretical concepts are taught together with practice, and because the average French student invariably has to repeat a year or two of his/her studies, hereby providing him/her with double exposure). Yet, because all of them have a similar training and they have also been conditioned to see translation classes as language training rather than translation training, few think of themselves worthy of a career as translators. Mass education has had perverse effects: few French universities offer hands-on training in machine translation as part of the curriculum, for example, as the number of computers is minimal (at the time of writing, November 1999). British students have less translation teaching as part of the general language curriculum and master fewer theoretical concepts: the adoption of the communicative approach which supplanted the introduction of grammatical concepts for language teaching had a snowball effect: grammatical description was no longer used as a teaching vector, therefore, not being in current use, could not be exploited for other purposes. The early decline of Latin and Greek in mainstream secondary schools also contributed to the lack of exposure to grammar concepts. Conversely, translation is taught as Translation more often than in France, and practical elements are offered, such as

- working with translation Internet resources, machine translation courses, corpus building as learning and assessment tools,
- work placements in translation agencies as part of the Year Abroad ECTS,
- supervision of a variety of translation-based undergraduate dissertations, individual tutorials as translation assessment feedback,
- contacts organised with working translators,
- not forgetting teaching with smaller groups (typically under 20 students in Britain vs over 40 in France at undergraduate level).

British students are therefore more likely to think of translation as a possible career, since most 'practical aspects' mentioned above are not part of the core language course and have to be actively selected. As we well know, British universities now have to be student-centred for survival, whereas French universities, even though numbers have started to fall on popular courses such as English, still have the upper hand and see demand exceed supply. They can therefore still concentrate on quality (as measured by the providers) rather than on user needs.

Specialised Translation post-graduate courses: student-centred or customer-centred?

With the growth in need for quality translation (globalisation, international business, international NGOs, the opening of Central and Eastern Europe and future EU enlargement in particular), Brussels is becoming the most important translation centre of the Western world,

[1] Survey done during the academic year 1998-1999 at the University of Portsmouth, on 73 undergraduate students of French: as part of their French language programme, final year students have to have individual or small group guided conversations each week with their **language partner**, who is usually a French exchange Erasmus student and they have to hand in a written 200 words report of the said conversations.

with more translation agencies, translation activity and translation professionals than anywhere else in Europe, a fact that is revealed or confirmed by opening the city's business directory, *Guide de GIDS 1999*, which lists 332 translators or translating agencies. British students still consider that university undergraduate and postgraduate degrees are worth having, not because everybody else has them too, but because they should help one find a career related to the subject studied[1]. Given that mostly, native speakers of British English will study in Britain, British universities are now responding to demand, and established postgraduate degree courses in Translation have been complemented by newer ones. In France, only Translation schools such as ESIT make the explicit claim that they train students for the translation professions. In Britain, the 23 universities offering postgraduate degrees in Translation all make this claim, with more or less conviction, in their current brochure. Here are a few of the excerpts found in current brochures:

> The MA programme offers an exciting development in the field of professional training of translators. (University of North London)

> The MA Translation provides scope for the practising or intending translator to gain a postgraduate qualification in translation. (Middlesex University)

> We take good language graduates from all over the world and help them to develop academic and vocational skills that will enable them to become professionals. (University of Salford)

> The programme will provide you with both the practical advanced translation skills necessary to compete for work as a professional translator, and the theoretical base ... (University of Leeds)

> As well as job opportunities in the translating profession, students will have open to them employment in branches of Government service ... (Heriot-Watt University)

> The MA [...] is a prized qualification. Its possession is evidence that you are qualified to work at the top of your chosen profession and should help you earn a higher salary. (University of Newcastle)

> The MA in Literary Translation is designed to provide an academic qualification for those intending to become (or who already are) professional translators. (UEA, Norwich)

> This programme is designed to meet the demands of commerce, industry, and public service for high-quality translation. (University of Kent)

> The course [...] is designed to enable graduate linguists to develop the skills of interpreting and translating to a professional level.(University of Bradford)

> The MA [...] aims to prepare linguists for careers as interpreters and/or translators. (University of Bath)

Since British universities have Career Offices which collect data on graduates' employment, one can estimate that claims are based on actual statistical evidence. But University courses are not yet products like cars or life insurance, and consumer groups do not examine and

---

[1] Portsmouth University Careers Office has established statistics concerning employment records which show a high number of graduates, including language graduates, find employment where the subject(s) they studied at a British university are relevant.

compare, nor have they (yet) sued an institution for misrepresentation about employability records. The way to know if courses match expectations include the now traditional combined methods of peer assessment (for example in a forum such as this one where teachers can compare and discuss their methods, as well as departmental staff seminars, discussion and exchanges), student feedback (through tutorials, end of session questionnaires and Boards of Studies) and comments made by overviewing bodies, such as colleagues at Unit Boards and Boards of Examiners or External Examiners.

Graduates in general have been suffering from the effects of unemployment, and obtaining a further qualification after their degree is seen as adding to the statistical probability of entering a study-related career. First Destination Statistics state that in the UK, 68.5% of graduates were employed within one year of their graduation[1]. A recent local survey indicated that about 54% of language graduate respondents were employed in posts closely relevant to their studies[2]. In countries where the number of graduates as a percentage of the population is already high, like France, the direct relationship between course and employment (except where very high skills or areas of professional shortage are involved) is not viewed with the same expectation and optimism.

* In effect, the provision of extra MA courses, in universities situated near enough to allow students with jobs or family commitments to combine their various occupations is clearly student-centred, allowing improved access.

* The fact that courses on offer provide a variety of emphases (e.g. translation with interpreting at Bath and Bradford Universities, preparation for translation research or special training in machine translation at UMIST, availability of lesser taught languages such as Greek at Portsmouth or Chinese at Newcastle Universities) is a clear message of market segmentation which also helps students select their preferred combination of options (whenever geographic mobility is not a problem).

* In addition, the vocational element, which must be one of the main selling points in postgraduate courses in Translation, is reflected in the fact that out of these 23 institutions offering postgraduate training in Translation, four offer MSc qualifications rather than (or as well as) MA or PgDiplomas, the 'proof' that translation studies can be and are increasingly regarded as science.

In marketing terms, the above (the provision of a number of translation courses, the details of which are available to prospective students by way of colour brochures or websites, the variety of options and approaches, the opportunity for student feedback) cover the main elements of what is known as the 'marketing mix': continuous quality control, product specification, distribution (or local availability), and communication (packaging).

One aspect is missing: price. The price of a commodity is the amount customers are prepared to pay (British people consider that £25 per night for a single hotel room is cheap. French people, who can have access to cheap hotel chains even in Paris, where three people can stay for less than £20, would not consider it cheap). Even with indirect governmental subsidies, registration costs for EU students are often seen as high. Not too high yet compared to

---

1 Figures provided by the Careers Office at the University of Portsmouth for the year 1998-1999

2 Association of Graduate Recruiters Survey, 2000 (KPMG/UCAS), figure obtained by adding different categories of occupations and weighting them.

product benefits, such as employability, but we should think of short-term and long-term competition which are going to make certain courses less attractive to students:

* Even if British students have the specific advantage of being native speakers of English (which protects them from competition from non-native speakers for translation work into English), British courses recruit students of other first languages who necessarily have a wider geographical understanding of study location. Erasmus student exchanges, as well as temporary Erasmus teaching exchanges between partner institutions in Europe will certainly contribute to raising the level of awareness - of their competence and their shortcomings - ensuring that European students outside Britain become better prepared as competitors.

* Also, native English speakers are lecturers in institutes, translation schools and universities in other EU countries and the market is not a national one. Secondary aspects such as the cost of living and affordable accommodation will also be decisive factors for mobile students. 'Our' students might therefore choose to study abroad in future.

* For those who are not, or who prefer not to be, Internet courses and other distance-learning packages from new-comers (on a national or international scale, such as courses available from the USA) have already advertised their services.

* In addition, translation and interpreting services are now managed and sold by a large number of firms with experience, contacts and ideas. The 'buddying' or shadowing service is offered by some of them as a personal apprenticeship which will give aspiring translators practical experience in a given field, genre, or in a range of activities.

* It is also worth noting that many organisations - the International Institute of Hospital Engineering for one - now prefer to employ experts in specialised fields who have a sound command of one or more foreign languages even if they have no formal translation training (Haggett 1997).

Conclusion: the need to redefine the emphasis

This is not to say that translation courses in British universities are doomed because they are slowly becoming redundant. They already have evolved from being text-centred, concentrating primarily on translation theory, linguistics, problems of translation, to becoming student-centred, with better access (more local courses, more variety, more languages covered), better opportunities (part-time studies, placements), better quality-control and responsiveness to student criticism and constructive suggestions (such as offering training in accountancy and other professional aspects of translation). In the long term, there is a need to look at global work opportunities, global communication, as well as dark corners. The documentation is already being processed and signed for EU enlargement for example, yet neither Hungarian or Polish are listed anywhere among the working languages available in a single University in Britain. Courses must move to the next step, the third one if one considers that the first generation of courses were text-centered. They will have to change their emphasis from student-centred to translator-centred: not just the student on a course, but the future working translator within the student. This is the perspective chosen for the following survey.

There is not one single end user of courses available on the market, but a composite end user. The student constitutes a large proportion of this multi-entity, because it is the student who is attending classes, having to pay living expenses, receiving marks, then applying for jobs, but there are other elements to be included too. MA/MSc courses of the future need everything : an excellent theoretical framework, numerous practice opportunities, intellectual rigour and adaptability, stability, predictability and innovation. They need to react to competition by looking out and offering new attractive features, new tools: *le beurre et l'argent du beurre*.

References

Maréschal, G. *Repérage d'unités terminologiques dans le contexte de l'enseignement de la traduction spécialisée*, Meta, 1989, 34 (3): 377-80.
Haggett, G. *Translation Today*, The Linguist, 1997, 36 (6): 168-6.
El-Shiyab, S. *The importance of teaching translation theory,* Babel, 1996, 3: 166-73.
University of Bath, *Student Prospectus, 1999-2000*
University of Bradford, *Student Prospectus, 1999-2000*
Heriot-Watt University, *Student Prospectus 1999-2000*
University of Kent, *Student Prospectus 1999-2000*
University of Leeds, *Student Prospectus 1999-2000*
Middlesex University, *Student Prospectus 1999-2000*
University of Newcastle, *Student Prospectus 1999-2000*
University of North London, *Student Prospectus 1999-2000*
UEA Norwich, *Student Prospectus 1999-2000*
University of Salford, *Student Prospectus 1999-2000*
BELGACOM, *Le Guide de GIDS,* 1999 (1742)
Careers Office Publications, University of Portsmouth, *First destination Statistics,* Portsmouth,1999
Association of Graduate Recruiters, CUS in association with KPMG/UCAS, London, 2000

Two practical techniques for teaching specialised translation to non-specialist students

Begoña Rodríguez de Céspedes and Caterina Jeffcote, University of Portsmouth

Abstract

This paper presents a task-based approach to teaching specialised translation on an MA Translation Studies course without specialised knowledge units. It features classroom procedures for approaching a given type of text. In the first instance, the use of pre-translation exercises, often disregarded in conventional specialised courses will be advocated. A methodology based on the functional approach and *skopos* model whereby texts are not analysed in isolation but within a situation and a given context will be considered in regard to the translation of instruction manuals from Spanish into English and English into Spanish. Bottom-up/top-down procedures are designed to develop a full understanding of the text and its relationship to its context, and modelled on the best practice of professional translators.

The second part of this paper presents an approach to the translation of economic texts from English into Greek and vice versa, assuming no specialist knowledge of economics. The examination of terminology in and out of context, the use of parallel texts in the SL and especially in the TL, and the compilation and use of extensive glossaries are evaluated. Bearing in mind that most MA courses last only one year and allow little time for the development of a wide range of specialist knowledge, these exercises are designed to enable budding translators to develop confident and effective strategies for tackling specialist texts despite having insufficient conceptual knowledge of the field from which they are drawn.

Introduction

This paper outlines two practical, task-based classroom techniques for the teaching of specialised translation. The first technique stresses the importance of using pre-translation exercises before students attempt the actual translation. It is based on a specialised translation workshop where students translate from both Spanish into English and vice versa. The second technique examines the use of terminology in and out of context in an attempt to familiarise students with specialist economic texts. The source language in this second example is English and the target language is Greek.

Using pre-translation exercises and parallel texts in the translation of instruction manuals

The suggested methodology of this technique is based on the *skopos* model and functionalist approach[1] whereby texts are analysed not in isolation but within, and for, a given situation or context and for a specific purpose. Whereas the basis of the functionalist model is the notion of equivalence between texts, the *skopostheorie* underlines the importance of the purpose of texts. Both approaches have received support since they were first propounded by Reiss (1977) and Vermeer (1978) (members of what is known as the 'German School').

According to *skopostheorie*, the purpose of a translation is dependent on the expectations, knowledge, norms and values of target readers influenced by situations and culture. ST analysis and translation criticism are considered to be fundamental exercises in the training of translators. These are part of what might be called pre-translation stages whose main purpose is to compare both ST and TT in order to highlight both common and differing characteristics before the student attempts a translation. Normally, the use of parallel texts proves very

---

[1] Functionalism: In translator training, a methodological approach where the translator's decisions are governed by the intended function of the target text or any of its parts. The most important theory on which functionalism is based is the *skopostheorie* developed by Vermeer in 1978. Nord (1997: 138)

practical in the search for target text conventions, that is, equivalents in each of the cultures under analysis.

The first part of this approach uses procedures to analyse and translate a given type of text- in this case instruction manuals.

Why use manuals and instruction booklets in a translation class?

* It is a good starting point for the trainee translator because the texts are not highly specialised.

* Manuals are consumer-oriented texts that students come across in real life, such as household appliance manuals. Hence students are familiarised with this type of language.

* They share the same communicative function, that is, instructions addressed to the consumer on how to use a given product.

* Manuals are often multilingual, and normally a given ST is translated into different TTs so they present the same reality to different contexts and cultures. However, some readerships might know more about the product in the manual than others. For example, a kettle is a common appliance in every British household but not in Spanish ones.

* One problem that manuals illustrate very well is that when texts are presented through inadequate translations the reader can tell if the SL text is the 'real' ST or a generated one. In the latter case, the expectations, values and norms of the target reader are not 'respected', either because the translation was undertaken by a non-native speaker or, in the case of some STs, because they were not linguists or specialists. It is often the case that whilst all texts in a manual seem equal at first glance yet one can usually spot the ST because one or more of the TTs does not work idiomatically.

The peculiarity of these types of texts is attractive to the translation teacher. As Trosborg (1994: 25) notes "It can be said about the translation of technical brochures that it is far from being a mere transcoding process, but ... a cross-cultural event" and that "Industrial translators must produce texts that seem so natural (in fact), that translations are indistinguishable from originals." (67). Relatively few translations of brochures and manuals meet this demand.

Pre-translation exercises

It is often difficult to present these issues to the translation student who has had no contact with specialised translation, or indeed, no practise of translation at all.
Producing samples of Spanish and English texts on the same page and from the same manual enables the 'parallel' comparison of both ST and TT. Parallel because the texts have the same function and same graphic format but different cultural conventions. Below an example of a text carrying these characteristics.

Ceramic hob manual

OLLAS Y CONSEJOS	POTS AND TIPS
Utilizar sólo ollas y sartenes con fondo plano, fuerte y lo más grueso posible.	Use only pots and pans with even, firm **bases as thick as possible.**
Esto se aplica en especial al cocinado con elevadas temperaturas (por ejemplo, al freir).	This applies particularly for cooking at high temperatures (e.g. deep frying).
Los fondos desiguales alargan el tiempo de cocción y aumentan el consumo de energía.	Uneven bases lengthen the cooking time and increase the energy consumption.
Las ollas no han de ser **tampoco** más pequeñas que los quemadores.	
!Poner siempre las tapas y cerrar!	**Pots should not the lid and close!**
Al cocinar sin tapa o con tapa desplazada, se desperdicia la mayor parte de la energía.	Cooking **without or with** shifted lid wastes the most energy.
Evite el **cocinado en vacío** con ollas esmaltadas. Al hacer eso, los fondos pueden estropearse y al moverlos rayan la superficie de la cocina. Igualmente producen rozamiento los fondos de las ollas y sartenes con rebordes y aristas.	Avoid any **empty cooking** with enamel pots. The bottoms may be damaged and can cause scratches on the hob top when being moved. Bottoms of pots and pans with rims and edges can also have abrasive effect. Pay attention that no hard or pointed objects - e.g. spice-bottles - fall onto the hob top. It can be damaged.
Los **granos de arena**, por ejemplo de las **tarteras**, también pueden **producir rayas.**	**Grains of sand** – e.g. from cleaning vegetables- may be the cause of scratches.
!Atención! No poner objetos inflamables (sprays) o **cosas** que puedan arder debajo de la encimera.	Caution! Do not put inflammable objects (sprays) **or things** which can burn **under the hob top.**

(Extracted from BALAY's ceramic hob instructions manual).

Since the classes involved in this case study included both Spanish and English students working into both languages, each contingent is asked to analyse their L1 text first, before discussing what the main characteristics of both texts are. Successful and unsuccessful translations are also analysed. The text above is an example of the latter.

Both top-down and bottom-up exercises are used at this stage as with any other type of text. Examples of top-down exercises are intralingual and gist translation whereby students either paraphrase the content of the text in their own words, or summarise it in their mother tongue. These activities serve a purpose, that is to gain an overall understanding of the ST. Another top-down exercise that is used in class is the production of what is known in functionalist terms as translation brief, or macro-analysis i.e. what is the communicative purpose of the text? What are the extratextual characteristics? Who is the target audience? What is the purpose/motive of the text? What will be the time and place of text reception and medium?

Bottom-up exercises include the analysis of the source text in specific areas, known as intratextual analysis or micro-analysis, such as: standard format, paragraphing, punctuation, register, syntax, lexis, style. The pedagogical aim here is for the student to infer the characteristics of a given source text. This is where the production of a corpus of parallel texts (or indeed different samples of TTs) is very useful since the student becomes familiarised with both genre and style.

After a linguistic and contextual analysis has taken place, criticisms of both SL texts and TL texts are carried out. The purpose of these activities is to make the student aware of all linguistic and extralinguistic factors to bear in mind when attempting a transfer from one culture to another.

Instruction manuals are excellent tools for this type of pre-translation analyses because one can readily see and compare the pitfalls of a bad translation. They raise the following key questions for translators:

1. Has the TT been translated from a given ST, and then into a third language?

2. Is it a genuine ST? Or, indeed, a genuine TT? Does it sound correctly in Spanish/English?

3. Is it a successful/unsuccessful ST/TT? i.e. Do both texts share the same communicative purpose and conditions to be regarded as a good translation?

The use of such exercises is an effective way of training the future translator. Students develop instincts from texts and contexts. They do not feel daunted by the text because they are not asked to produce a translation straight away and their confidence increases as they exploit the features and purpose of the ST. Another advantage of these exercises is that by looking at poor translations, the student, as a future translator, is made aware of both good and bad translation practice.

Teaching the translation of specialised economic texts to non-specialist students

This second technique was developed for the teaching of economic translation from Greek into English, to Greek students who have never studied economics. The student profiles, the types of text used for this purpose and the methodology used for teaching translation of this type, namely, the use of economic theory derived from specific terms in the text, are looked at. In addition, the use of terminology in and out of context are noted in terms of encouraging students to make their own very extensive terminological glossaries. Finally, the problem of untranslatability is given particular attention in an attempt to highlight a very common problem for specialist translators.

Students who decide to undertake a postgraduate course in Translation studies are usually from varied academic backgrounds. They are usually language students with a clear interest in developing particular skills that will enable them to exploit their linguistic knowledge in a more concrete manner. In some countries, and Greece is certainly one of them, there is a clear distinction between students who complete a Higher Education course in certain scientific disciplines such as medicine, engineering, computer studies, economics etc., and those who decide to study languages. The difference lies in the fact that, once in the job market, the former group of students very rarely decide to exploit their specialist knowledge by translating specialised texts of their discipline. They usually opt to work in an industry directly related with their course of studies, in most cases, after having completed a postgraduate course that offers them further specialisation within the discipline. At this stage it should be noted that Greek students very often study one or more languages in parallel with their university degree, as foreign languages are often considered a prerequisite for future employment.

On the other hand, language students, once they have completed their first degree, are faced with a dilemma. They can become part of a long government list which will allow them to be absorbed by secondary education institutions in which they can teach the language they have studied (in ten or in some cases twenty years time!) or they can embark in the search for alternative employment hoping that they can employ the linguistic skills they have acquired during their four years of study. This is when a postgraduate qualification in a specialised linguistic discipline becomes imperative. Whilst literary translation is, in most courses, routinely taught at undergraduate level as a means of language learning, no other type of translation is undertaken in class as it is often regarded as irrelevant for the purpose of the particular course. Furthermore, the Greek job market is more than saturated with literary translators (in many cases self-appointed ones) who accept to translate fiction for a very low price. Needless to say, the quality of this work is, more often than not, questionable.

As a result of the above, students wishing to find a particular niche in the languages market, find themselves studying specialised translation, in the hope of acquiring sufficient extra-linguistic knowledge in at least two fields which should enable them to confidently tackle texts of a very specialist nature. As most British full-time MA taught courses in translation span one academic year, the following questions should be given particular consideration:

1. Is a year enough for students to become specialist translators?

2. Can specialised translation be taught to non-specialist students?

3. Should these students be granted a qualification of this weight, merely on the basis of 'familiarisation' with the subject?

Classroom strategies

This approach was used when teaching economic translation from English into Greek and utilised one type of journalistic economic texts, specifically, texts taken from *The Economist* magazine. The reason for which *The Economist* was chosen is because the purely economic texts in it offer themselves for their expressive language and therefore render the task of translating them more challenging as well as more satisfying. However, the type of expressive language used in these texts is not examined since the aims of this workshop are to focus on the way language for specific purposes, in this case economic terminology, is exploited to introduce students to various economic subjects, concepts and terms.

When language graduates first come into contact with an economic text of this type, they tend to exhibit various degrees of panic. The text is too specialised, too difficult to comprehend and certainly too difficult to convey. They are totally unfamiliar with some of the idiomatic language used and, even though native speakers can be of use to clarify such ambiguities in meaning, the terminology poses problems in itself in terms of decoding its meaning before encoding it in the target language. My response to such initial panic attacks is a slow desensitisation strategy.

Students are introduced to one main subject per text. In the following example it is unemployment:

> From Gloom to boom
> Europe's economies are booming more loudly than anyone had expected. But growth alone will not cure Europe's high unemployment and fiscal profligacy.
> (The Economist, December 24th 1994-January 6th 1995: 41).

Students are naturally puzzled with allusive titles. Once the particular allusion is explained, however and a first translation is attempted, focus is then directed to specific terms and their definitions as opposed to their translations only. For example:

* A period of economic boom is characterised by a rise in prices and an increase in employment. The synonym expansion is often encountered to express the same term. The students are asked to think of a possible translation of the latter.

* Similarly, a period of prosperity is characterised by an increase in output and consumption. These terms are also explained in simple terms.

At this point an opportunity is taken to discuss the various stages of an economic long-cycle, and the terms expansion, contraction, recession (gloom) and depression, which are part of such cycles, are explained. A brief discussion normally follows on the economic and social reasons why economic long cycles occur. The students are asked to reflect on the shape of economic long-cycles as well as their frequency and length (approximately every 50 years).

The aim of this slight deviation from traditional translation in-class techniques is to provide students with an understanding of economic theory before proceeding to translate words or sentences. Thus, by the end of each session, students increasingly acquire familiarity with their subject and are armed with transferable skills to research texts by virtue of their terminology.

At this stage, it would be important to mention that the texts used are not seen merely in respect of their terminology. As this is not literary translation the following techniques should be respected:

* Faithfulness: students are, at all times, advised to adhere to the source text. Although they are dealing with non-authoritative texts, for the purpose of the exercise and for the length of time they are in class, they should not deviate from the ST or feel that they are allowed to paraphrase. Translation theory literature is referred to and students are encouraged to become conscious of the techniques used to convey various units of translation.

* Succinct style: students are at all times encouraged to produce good writing. Long sentences are, where possible, avoided and so are their own neologisms and loan words. The purpose of the exercise is to train students to produce good prose and, as this type of text is considered to a certain degree technical, then rules governing technical writing should be adhered to. After all, what their work is aimed at is a clear, easy to comprehend communicative Target text.

* Collocations: students unfamiliar with texts of this type are often reluctant to translate that "a sector of production shrinks", or that "labour markets can be deregulated", or that "fiscal and monetary policies can be loosened" and tend to look for synonyms. Similarly

"economies recover", "exports boom" and "benefits are trimmed". Familiarity with such language and its appropriate translation leads students to acquire knowledge of the fact that specific translations of these rather strange expressions do exist and are some times identical in meaning to the English ones.

* Terminology : students learn that dictionaries are not always a reliable source of information for terminological solutions and that they should check terms in more than one sources and, if at all possible, with what translators call 'living dictionaries' in other words, experts.

All the foregoing is aimed at teaching students transferable skills that will enable them to translate a variety of texts. We should, however, pay particular attention to other aspects since terminology in context, and terminology out of context, should be considered in their own right.

Whilst terminology in context is used to highlight terms found in a particular text and translated in a particular way, terminology out of context is used to inform students on a different use of the same term, possibly with other qualifying adjectives or terms attached to it. In the foregoing example "Gloom to boom" the term unemployment is used and translated. The students are then asked how may types of unemployment they are aware of. They tend to find this question puzzling as they are usually aware of one type of unemployment only - the one where people don't have a job! Then it is explained to them that there are vary many types of unemployment but due to constraints in time, only eight types are going to be mentioned in class. The presentation is made in the form of a game whereby the students are presented with the term and are then asked to provide a possible solution in the target language and what they think that the term means. Definitions are subsequently provided and the students have a chance to make a note of them.

- Economic unemployment : where the workforce cannot be absorbed due to adverse conditions with the economy.

- Technological unemployment : due to technological developments such as automation

- Cyclical unemployment : due to cyclical variations of the economy. (By now students have a fairly good idea what an economic cycle is.)

- Frictional unemployment : is due to imperfect organisation of the labour market, excessive supply of labour or skills in one place, insufficient supply in another, non-systematic informing of interested parties for the existence of effective supply and demand.

- Hidden unemployment: occurs when the levels of unemployment are higher than thought. An example is given relating to the Greek economic situation whereby, people who are unemployed are not always registered as such, as they are often not entitled to benefits.

- Disguised unemployment: occurs when employees are not fully occupied, in other words, production could have been achieved with a lower number of employees. An example is again given of the Greek civil service, a part of the population that are particularly notorious for both the security of their positions and the inefficiency of their work.

- Seasonal unemployment: occurs when employment is reduced for a certain period of time due to seasonal circumstances. For example, the Greek tourist industry, where part of the population work for the summer months only, say from May to late October, and are registered unemployed for the rest of the year.

- Structural unemployment: due to the way the economy is structured in general, or, perhaps, to the imbalance between the skills supplied and those demanded. A very relevant example is given with the dearth of technical and economic translators in the Greek market and the abundant supply of literary translators.

The above examples demonstrate that although only the term unemployment was provided in the title and only structural unemployment is mentioned further on in the text (terminology in context), the other seven variations of the term may be found in different texts (terminology out of context). Thus students have, by now, become further familiarised with aspects of economic theory. However, this is not the sole aim of teaching economic translation in this way.

The idea that every translator should have their own terminological bank is generally acknowledged. Dictionaries and terminological databases do not always meet a translator's needs sufficiently. Furthermore, they may not always be readily accessible, or they may even be confusing with regard to the appropriateness of the terms provided. Consequently, students are encouraged from a very early stage to produce their own terminological glossaries and to make them as extensive as possible. They are encouraged to list the terms in columns and in alphabetical order with, or without, definitions, but certainly with the translation of the term listed at an opposite column. They are also encouraged to compare their glossaries with those made by fellow students, a practice which also helps them consolidate their knowledge of terms.

If students are to be examined in due course, they can easily and confidently refer to their own glossaries which act as time-saving devices and enrich their linguistic knowledge of the subject matter. These glossaries can at a later stage be enriched even further, with the addition of terms encountered in texts they may undertake as budding professional translators.

Problems of untranslatability

In the world of micro and macroeconomics there are more or less universal rules governing theoretical subjects and therefore equivalent terms in the Target Language are rarely a problem. In the area of finance, however, this is not the case. Non-equivalence is more likely the case than not, and students, as well as qualified professional translators are often faced with terms or even entire sentences that cannot be conveyed successfully in their mother tongue. This is because a specific term has never been translated before, or, the notion described by it simply does not exist in the target culture. Let us take a particular text as an example:

> <u>A New PEP Manager for the New Year?</u>
>
> Transferring your Pep can transform the performance you get, but investors need to be careful that they don't inadvertently fall foul of the Inland Revenue.
>
> Sometimes investors don't have a choice about moving their personal equity plans (Peps).
> (Extract taken from: *Investors Chronicle* 6 January 1995: 34)

The only culture-specific term that does not seem to be posing problems here is ' Inland Revenue'. Once it is explained to students that it is the equivalent of the Greek Tax Office, then a solution is worked out as to whether it should be transferred, or translated with a footnote.

The problem, however, lies with the key term of the text 'PEP'. Peps do not exist in Greece. They have certainly never been translated before as such, as methods of investing are entirely different and have traditionally consisted of government bonds and high interest deposit accounts. The purchase of shares, can be done either directly at the Athens Stock Exchange (a very popular institution with the Greeks) or through a financial advisor who tends to be independent. Asking Greek students to convey the term in their mother tongue, entails a lengthy preparation with regard to British personal investment traditions and culture. A parallel text may then be used to provide further details on Peps and the way they can be employed to finance potential long term needs of a household, including the purchase of a property. Additional information is also provided on the fact that Peps have now been phased out and substituted by ISAs.

On the whole, teaching economic translation to non-specialist students, whilst it can prove initially daunting, can ultimately a very rewarding task. Through the use of terminology in and out of context, students acquire a grounding in economic theory and a set of skills which they can employ later on in their careers as specialist translators. During the length of one academic year they continuously practice these skills and undertake similar tasks both at home and in the classroom. Eventually, they may decide to transfer this practice to other areas of expertise. As Verrinder put it,

> "Most freelance translators will spread their eggs around as many baskets as present themselves and are quite resigned to the fact that to achieve a reasonable standard of living from an almost endless flow of work, they have to commit themselves, body and soul, night and day, to as many as half a dozen work sources, together with that supreme prize, if they are exceptionally lucky, of being able to work direct for a private client, getting almost as much as the agency itself would."
> (Verrinder in Picken 1983: 33)

References

Brislin, Richard W. 1976. (ed.) *Translation: Applications and Research*. New York: Gardner Press.

Dollerup, Cay and Loddegaard, Anne. (eds.) 1992. *Teaching Translation and Interpreting: Training, Talent and Experience*. Philadelphia: John Benjamins.

Dollerup, Cay and Vibeke, Appel. (eds.) 1996. *Teaching Translation and Interpreting 3: New Horizons. Papers from the Third Language International Conference Elsinore, Denmark 9-11 June 1995*. Amsterdam: John Benjamins.

Gile, Daniel. 1995. Basic Concepts and Models for Interpreter and Translator Training. Amsterdam/Philadelphia: John Benjamins.

Kinsella, Valerie. (ed.) 1978. *Language Teaching and Linguistics: Surveys*. Cambridge: Cambridge University Press.

Kussmaul, Paul. 1995. *Training the translator*. Amsterdam/Philadelphia: John Benjamins.

Newmark, Peter. 1988. *A Textbook of Translation*. London: Prentice Hall.

Nord, Christiane. 1991. *Text analysis in Translation: Theory, Methodology and Didactic application of a model for Translation-Oriented Text Analysis*. Amsterdam: Rodopi.

Nord, Christiane. 1997.*Translating as a Purposeful Activity: Functionalist approaches explained.* Manchester: St.Jerome,
Picken, Catriona. (ed.) 1983. *The Translator's Handbook.* London: Aslib.
Picken, Catriona. (ed.) 1985. *Proceedings from the 6th Translating and the Computer Conference*. London: Aslib.
Toury, Gideon. 1995. *Descriptive Translation Studies and Beyond.* Amsterdam/Philadelphia: John Benjamins.
Trosborg, Anna. (ed.) 1997. *Text typology and Translation.* Amsterdam/Philadelphia: John Benjamins.
Wilss, Wolfram. 1996. *Knowledge and Skills in Translator Behaviour*.
Amsterdam/Philadelphia: John Benjamins.

Topic related and linguistic matter

Connotations in public and political discourse

Eve-Marie Aldridge, University of Portsmouth

Abstract

Translating oral language may at first seem slightly easier than translating written language, since the meaning of an oral message can be further conveyed and/or emphasized by accompanying extra-linguistic features such as accentuation, intonation, body language, physical environment, etc. However, when it comes to translating an address given at a contemporary political party conference, the specificity of the situation in the SL is so highly culturally-bound and anchored so deeply in the here and now of the social and historical context, that it usually causes the semantic value of words and expressions to cascade into affective and emotionaly charged lexemes and utterances within that culture. These cannot translate well in the TL where they may well hang in the air like some uprooted alien entities, since the TL audience will normally operate within a semiotic perspective where, given a portion of reality, it will apply different and sometimes contradictory filters to the SL. Hence connotations in the political discourse of a conference address are bound to develop into a cascade of meanings related to the social and economic climate of the time within the semiotic universe of that language, leaving the translator with the particularly hard task of having to translate both the text and its specific semiotic and pragmatic environment, and often make explicit the myth, in the sense that Barthes uses the term, which is being addressed.

The discourse of public and political bodies has been fairly extensively researched. According to their personal interest and political agenda, researchers have adopted different perspectives on the topic, from Van Dijk's pragmatic approach (Van Dijk, Teun A.1977), Austin's speech as action (Austin 1975), Searle's context and situation approach (Searle 1969), the social construction of reality through language and social interaction (Vigotski 1986), the marxist analysis of language (Calvet 1977), the lexicometric research (Lafon 1985), the contemporary CDA (critical discourse analysis) (Fairclough 1989), right up to the angry political oppositional stance (Raban 1989). However, only a few historical or political speeches have ever been translated: among those that have, Martin Luther King's "I have a Dream", comes to mind. Most of the thousands of speeches delivered everyday by politicians and officials are offered for immediate consumption to the audience to which they are addressed, and remain as ephemeral as the newspapers which may, or may not, report them. Most political speeches, such as the (US-American) Presidential Address to the Nation, tend to follow a set pattern. They can be sub-divided into a number of sub-genres, according to the occasion in which the speech is delivered and the audience to which it is addressed. Today, the study of public and political discourse still attracts much attention from linguists, sociolinguists, historians and communication experts. The interest is still not so much on what is said but on how it is said. The Annual Conference Address of the leaders of each of the three main British political parties, which are widely reported and analysed by the British media is one such sub-genre which I am looking at in this paper.

What are the specific features of a party political Conference Address? It is, for the leader of a political party, the ideal platform to review the progress made over the past twelve months, to praise what has been achieved, to send messages to foreign leaders abroad, to give some indication of the direction towards which they intend to veer their party. It is used to criticise all other parties, to rally their own troops - wooing the general public at home for votes when the conference season takes place near the time of a possible general election, and hopefully, help them achieve a not too distant political, social and/or economic goal. What is the specificity of this sub-genre? It is carefully written but delivered orally to the party faithful, from a carefully set stage. It is broadcast live on radio and television. It is an annual ritual. It is a one man/woman show: the only interaction from the audience is the applause, a "substitute mode of response", according to Gunarsson (Atkinson 1984), which punctuates parts of the speech.

The text of the address itself is heavily anchored in the contemporary political, social and historical context, and therefore connects extensively with many co-texts and co-references. It is peppered with jokes and puns at the expense of political and ideological opponents. It has many repetitive elements, assimilations and appropriations. It has to allude to the latest popular concerns of the day, whether these represent important national issues or not. It must seem genuine and passionate. It is a weapon to win support and to win votes. It is written in short punchy paragraphs, full of catch-phrases and journalistic 'sound-bites' which the media love. It is a key moment in the party's 'organisational culture' which helps to reinforce its corporate identity, and even at times, create a new one (Gunarsson 2000). Like praying, using proverbs and popular sayings or re-telling well-known jokes, it has a participative redundant function. It has been prepared for weeks by a whole team of co-writers and is often modified until within a few minutes, if not seconds, of its delivery. It is thus deeply culturally bound and its translation is very likely to pose problems on that score. In this article, I will be looking at some translation issues, namely humour, biblical references and narratives, from extracts drawn mostly from annual Conference Addresses which the leader of the Labour Party, Tony Blair (TB), delivered between 1994 and 1999.

Humourous remarks and jokes.

Talking in 1994, in his first speech as leader of the Labour Party, about what he considered a strange word from the mouth of a conservative minister who had attented the TUC Conference that same year, TB declared :

> Most absurd, 'full employment' was tried by daredevil David Hunt at the TUC.His reward - the most humiliating demotion imaginable: one day, counting the employed ... the next, he's counting traffic cones.

Let us try to render this in French:

> *Le plein emploi. Un terme tout à fait absurde dans la bouche d'un ministre conservateur. Et pourtant, en véritable casse-cou, c'est bien le terme que David Hunt a utilisé devant le TUC. Et rappelez-vous qu'il l'a payé bien cher: du jour au lendemain il s'est retrouvé à compter les cônes au bord de la route au lieu de compter les chômeurs. Une humiliation et un limogeage sans précédents.*

Not too much of a problem in this case, but this alerts us to the problem that some words and expressions may fall more naturally into an 'ideological' camp than in another. In his essay on W.B. Yeats, George Orwell (Orwell 1994) writes:

> One knows, for instance, that a Socialist would not write like Chesterton or a Tory imperialist like Bernard Shaw, though how one knows it is not easy to say.

Some words and expressions are 'owned' by a party, a religion, a fashion trend. If the opposite camp tries to borrow them, the attempt is usually frowned upon and/or ridiculed. This does not prevent words or expressions to 'shift' their meaning as part of a more general extension of certain types of discourse and semantic engineering, especially on the part of governments and ministers (Stubbs 1996).

Further on, talking in the same address about the Eurostar, and the failure of the Conservative government to provide adequate railway lines between Dover and London, TB declares:

> Now it's up and running ... trains speed through France at 185 miles per hour, through the tunnel at 85 miles per hour, and then go through Kent ... at 47 miles per hour.
> The French got the high-speed link. We got the slow coach link.
>
> *Maintenant il roule enfin. Il traverse la France à 300 km/heure, le Tunnel sous la Manche à 140 km/heure, puis le Kent ... à 75 km/heure.*
> *Les Français ont le TGV. Nous, nous n'avons qu'une vieille Micheline.*

The funny opposition (high-speed link/slow coach link) is somewhat lost in the translation, even if the main idea is retained: that the UK, which, in the past, has led the industrial revolution and been at the forefront of industrial development, did not manage, because of Mrs Thatcher's opposition to the scheme, to achieve what the French seem to have been able to achieve.

A bit further, we find:

> Michael Howard, the man in charge of prison catering. Last year he told the Tory conference he was building six tough new prisons.
> Butlins wouldn't win the contract, he said.
> He was right.
> The Savoy got it.
>
> *Michael Howard, celui qui s'occupe des cuisines dans les prisons. Il avait déclaré lors de la conférence du Parti Conservateur l'an dernier, qu'il allait construire six nouvelles prisons.*
> *Ce n'est certainement pas les camps de vacances Butlins qui obtiendront le contrat, avait-il déclaré.*
> *Il avait bien raison.*
> *C'est un hôtel de luxe cinq étoiles qui l'a obtenu.*

Here, the opposition between the fairly cheap family holiday camps Butlins and the top luxury hotel, the Savoy, is more difficult to transfer, as Butlins does not have an exact equivalent in France. The connotation which springs to mind when the cheap and cheerful holiday camps Butlins is mentionned and the resulting comparison between the new prisons and the luxury five star London hotel are somewhat lost. The derogative 'labelling' of Michael Howard as the chief caterer of prisons, rather than by his proper title, Home Secretary, is both impertinent and funny, and one has to be familiar with the political responsibilities of the persons mentionned in such speeches to fully appreciate this type of humour.

In his 1995 Conference Address, at a time when the popularity of the Conservative Party seemed at a very low ebb, making fun of senior Conservative MP's trying to find "safer" seats to be re-elected, TB said:

> But then again, what is a winnable Tory seat? Peter Lilley, MP for St Albans. Majority 16,000. Unsafe. Lilley on the chicken run to Hitchen and Harpenden. Tory chairman, Brian Mawhinne ... Majority 5,000. Unsafe. On the chicken run from Peterborough to Cambridgeshire. And Basildon man himself, David Amess ... on the chicken run to Southend.
> Why did the chicken cross the road? To get a safer seat.
>
> *Comment peut-on être candidat conservateur et sûr de son siège aujourd'hui? Même Peter Lilley à St Albans. Une majorité de 16.000 votes la dernière fois. Aujourd'hui, il se fait parachuter à Hitchen et Harpenden. Et Brian Mawhinney, lui-même, le numéro deux du parti conservateur. Une majorité de 5.000 votes à Peterborough aux dernières élections. Parachuté ailleurs. Et notre fameux David Amess, l'homme célèbre de Basildon. Parachuté à Southend.*
> *De quoi ont-ils donc tous si peur? Du verdict des électeurs.*

A 'chicken' does not have the same connotation in English and in French. The above translation does not render all the pejorative innuendos which the words "chicken" or 'chicken run', repeated four times in five lines, contain, nor the image of senior conservative MP's with huge majorities at the previous election, running around the country in all directions in order to secure a safer seat than the one they hold, in order to be re-elected. It does not indicate either that the towns where these MPs were formerly elected are normally rather safe conservative strongholds, implying that the usual conservative electorate is fast abandonning the Conservative Party. The familiar 'structure' of the joke: "Why did XXX do YYY?" is also very difficult to render in a funny way. We could think of something like: *"Quelle est la différence entre X et Y?"*. We could not use the term chicken (*un poulet*) as this would normally evoke a policeman in French. And, in the French imagery of La Fontaine's *Fables*, even those animals who end up beaten up, eaten up or come to a sore end are never depicted as natural cowards. We could attempt to use the image of *'poule mouillée'*, which implies a great degree of physical cowardness and much contempt in the value-judgement of the utterer. But this may lead the hearers to infer that it is the speaker who judges the conservatives to be so, not necessarily the electorate. We could also try to resort to familiar expressions of the type:

> *Comment/Pourquoi fait-on XXX dans/en YYY?* (For instance: *Comment fait-on entrer quatre éléphants dans une 2CV?*).

> *Pourquoi courent-ils dans tous les sens? Ils ont peur des électeurs.*

This is not quite as funny as the original quote but keeps the image of the conservative candidates running around the country to secure a safe seat.

The Biblical references The Biblical referencesThe Biblical referencesThe Biblical referencesThe Biblical references

One of the trade marks of Labour speeches in general, and Tony Blair is no exception, is the use of biblical and religious allusions. Mrs Thatcher, due to her Methodist up-bringing, also made wide use of biblical and religious references, but among the Conservative leaders, she was rather an exception.T.B. starts his 1995 speech with an allusion to Genesis where, after Cain killed his brother Abel, God asks him "Where is Abel thy brother?" To which Cain replies: "I know not. Am I my brother's keeper?".

In his address, T.B. turns this interrogation into a statement:

> I am my brother's keeper,

to imply that he is a caring person whom people can trust. This sentence poses quite a problem in French. Can we translate TB's quote by using the assertive form of the French translation of Genesis and say :

> *Je suis le gardien de mon frère.*

This would not mean much to a French-speaking audience who would probably not be familiar with the biblical reference. Such an audience would be more familiar with the Parable of the Good Samaritan and are more likely to use this expression to describe someone who shows compassion and is kind to someone in need, who physically and materially helps him/her and, above all, shares some of his possessions with that person. Furthermore, the word *gardien* is more likely to evoke a prison guard or a *'gardien de la paix'*, a policeman, which is not the way TB wants his audience to see him. What about :

> *Je suis/ serai le bon Samaritain.*?

That does not sound quite right either as TB never intends any 'personal' sharing. In fact, his brand of caring is more likely to make him point his brother in the direction of the nearest Charity Shop. This leads us to wonder what the exact meaning of that phrase in English means, and, if translation has to be faithful to the original, to what extent is it possible to translate the vagueness of the language which many politicians adopt?

If we attempt to translate it as,

> *Faites-moi confiance. Je suis un bon Chrétien*

this is more inclusive of the qualities which a good Samaritan displays, but it may sound rather strange to a French audience. There is an official divide in France beetween public life and religious practice, and laicity is the official position of the State. This, added to the revolutionary background of the socialist ideology of the Left, would not allow a French socialist audience to include the label "Christian" as part of its recognised lexicon. It would also probably be counter-productive and maybe even laughed at, since the Catholic Chuch hierarchy has often been (and to some extent, still is) associated with very conservative and reactionary attitudes, as it is generally perceived of approving, or at least happy with, an inegalitarian society, in other words, a position which is the exact opposite to the declared socialist ideoly. We are here confronted with a problem mentioned among others by Venuti (2000).

> Translation never communicates in an untroubled fashion because the translator negotiates the linguistic and cultural differences of the foreign text by reducing them and supplying another set of differences, basically domestic, drawn from the receiving language and culture to enable the foreign to be received here.

The problem we have here is, of course, that 'political parties' and political ideologies are very specific to any one country, and cannot be exported or 'translated' directly into a foreign environment. Although Labour is usually associated with the left of the political spectrum or with a socialist ideology, TB has, from the beginning, dissociated himself from 'socialism', even though the term does not carry the same revolutionary connotations in the UK as it does in most parts of the world. If used at all by TB, the word tends to be somewhat 'tamed', as indeed it is in that same address, where TB gives a personal definition of what he means by socialism:

> We aren't simply people set in isolation from each other, face to face with eternity, but members of the same family, community, the same human race. This is my socialism.

> *Nous ne sommes pas des individus seuls, isolés les uns des autres, face à l'éternité, mais nous appartenons à une même famille, à une même communauté, à la même race humaine. Voilà ce que j'entends par socialisme.*

The meaning of 'socialism' has been here localised and custom-designed to empty it of any of its historical, revolutionary, connotations and most politicians of most political parties could now safely adopt it if they wished.

The word 'eternity' is another example of the non-transferability of at least part of the meaning of a word to a foreign context: it would probably not only refer to the earthen part of someone's existence, but also include the after life, the final judgment, the day of reckoning, his/her 'eternal life' as a Christian. It is a subtle and quasi automatic way of linking civil society and religious life: the British sovereign is still temporal Head of the Chuch of England, and the link between the civil and religious authorities are centuries old and well established. Therefore the word does have some vague religious connotation attached to it which a French audience/social body, who considers *eternity* as a simple linear time expression, would not necessarily pick up.

Another biblical borrowing, this time to be found in the 1999 Address, is the meaning associated with the word 'free' and the recurring expression 'set the people free', and idea which both starts and ends this address. It is even expanded several times to "set your/the people's potential free". This expression would almost automatically remind a British audience of Exodus, of the long-drawn battle of will between Moses and Pharaoh, and of the hundreds of films, plays, songs and musicals which have been produced around this very popular story. In TB's address, it is New Labour who has to undertake this 'historic mission', liberate and set free the British from the "forces of conservatism":

> You know them, the old elites, establishments that have run our professions and our country too long. Who have kept women and black and Asian talent out of our top jobs and senior parts of Government and the Services. Who keep our bright inner city kids from our best universities. And who still think the House of Lords should be run by hereditary peers in the interest of the Tory Party.
>
> *Vous savez ceux dont je parle: les élites, les groupes qui contrôlent le pays et les professions libérales. Qui refusent systématiquement l'entrée des femmes, des Noirs, des Asiatiques dans les échelons supérieurs des Ministères et des Armées. Qui refusent l'entrée dans nos universités les plus prestigieuses des jeunes originaires des banlieues populaires. Et qui croient encore que tous les membres de la Chambre des Lords devraient être des pairs héréditaires et défendre les intérêts des Conservateurs.*

Getting rid of these awful forces of conservatism does indeed sound like a Herculean task, comparable to that of Moses getting the enslaved people of Israel out of Egypt. Until one remembers that with a majority of over one hundred MPs in Parliament, it shouldn't be too hard for any government to pass laws to remedy this sorry state of affairs, if one wished to do so, in order to drive its people into the Promised Land of milk and honey. In so far as the translator renders the information given in the original, s/he may feel satisfied with a surface translation of such a text. I believe, however, that, when translating public and political discourse, some comments can be made about the original text, in the same way as literary translators do at times explain differences between the source and the target cultures, enabling target audiences to better appreciate the original. This would be a way of situating the specific speech or text in a wider contemporary 'discourse'. It may well depend on the aim of the translation and who is interested in finding out who says what, when and how. But co-texts and co-references play an enormous part in politics. Leaving the translated text in this sphere without annotations can, in my opinion, be fairly misguiding.

Narratives and personal experiences

Short narratives are to be found in most contemporary British Conference Addresses, whatever the political party. They have different functions as illustrated below. In his 1999 Address, talking about the extreme views and attitudes of the Conservatives, TB says:

> Far right, far out.
> But not far enough for some. Like the letter I got last week from that bloke who said did I know the Tories had been listening to Britain. They can't have been listening too hard. They're still here.
>
> *Des idées extrémistes. D'un autre monde.*
> *Comme dans cette lettre que j'ai reçue la semaine dernière d'un électeur qui m'écrivait pour me demander si j'avais entendu dire que les Conservateurs étaient à l'écoute du pays: ils sont sûrement sourds, me disait-il, puisqu'ils sont encore ici!*

This short narrative is included as a proof that, with their extreme right-wing policies, both TB and the majority of the electorate, believe that the Conservatives should disappear once and for all. But the use of the word "bloke", a low register, popular, story-telling type of word, cannot be easily rendered in French by any of the words which would normally translate it: *type, gars, petit gars, brave type*, etc. The reason is that it is difficult to imagine a French Prime Minister or a French President, addressing formally his supporters, ever using this level of register. Only the most 'populist' politicians, at a lower echelon of the national political hierarchy, might. Nor does one imagine a French ordinary citizen writing to the PM or the President to share such a trivial comment, nor, if s/he did write, this comment being reported in such anectodal terms on such an occasion The recurring of these short narratives in most contemporary conference addresses is a good illustration of how the speakers build their identity and position themselves in relation to others (Wetherell 1987). Here it helps TB to prove that, as well as doing important things which a PM has to do, he is the one who takes time to listen to the ordinary man. He is the man in charge but also the man in touch. This again may be a cultural difference between a British and a French context: in the latter, politicians are supposed to keep in touch (it is indeed the main reason why they are elected), and they often do in fact keep in touch, whether they want it or not, as French politicians tend to accumulate several 'mandates' at local, regional, national and/or European level.

A bit further on in the same Address, TB gives another short narrative:

> My grandfather's generation was strong on values. Respect for people. Good manners. Horror of crime. But it was a generation also of deference and of prejudices: racial, sexual, social.
>
> *La génération de mon grand-père avait certaines valeurs: respect des individus, bonnes manières, respect de l'ordre établi. Mais c'était aussi une génération pleine de déférence pour l'ordre hiérarchique et imprégnée de préjugés raciaux, sexuels et sociaux.*

The function of this short narrative, apart from portraying TB as a 'family man' who can go back at least two generations (in a country where relatively few people keep in regular touch with their immediate family), is to offer him an occasion to proffer a value judgement on the changes in mentality and attitude which have swept across the country in such a short time. He is here constructing his identity as moral expert who knows what is best for the country and which values can be retained or changed. It is however doubtful if a French audience, or anybody looking at the rhethorical value of the text, would understand why having "good manners", which belong to the private sphere of people's life, hardly a matter of concern for a PM, should be perceived to be at the same level as "prejudices", which can have serious consequences on some parts of society. "Good manners" is also one of those very vague terms which can cover a multitude of sins. The whole narrative seems to be such a sweeping generalisation of what people used to be like in those days that it is hardly believable: a sort of effort to re-construct the social history of the period. Should "horror of crime" become - and really mean - "*peur du gendarme*" for instance? The expression "horror of crime" puts victims, perpetrators and the public at large in the same category and does not discriminate between them. Is it a gene that people possessed in those days which today's generations have lost? Furthermore, the literature, magazines and newspapers of the period TB is referring to, do not, on the whole, display either good manners, horror of crime and respect for people, as the staple diet of that generation.

So, the question here again is: should the translator 'fill in' some comments, if s/he feels that the text being translated might seem a bit odd to a target audience who would view the role and the function of PM in a different light, and whose view and perception of history/social history is greatly at variance from that of the original audience? This would of course depend on the aim and function of the translation, and the level of knowledge the intended target audience would have of British society. But once a translation has been produced, it may well be borrowed and used by a different target audience, and the discrepancy in knowledge of that audience may be wider, leading to a different interpretation of the original.

Conclusion

In the above examples, we have looked at some of the issues which translation of a sub-genre, the UK Conference Address, gives rise to. These issues turn around how best to translate those parts of a discourse which display embodiments of a culture, including narratives, jokes and the use of religious literature. The choice for the translator between formal, literal, equivalence, and dynamic equivalence, that is the relative equivalence of effect on the reader or listener, will normally depend on the final aim of the translation. Dynamic equivalence, or as Newmark (Newmark 1981) prefers to call it, the "semantic and communicative" translation attempts to render the exact contextual meaning of the original. All translations are communicative to a degree. The translator will have to consider each issue in terms of the degree of motivation of particular strategies, and judge which one to adopt to achieve the greatest adequacy for the task in hand (Goddard and Wierzbicka 1996).

The political address comes under the umbrella of the 'discourse of power'. It expresses ideologies which use a number of keywords, expressions, historical references. These are a recognisable feature of an often emotive and committed discourse. This discourse, based on emotion more often perhaps than on reason, can bring to the terms it uses and the ideas it evokes an important degree of semantic elasticity and distortion, as in the following passage of TB's 1999 Address:

> The forces of conservatism, allied to racism, are why one the heroes of the 20th Century, Martin Luther King, is dead.
> It's why another, Nelson Mendela, spent the best years of his life in a cell the size of a bed.
> And though the fact that Mandela is alive, free and became President, is a sign of the progress we have made …
>
> *Les forces du conservatisme, alliées au racisme, ont causé la mort d'un des plus grands héros du vingtième siècle, Martin Luther King.*
> *Ce sont ces mêmes forces qui ont été responsables de l'emprisonnement de Nelson Mandela, forcé de passer tant d'années de sa vie dans une cellule grande comme un mouchoir de poche.*
> *Et si M. Mandela est bien vivant, libre et aujourd'hui Président, c'est bien là la preuve du progrès que nous avons accompli…*

In this extract, the expression "the forces of conservatism" follow a long passage in which TB gives a very long list containing all the outdated attitudes and backwards policies which the Conservative Party has been guilty of over the past one hundred years: they held the nation back, they are prejudiced, they keep people down, they hold people back, they were against women's right to vote, against the creation of the NHS. Coming straight after these accusations, the expression "forces of conservatism" cannot but be taken for an exact synonym of the "Consevative Party" itself, infering that the party has been also responsible for Martin Luther King's death and Nelson Mandela's imprisonment.

This is not so much an extension of the meaning of the word "conservatism" as an example that signification in language is not restricted to discrete elements of that language nor to verbal language itself. It is constructed from a whole range of phenomena, including social structures, beliefs, historical and literary references, etc (Hattim and Mason 1990). Individual words move through a semiotic universe which gives them a slightly different signification every time they are used. Political discourse, with works within great emotive intertextuality, tends to stretch word meaning further maybe than other more rational types of discourse. The vagueness (or even absence) of the arguments presented and the vagueness of the lexicon used are intentional (leaders of political parties want to please and appeal to as many people as possible). Their success can be greater and easier perhaps in a two-party political system, such as found in the UK and the United States of America. In these countries, political discourse can rest on a fairly simplified Manichaen vision of the world ("I am right" versus "You are wrong", "I am the White Knight in shining armour" versus "You are the forces of evil", etc.). In countries where several political parties compete for power against each other, each one has to define more precisely its options, choices, strategies, in relation to each of the other political parties. As a consequence, would the discourse be as emotive, but the semantics, the lexicon and the rhethoric slightly less reductive?

References

Atkinson, M. (1984) *Our Masters' Voices*. London: Methuen.
Austin, John. (1975) *How to Do Things with Words*. London: Clarendon Press.
Calvet, J-L. (1977) Marxisme et Linguistique. Paris: Payot.
Fairclough, Norman. (1989) *Language and Power*. Harlow: Longman.
Goddard, C. and Wierzbicka, A. (1996) "Discourse and Culture". in Van Dijk, Teun. *Discourse as Social Interaction*. London: Sage
Gunarsson, Britt-Louise. (2000) "Discourse, Organizations and national cultures". In *Dicourse Studies,* 2,1. London: Sage Publications.
Hatim, Basil and Mason, Ian. (1990*) Discourse and the Translator*. London: Longman.
Lafon, P. et alt. (1985) "Lexicométrie et Associations Syntagmatiques: Analyse des segments répétés et des cooccurences appliquée à un corpus de textes syndicaux" in *Actes du Colloque 1983 de l'ALLC*. Paris: Slatkine-Champion.
Newmark, Peter. (1981) *Approaches to Translation*. Oxford: Pergamon.
Orwell, George. (1994) *The Penguin Essays of George Orwell.* London: Penguin.
Raban, Jonathan. (1989) *God, Man and Mrs Thatcher*. London: Chatto and Windus.
Searle, John R. (1969) *Speech Acts*. London: Cambridge University Press.
Stubbs, Michael. (1996) *Text and Corpus Analysis*. Oxford: Blackwell
Van Dijk, Teun A (1977) *Text and Context: Explorations in the Semantics and Pragmatics of Discourse*. London: Longman.
Vigotski, L. (1986) *Thought and Language.* Cambridge, MA: MIT Press
Venuti, Lawrence (2000) "Translation, Community, Utopia" in *The Translation Studies Reader*. London: Routledge.

Wetherell, Margaret. & alt. (1987) "Unequal Egalitarianism'" *in British Journal of Social Psychology*, 26 (1977) *Marxisme et Linguistique*. Paris: Payot.

The effects of cultural and culture bound language on political translation

Nicole Berry, University of North London

> Language has a setting [...] language does not exist apart from culture.
> (Katan 1999: 73)

Abstract

A culture is influenced by historical, political and sociological events. In the past two decades alone, the world has undergone radical reformation. The Soviet Union has been divided into separate countries, Germany has been re-unified, Yugoslavia has witnessed two major wars and as we approach the millennium, the United Kingdom is witnessing the devolution of Scotland and Wales, whilst paradoxically we move towards a United Europe. Events like these influence cultural behaviour and values, which subsequently influence language and the result is a wealth of new words and terms. For example, the creation of a centralised or Brussels-based Europe, has brought with it an entire lexical system of 'Eurospeak' and 'Euroterminology'. The Internet database, Eurodicautom is an example of how common linguistical ground is sought and of how Europe is being lexicalised.

Different cultures absorb different elements, and words and terms can therefore adopt new meanings. Every country has a different political environment and it is this cultural difference that causes translation problems in political translation. Politics and culture are inseparable and thus the languages of the two must inevitably merge. We shall attempt here to look at the inflence of this interdependence on the translation of political texts. In researching the effects of political language and values on the practices of translation (or intercultural transfer), several excerpts from French and English political texts will be taken as an example and any problems or points arising from these in terms of cultural language will be applied to the theoretical backdrop established in the first half of this research paper.

Introduction

The main aim of this paper, as its title suggests, is to explore the effects that cultural language has on the translation of political texts by applying practical issues of translation to a theoretical analysis of this research area. This will hopefully either prove or disprove the importance of cultural language in political translation and how cultural political language is. The area of cultural language with which this study is concerned is the lexical denotations and connotations of political language and how subsequently political language is affected by cultural differences. Syntactical and text-level problems will not be considered here.

The first part of the paper will discuss the notion of cultural language and the problems arising from this in translation generally. Then the aspect of political language will be discussed and any overlaps between English and French will be exposed. Once the theoretical framework has been established, issues arising from specific examples will be dealt with thematically and any correlation in results will be examined.

Cultural language versus culture-bound terminology and language

A distinction has been made between cultural lexis and culture-bound lexis. A culture-bound term or word is such that it is specific to only one of the two cultures in question, or has a specific meaning in one culture that differs from its meaning in another culture. For example, idioms, neologisms, eponyms and ideologies fit into this category. A political example could be *Thatcherism*. This eponym is culture-bound in that it is applicable to solely British politics. It is translatable through naturalisation. The suffix is made French and we are provided with the translation *Thatcherisme*. The basic formation of the term is unchanged but the meaning is much more value-laden in Britain. Cultural language on the other hand probably defines a large percentage of our everyday language – it is specific to our culture, and within our paraculture are the levels of diaculture and idioculture (Nord 1997: 24). That is to say that, for example, within the paraculture of England there are a multitude of sub-cultures (or diacultures). The following diagram illustrates this further:

Paraculture	**Diaculture (sub-culture)**	**Sub-sub culture**	*Idioculture*
England	Londoners Southerners Northerners	Westenders Eastenders	Mary Jones (an eastender)

If we apply this to the world of politics with which this paper is most concerned, the following results are produced:

Paraculture (a paraculture on its own or if seen in the wider scheme of things a diaculture)	**Diaculture**	**Sub-sub culture**	**Idioculture**
Political society	'New Labour' le PS (Parti Socialiste)	Blairists Backbenchers Les Jospinistes	Blair Jospin

On the broader scale of political society or England, although the language used is less specialised, it is cultural in that the individual creating the language belongs to a specific culture.

If two cultures are close together this perhaps makes it easier to translate. Thus translating between French and English may produce less cultural problems than translating between Arabic and English. David Katan talks of High Context Cultures and Low Context Cultures. The conclusion of his discussion is that High Context Cultures are far less accessible to 'outsiders' than a Low Context Culture. In a diagram showing his context ranking of cultures, he places Japanese and Arabic at the High Culture end, whilst English and French are juxtaposed in the middle. (1999: 183) However, in the boundaries of political translation between French and English, there are fundamental differences between both the political structures and mentalities of both countries. The French political system is closer structurally to that of America, than England and parties such as *'Le Front National'* have a more politically active role in France. These are just two examples of many.

All the literature used in research of cultural issues in translation agreed that the translator is a cultural mediator. There appear to be a range of definitions of culture, from that of the "functional correlation of different sign systems" (Hatim and Mason 1990: 105) to "objects, processes, institutions, customs, ideas particular to one group of people." (Newmark 1995)

The core idea is basically the same. The literature researched also converges on the link with culture specific language to translation problems. As stated earlier, cultural language is a part of almost any text produced. Christiane Nord supports this in her statement that:

> Cultural translation problems are a result of the differences in the norms and conventions guiding verbal and non-verbal behaviour in the two cultures involved.[...] they are present in almost every translation task [...]
> (1997: 66)

The exceptions may lie in structurally rigid texts such as declarations, where non-cultural technical terms far outweigh LGP (Language for General Purposes). An example of this can be seen in the following extract, taken from a European Parliament declaration:

> Implementation of Community-level measures for realization of the objectives of the White Paper on growth, competitiveness and employment [...].

Political Language

The next section will look at political language and any cross-language features that present themselves between political and cultural language. Perhaps the term 'politico-cultural' language could be used here, as out of the non-literary translation disciplines, law and politics is perhaps one of the most 'culture-bound', alongside media and the arts. Indeed an article appearing in the journal *Meta* (1990, n° 35) discussing issues of legal translation suggests that *"la traduction juridique est une traduction technique mais aussi culturelle; elle est scientifique mais aussi sociale."*

The term *juridique* could, in my view, equally be substituted by *politique* as political texts also create a juxtaposition of genres. We could perhaps refer to politics as a hybrid genre – containing elements of both literary and non-literary translation. Political texts are factual in content but sometimes literary in style. The following extract supports this notion and is taken from *Pouvoirs* (87: 1997), a French political journal article which investigates women and their link to democracy:

> *La démocratie tient sa force comme sa fragilité de ce qu'elle n'est pas un modèle figé. Lorsqu'elle ne se contente ni d'un simple mot d'ordre stratégique ni d'une simple table rase du passé, lorsque au nom d'une sorte de 'ferveur utopiste' elle prétend contribuer à l'indispensable 'invention' permanente de la démocratie [...].*

Clearly the discourse is political yet there are stylistic features of literary translation such as the idiomatic *une simple table rase du passé* which could be translated as *a clean sweep of the past*. However it would be wrong to make such generalised statements about political language. Some political texts possess qualities of technical translation and could not be considered as literary or cultural. Hatim and Mason (1990: 188) back this up with their view on the translation of certain political documents:

> Least modification seems to be called for in the translation of treaties, declarations, resolutions and other similar documents. These forms are not culture-bound.

An example of the above will be included in the next section of this paper which deals with practical issues of translation.

Political texts can not be linked to one specific genre or text typology and this is another problematic feature of political translation. This research paper will investigate the notions of cultural and culture-bound language in different text types and genres. The genres will include official documents, newspaper (broad sheets) articles, and journal articles. The latter can be broken down into the sub-genres of feminism, politico-economic and cold war. The majority of text types are a hybrid mix of argumentative and expository, whilst the official documents tend to be of an instructional typology (Basil and Hatim 1990: 154 –159).

Before moving on to look at specific texts I would like to consider political language a little further. An article appearing in *The Linguist* entitled "A Single Language for Europe" (1998: 162-167) made the following statement:

> Politics has played a major role in human languages since the beginning of time.

Is it any wonder therefore that political language possesses inherent aspects of a country's culture and ideological framework and as a result creates problematic cultural issues in translation? This leads onto the question of whether all political terminology is culture-bound and whether political terminology exists at all. Perhaps it would be more accurate to talk of value-laden words.

Terms according to Sagar, Dungworth and McDonald (1980), should be subject specific, monosemic, self-explanatory, and transparent. The meaning of a term should be independent of context. If we consider the abstract political term *democracy* and apply the above criterion we can see that *democracy* is subject specific. However, one cannot say that it is monosemic. Even within one culture such as England, there are so many diacultures that people's perception of what democracy is would not be the same. If we were to look at the medical term *myocardial infarction,* this can only have one meaning in any culture. The meaning of *democracy* is not necessarily independent of context as will be highlighted further on. Likewise if we consider the 'term' *fascism* a similar result is produced. However, Newmark in his book *About Translation* refers to *fascism* as a term. He does agree that it is culture-bound and says that he considers it to be "the messiest term in the entire world political vocabulary and the translator in certain contexts should try to resist its extravagant use by a narrower definition." (1991: 150)

If one was to accept that there is a case for political terminology then one would also have to accept that a political term has its own set of defining characteristics – namely: subject specific, polysemic in referential meaning (but with perhaps a general universal definition within one paraculture), ideologist and dependant upon context. What really makes it a term is the fact that if 'fascism' or 'democracy' were used in another discipline such as medical or scientific translation then it would be considered a subject external term. From here on this paper will refer to political terms.

The other question posed with regards to political language was whether all political terms and words are culture-bound. This paper has already made use of an example to refute this notion in the reference to treaties and official documentation which were considered to be non culture-bound. However if an official European document were to be translated into the language of a non-European culture it might be considered to be culture-bound. (However this begs the question as to whether this situation would ever arise). The literature researched seems to have conflicting opinions on this issue. For example, Peter Newmark suggests that political language is not all culture-bound but does contain a number of cultural deposits (1995). An example of how political terms can be culture-bound can be found in *Pragmatique du Discours Politique* (1994: 147). Different values associated with the term *communisme* with reference to supporters and non-supporters of the Italian Communist Party are considered. The same single term is associated with the following negative and positive meanings: *"synonyme du mal plus profond"*, *"synonyme de Léninisme"*, *"l'oppression"*, *"la foi enracinée dans l'histoire"*, and *"le rêve du cœur"*.

As stated earlier a number of examples taken from different text types and genres will be looked at to show the effects of culture-bound and cultural language in political translation. Once the effects have been shown, this paper will evaluate the results. The text will then look individually at the term *democracy* to show how connotations of this term differ in different text typologies within just two paracultures – France and England.

Lexical analysis

The lexical aspects that are particularly relevant to 'politico-cultural' language and that arose in the texts studied (even if only in limited numbers) are: collocations, neologisms (including eponyms), cultural equivalence, standardisation as a cultural threat, epistemology and lastly implicature of different terms in different cultures.

Collocation quite simply refers to the compatibility of words e.g. *law and order*. However this rather over simplifies and it is the deeper connotations of collocation with which this paper is most concerned i.e. culture-specific collocations. It is not uncommon for political language to contain a number of 'clichéd' connotations – for example we get used to hearing such terms as *democratic republic* – easily definable as a dictionary definition but this definition does not necessarily relate to reality. The media and politicians use collocates to avoid the 'real' truth at times and it is this aspect of collocation that can be culture-specific and affects the translation of political language. The translator must assume the role of cultural and political mediator. The text will now look at some specific examples which arose in translation practice.

Political language has many collocations, however they are not all cultural. The examples chosen for comment below are considered to be culturally laden but not culture-bound as they exist in both the source and target language cultures. However, their interpretation by different cultures could make them culture-bound. The first examples appears in a text which being linked to racist issues has political undertones. Discussing the possibility of a law to combat clandestine immigration, the collocation *en renforçant les contrôles d'identité* is used. For the author who is clearly in support of these controls this collocation has positive implications. For an immigrant struggling to become legal, this would seem negative. Similarly, the concept of political presence of Ankara in the Commonwealth of Independent States to which Russia is opposed, can have several connotations. Political presence can sometimes be masked under the guise of physical army presence, as in the contemporary Kosovan crisis. For Milosevic, 'political presence' is negative and for the refugees it is hopefully a means to an end. In political translation, the translator's target audience needs to be carefully considered.

This next paragraph will look at neologism as a cultural effect in political language. In Newmark's discussion of political language he comments that "political language is rich in neologism both ephemeral and permanent." (1991: 158) When does a permanent neologistic term loose this status and become accepted as a 'term'? For example Newmark makes reference to *Keynesians* and indeed we find the adjective *keynésien* used without explanation in French political texts. Perhaps this term is no longer a neologism and despite the derivation of the eponym from a British political economist, the meaning seems to be well known in Europe. This would make the term an issue of European culture and not of British culture.

A reference to *Gordon Brown* in translation may need the added 'Chancellor of the Exchequer' or the cultural equivalent. The reason for including this in a discussion of neologism is to draw attention to the verb 'to Gordon Brown it' which appeared in an article in the Guardian[1] and is synonymous for '*to dress down*'. This is to highlight the fact that political neologisms can create a problem culturally in translation. Another recent example could be *Blair's babies*.

One of the most interesting and problematic issues arising from the aspect of cultural language in political translation is the notion of 'culturemes'. This term is used by Christiane Nord and refers to

> a social phenomenon of a culture A that is regarded as relevant by the members of this culture and, when compared with a corresponding social phenomenon in a culture B, is found to be specific to culture A.
> (1997: 137)

The following are considered to be 'culturemes' but it could equally be argued that they should be included under the proceeding section on cultural equivalence. Let us for example take the French word *la banlieue*. The connotations inherent in this word are specific to the source language culture (French). There is a whole set of moral and cultural values that are associated with it, such as 'immigrant', 'racism', 'crime', 'poverty', 'lower class' etc. The word describes the area surrounding a city i.e. the suburbs. 'Suburbs' in the target culture (English) connotes 'middle – upper class', 'avenues', 'non-immigrant', 'desirable location', 'expensive property' and the list goes on. This should therefore be translated by a cultural equivalent such as 'council estate' or 'inner city'. However, it is felt that something of the target language culture is lost here and although English can provide an equivalent, *la banlieue* is considered to be quite specific to culture A. Viney and Darbelnet support this notion from a linguistic angle, by discussing the linguistic divergence of France and England in such concepts as *banlieusard*. They say that this has clashing social connotations with 'suburban'. (1995: 279)

The next term taken as an illustration is distinguished as a political term by its suffix 'cracy' (and '*cratie*' in French) and appears in a feminist text[2]. Gynaecocracy will be looked at as 'cultureme' from the point of view of the term being specific to culture A (Western culture) and referring to culture B (middle-eastern culture). The dictionary definition of gynaecocracy is "government by women or by a single woman" (Collins 1998: 690). I am not claiming to know the following to be true, merely voicing my personal expectations. This is not a particularly widespread term in French or English but nonetheless is not such an alien concept e.g. Thatcher's Britain. In certain mini-societies within a paraculture e.g. feminist groups this term could be applicable. However in a culture where women do not even have the right to vote, it would be surprising if this term exists, and if it does exist in a dictionary, it may lay dormant in its pages. As a political concept, it is 'alien' to culture B.

---

[1] *The Guardian*, Tuesday December 23rd 1997. The article states that in the November of this year, the verb '*to Gordon Brown it*' 'crept into English due to the fact that he had worn a lounge suit at the Mansion House'

[2] Pisier, Evelyne & Varikas, Eleni. 'Femmes, République et démocratie. L'autre dans la paire'. In *Pouvoirs*, 87: 1997.

Cultural equivalence is not necessarily a major translation problem, but nonetheless can distort the meaning of the source text on a lexical level. A few phrases taken in journalistic articles will illustrate this. From a simple transfer such as *élections législatives* to general elections (this due to the differences in the political structure of France and the United Kingdom) to White Paper which translates as *livre blanc*. The term shopfloor which is partially redundant now due to the effects of Thatcherism on trade unions in the eighties, or at least has lost some of its connotative meanings, not surprisingly has a cultural equivalent in France – where *syndicats* are still fairly militant. The emphasis in the French term *ouvriers* is on the group of people, whereas in English we refer to the place. This has subtle differences in meaning.

The introduction to this part of the thesis talked of standardisation of language as a 'cultural threat' and this is with particular reference to Europe. In theory, the more specialised a language is, for example the language of technology or the Latin based nomenclature system of medical language, the less cultural interference there is. As mentioned earlier, political discourse is one of the least specialised areas of translation in terms of terminology and is subsequently more culture-bound. However, the apparent need to standardise 'euro-terminology' and the language of European documentation eliminates certain cultural issues arising between Western cultures. However, non-European translators would still find cultural issues a fundamental problem. As this essay is most concerned with French and English, we can discuss standardisation as a 'cultural threat' in European political discourse. An article from *The Linguist* (1998: 154-159) embraces the idea of a Single Language to juxtapose the Single Market and the Single Currency, which in itself has enormous cultural implications. Hatim and Mason (1990: 11) suggest that

> In the field of translating for international organisation, for example, there have to be strict in-house rules for such matters as the names of sovereign states, variants of which inevitably reflect ideological attitudes.

In other words, any possible cultural interference needs to be 'neutralised' or 'ironed out' from the pre-translation stage. Recurrent instances of European language appearing in French political texts are *euro*, *mécanisme de change* and *déficit public* which are naturalised and grammatically altered to English but are basically identical. *Eurojargon* is a document by Anne Ramsay (1994) containing terminology, acronyms, and abbreviations concerning Europe – for example, the *PPE* (the European People's Party*)* and *V* (the Green Party of the European Parliament) are neologistic acronyms and show how a whole new language has evolved which is aiming to neutralise all European cultures into one 'supranational culture' (Nord 1997) – linguistically speaking.

Epistemological translation problems are a feature of any translation field – politics being no exception. Just to divert your attention back to an earlier citation from *The Linguist*

> politics has played a major role in human languages since the beginning of time.
> (1998: 154-159)

Political discourse therefore is considered to possess historical and cultural values which underlie words and terms. Political texts can contain examples of historically and culturally bound political references. Hence, the expression *au nom du principe fondateur* which is culturally more appropriate to France than to England as it has constitutional undertones. Similarly, in a discussion concerning the European common foreign and security policy, *regional round tables* are mentioned[1]. *Round tables* has historical, cultural and political undertones, namely, chivalry, honour, Arthurian, and 'mini democracy'. Although the story of King Arthur is generally known worldwide, the connotations of the expression may not be so evident and therefore perhaps an additional footnote could be added in translation.

The final linguistic grouping discussed here is implicature in political translation and its cultural implications. Two items will be considered here, the first being the term 'regime' and the compound matrimonial regime[2]. Peter Newmark is of the opinion that loan words adopt a negative meaning and says that *régime* in English and German has authoritarian tones, whereas it does not in French. (1991: 152) The implications of regime in England are 'military' 'discipline' and 'order'. In Spain the implications are perhaps even more negative e.g. Franco. In France there is no underlying surface meaning. The differences in meaning derive from cultural experiences and how the word has been manipulated by politicians or how it has been used as a label and then has retained this meaning. In their article, Evelyne Pisier and Eleni Varikas refer to a *régime matrimonial* which is used as an analogy to monarchic power and actually has a negative connotation as it refers to a man's right to 'govern' the family. Here *régime* has a negative meaning which highlights the fact that political terminology is connotative as opposed to denotative. Putting the terminological phrase *régime matrimonial* into the European database 'Eurodicautom', the English equivalent provided was "rights in property arising out of matrimonial relationship." That does not mean that this is a suitable translation, but that *régime* is not generally translated as regime in this context, but as rights or rules. However, due to the argumentative text typology and the open criticism of women's place in society at the time, perhaps regime would best convey the intentionality of the author.

Sensitivity to immigration issues can also be revealed through translation. For example, in the French press, the recurring link of *étrangers*, *récidivistes*, and *criminels* (which obviously become collective nouns referring to the same group of people) has implicit tones, but the use of punctuation is equally relevant. When journalists write any word connected with immigration and immigrants, they can use inverted commas, thus highlighting such phrases as '*appartenance raciale*', '*étranger*', *identité* '*réelle*'... This draws attention to the words and singles them out – a deliberate syntactical feature. As a translator into English in this era of political correctness, perhaps a decision would be made to remove this punctuation feature. Teun A. van Dijk in his essay on "Discourse, Power and Access" (1996: 92) discusses minority groups within political society and highlights different cultural attitudes towards political representation. The Netherlands seem to allow, albeit minimal rights to non-Dutch citizens having lived in the country for five years – a 'privilege' which he says is "fiercely opposed in [...] France and Germany." (1996: 92). He goes on to add that

> minorities are frequent topics of political talk and text, but this form of passive access is hardly controlled by them: they havevirtually no influence on this 'representation' in political discourse.
> (1996: 92)

Race is obviously a sensitive issue in translation – even within European cultures, conflicting opinions and attitudes exist. This aspect of political language has obvious cultural implications. We perhaps would all like to think that as a translator we could in some way

---

1 'Common Foreign and Security Policy', http://www.diplomatie.fr/frmonde/euro/eu25.gb.html

2 This is considered within the context of the abovementioned article, 'Femmes, République et démocratie', *op. cit.*

lessen the impact of racist discourse which is also a cultural issue. For example, Victor Chapple, a journalist for *The Sun* obviously felt (in 1989) that it was acceptable to write the following article about illegal immigrants which started with the title *Get Lost, Spongers*. His use of BLITZ in capital letters in the opening sentence as in "A BLITZ on illegal immigration is being launched by the Government" could perhaps be interpreted as a link back to World War Two discourse. (Caldas-Coulthard 1996: 96) Political racial discourse could be considered as an issue of 'idioculture' and not 'paraculture' as so many conflicting opinions exist.

The above paragraph leads nicely into this next aspect of cultural effects in political translation. Translation of medicine and computing could be considered to be fairly static in that new developments in both fields will obviously require frequent terminological updates, which having become part of the respective discourses will then remain in a 'vacuum of meaning'. However, whilst political discourse maintains the same ideologies, their meaning and appropriateness change from culture to culture, from decade to decade and maybe even from year to year. For example – *Labour* versus *New Labour*. It will be interesting to compare the meaning of *democracy* in different text genres, to show how the effects of cultural language on political translation are of fundamental importance. As a point of departure, this paper will give a dictionary definition of democracy:

1. government by the people or their elected representatives
2. the practice or spirit of social equality (Collins 1998: 417)

The uses of democracy in the source texts used for research do not conform to the above definitions.

Democracy is not denotative as a term as there are too many cultural undertones influencing its meaning. A brief reference was made earlier to the almost 'clichéd' collocation *democratic republic*. The feminist text mentined above[1] through its exploration of democratic trends in France, reveals democracy to be almost hypocritical, having one meaning in theory and another in practice. The authors of the text themselves, argue that republic and democracy are often misused terms, adding only confusion to their 'true' meaning. The cultural issue here arises in the argument that; if democracy had not been used to describe 'unequal', sometimes even totalitarian states, then perhaps there would not be such a diversity of ideological interpretations. It is almost ironic for a country to have been constitutionally named a 'democratic republic', when women did not have the vote or were not really considered as people in their own rights.

The article on "Common Foreign Policy and Security Policy" previously referred to states that one of the initiatives agreed on by member states (no doubt in a democratic meeting) is the "monitoring of and assistance for the democratic transition in South Africa." In this case the term is used, in contrast to the above examples, in a positive way – this will be a positive transition for South Africa. The cultural differences are huge. Those countries considered to be 'undemocratic' strive to become democracies and "democratic countries" struggle with its meaning.

Whilst 'democracy' would probably be translated as 'democracy' by most translators, it is important to be aware of cultural differences. If a translator is aware of cultural differences in a term then any implied information can be interpreted more clearly. One of the effects of

[1] Pisier, Evelyne & Varikas, Eleni. 'Femmes, République et démocratie', *op. cit.*

cultural and culture bound language in translation in general is that implicit information in the source culture often has to be made explicit in the target culture.

The aim of this paper consisted in proving or disproving the importance of cultural language in political translation. It may only have touched upon a vast theoretical area, but the following points are an interpretation of what I consider to the outcomes of the research to be:

* Loss of source language meaning – not necessarily due to bad translation, but to lack of cultural equivalence;

* Political terminology is connotative. The meaning of a term can change from culture to culture, from diaculture to diaculture and thus the translator needs to be aware of the target audience. What is implicit in the source language text may need to be explicit in the target language. Due to the connotative aspect of political language, a certain amount of sensitivity may be required in translation, especially in certain genres e.g. racial discourse;

* Due to the above and related translation problems, we begin to see the standardisation of terminology. For example, translation within the European Union can not be left 'open to interpretation'. However standardisation would only work in certain text typologies i.e. instructional and perhaps expository. In argumentative texts (many political texts can be classified here) this would prove to be impossible. It is the translation of argumentative texts that are most affected by cultural and culture-bound language.

Just between two European cultures, this paper has shown there to be some noticeable effects on the use of and the translation of political language. This study would benefit from further research into other associated areas. For example, it would be interesting to explore politico-cultural language in a non-European language and culture or perhaps make a closer study into the differences between French and English political culture and behaviour. It might also be thought that concentrating on just one effect would have been more concise. Yet, in provoking thought on the subject and showing the extent to which political language could be affected by cultural issues we hope to have opened the door to more stimulating ideas.

References

Baker, Mona. 1992. *In Other Words*, London: Routledge

Burton and Carlen. 1979. *Official Discourse*. London: Routledge

Van Dijk, Teun A. 1996. "Discourse, Power and Access". In Caldas-Coulthard, Carmen Rosa. *Texts and Practices*. London/New York: Routledge: 84-104.

Collins Dictionary. 1998. New York: Harper Collins.

Collins English Dictionary . 1998. 4th edition. New York: Harper Collins

Dallmayr, Fred. 1984. *Language and Politics.* Chicago: University of Notre Dame Press.

Guivarc'h, P and Fabre, C. 1989. *A Companion to Economic Translation,* Masson.

Hatim, Basil and Mason, Ian. 1990. *Discourse and the Translator*, London: Longman

Hatim, Basil. 1997. *Communication Across Cultures,* Exeter: University of Exeter Press

Katan, David. 1999. *Translating Cultures* Manchester: St. Jerome,

Newmark, Peter. 1991. *About Translation*, Clevedon: Multilingual Matters

Newmark, Peter. 1988. *A Textbook of Translation.* London/New York: Prentice |Hall

Nord, Christiane. 1997. *Translating as a Purposeful Activity.* Manchester: St. Jerome

Ramsay, Anne. 1994. *Eurojargon,* (4th edition). Amsterdam/Philadephia: John Benjamins Publishing Company

Shapiro, Michael.1984. *Language and Politics.* Oxford: Basil Blackwell.

Trogan, A and Larrue, J. 1994. *Pragmatique du Discours Politique*. Paris: Armand Colin.
Viney, Jean-Paul and Darbelnet, Jean. 1995. *Comparative Stylistics of French and English,* Amsterdam/Philadelphia: John Benjamins Publishing Company

Journals
The Guardian. Tuesday December 23rd 1997.
"A Single Language for Europe?" *The Linguist* 1998, vol 37, n° 6.
Meta 1990. n° 35. Montreal
Meta 1992. n° 37. Montreal

Websites
1. http://www.les.aston.ac.uk/hybridhypotheses.html
2. http://www.diplomatie.fr/frmonde/euro/eu25.gb.html
3. http://cc.uab.es/~iuts0/barna.html
4. http://www.inter-nationes.de/d/ueberset/ibf.html

With thanks to:
Eve-Marie Aldridge and Mona Baker for their recommendations on research literature.

Culture-bound terms in institutional-type texts

Graham Ketteringham, University of North London

Abstract

I intend to examine and analyse the phenomenon of culture-bound words, terms, and phrases in translation comparing and contrasting the latter in French, Italian and Spanish with English. The lexical field I wish to explore is institutional texts which will include the subject areas of politics and administration, law, health and social welfare and economics. In some case these will merge depending on context. I shall define 'culture-bound term' and discuss the concept of correspondence and equivalence referring to the translation of certain terms into English. I shall also compare common linguistic features between the languages in question. I intend to explain and specify the difficulty in achieving comprehensible transfer due to cultural boundaries and both connotative and denotative forces. I shall deal with semantic divergence and convergence of term equivalence comparing and contrasting French, Italian and Spanish mentioning etymological similarities and where synchrony has caused semantic differences to intervene with cultural factors which can lead to confusion and may give rise to incorrect transfer of concepts or ambiguity. The main linguistic and cultural groupings in the above languages relate to a common cultural and linguistic heritage of a catholic and greco-latin base in the case of French, Italian and Spanish, and a protestant anglo-saxon one in the case of English. I shall finally offer some solutions to the the issues raised depending on term equivalence or correspondence, the need for expansion of the equivalence in footnotes or couplets or both, and discuss the purpose of the translation of such terms with regard to the target audience.

Translation and culture.

Translation as a concept is often seen in a concrete sense as a bridge between languages and their cultures. Such bridges are sometimes difficult to build when terms, concepts or expressions relating to one culture do not exist in another or the concept may exist in a similar form but with a different denotative or connotative force. Here there may be a divergence of etymology and semantics especially in the case of languages with a common cultural heritage, for example French, Italian and Spanish. They all share a greco-latin linguistic origin and a christian-catholic social culture. English on the other hand, has some elements of greco-latin cultural linguistic heritage but also owes a lot to its anglo-saxon past, especially in the case of its linguistic origins. It is a hybrid language. The socially determining factor in its culture belongs to a protestant-christian base at least over the last four hundred years. These factors have left their mark linguistically and culturally in the historical development of its society and institutions.

These linguistic and cultural origins are instrumental in forging all contemporary cultural phenomena and their manifestations. Culture in terms of translation are those manifestations of a way of life "that are are particular to a community or nation that uses a particular language" (Newmark 1988: 94). The cultural transfer that takes place in translation must take heed of the cultural message or reality of the source language and its equivalence or correspondence in the cultural framework of the target language. Nida (1974: 199) states that cultural translation "is a translation in which the content of the message is changed to conform to the receptor culture in some way and in which information is introduced which is not linguistically implicit in the original". This, as Nida admits may lead to cultural adaptation. Newmark says that the translator must "mediate cultural features not so much in terms of target language cultural features (cultural equivalents) which are pragmatically vivid but usually inaccurate, but in terms of universal experience and ultimately common humanity." I agree with both of these definitions relating to cultural translation. There may be grounds for preferring one to the other in specific cases depending on the availability of linguistic and cultural terms in the target language. In institutional texts where one wishes to transfer the name and concept inherent in the particular organisation or entity one may adopt one or several translation techniques. Depending on the precise terms used in the designation of the institution, one may translate semantically or communicatively bearing in mind the existence or not of a corresponding term or cultural equivalent. The notion of correspondence or equivalence is fraught with danger and ambiguity. Equivalence may refer to the linguistic semantic equivalence or to the functional connotative meaning inherent in the name of an institution or particular term. The transfer of the term from one language and culture to another must take meaning into account but also the form; however, if respect for the form leads to ambiguity or confusion it should be sacrificed. Nida again makes the valid distiction between 'dynamic equivalence' and 'formal equivalence'. Dynamic equivalence refers to equivalent effect in the receptor language. The reader or audience would understand the intention of the source term, even though a semantic shift may have been introduced to accommodate the term into the target culture. The form of the source text is modified to preserve its meaning. Dynamic equivalence is relevant as it permits meaning to be transferred from one language and culture to another irrespective of the precise form. Formal equivalence is closer to a literal or semantic translation as it focuses on the correspondence of forms of the source text and target languages but is unlikely to convey meaning even partially or otherwise. At worst no comprehensible meaning, confusion or even ambiguity is the result, which is disatrous for the audience (user or client).

Nida also admitted that dynamic equivalence might cause misunderstanding by adapting the source too far to fit into the receptor culture and thereby corrupt the message or remove a connotative force. The term 'functional equivalence' is a "middle ground between dynamic and formal equivalence and emphasises the communicative function of translating to avoid misunderstanding." (Nida 1986). Nida's functional equivalence implies that forms should not be disregarded if they transfer meaning adequately. This, I think, is one of the main dilemmas facing a translator of institutional texts; there is a temptation to adapt the terms of the source text too far in the quest for transferring meaning and using cultural equivalents of the target culture when they may well be 'equivalents' but not exact similarities. In such cases the translation couplet is a valuable device. In all instances, referential accuracy must be paramount.

Culture-bound terms and equivalence

A culture-bound term is one which has a specific denotative and connotative meaning in a language referring exclusively to the culture of that language. It is usually a noun or nominal group referring to a large field of cultural phenomena belonging to a nation or linguistic group with a common culture. In this paper I shall limit myself to institutional terms and phrases of the lexical fields of politics and public administration, law, health and socal welfare. In many cases these areas overlap. As I have stated I shall refer to such terms in French, Italian and Spanish in comparison and contrast to English and to each other from a lingusitic and cultural point of view referring also to the concepts of dynamic, functional and formal equivalence. In the sentence: "Downing Street makes a decision", "Downing Street" is a culture-bound term, metonymy, with connotative and denotative force. It refers to the Prime Minister's official residence, the Prime Minister himself, but is most likely to mean the British government with the connotation of the Labour Party's policies as ruling party in the government. To a French target language audience the name 'Downing Street' could be rendered as a couplet: Downing Street (*siège du gouvernement britannique*) or, (*résidence officielle du Premier Ministre britannique*), depending on context.

Here we have a functional transation. The cultural equivalent in a dynamic sense would be '*Hôtel Matignon*' but it would be culturally out of context to translate it as such. I would suggest in any case, appending a footnote stating the cultural equivalence in some detail depending on the readership. Similar comparisons could be made with Spanish in which case the dynamic equivalence would be '*el Palacio de la Moncloa*' the official residence of the Spanish Prime Minister. The dynamic equivalence has its place but only if accompanied by a communicative translation to convey the function of the corresponding institution. Examples of the names of Italian governmental institutions, translated functionally into English would be: '*Il Quirinale*' as 'Official residence and headquarters of the President of the Italian Republic'. '*Palazzo Montecitorio*' the Italian Lower House of Parliament, '*Palazzo Madama*' the Senate, '*Palazzo Chigi*' the seat of the Italian Government.

The plethora of political parties and groupings and their acronyms can cause confusion and irritation to the reader of a translation of a political text - even though the reader may have specialised knowledge, of the subject and it could be argued that s/he is aware of the acronym. Occasionally the precise names hide a connotation that does not exist in the target language. Some translations given are literal and do not convey the meaning or implication of the name from its local culture. The nature of politics and political culture in France, Italy and Spain is such that political parties reform, change and merge and hence change their objectives, names and acronyms quite frequently. Rendering them in English in a meaningful way can be challenging to say the least. Superficial or literal rendering is insufficient, a functional approach is far more effective. It is quite unhelpful to leave the French R.P.R. as 'Rally for the Republic'; to assist the reader whom one cannot assume knows exactly the position of this party on the French political spectrum or its connotations, a footnote should be provided stating that it is the principal party of the Right in France, roughly equivalent to the Conservative party in Britain. It is also the party of Jacques Chirac, the French President of the Republic. The Spanish '*Partido Popular*', if rendered literally - which has been done - is not a great help to the reader, as it conveys nothing in the target culture. Again a brief footnote should be appended stating that it is the ruling right-wing party of government in Spain whose leader is José María Aznar and is the Spanish Prime Minister. A similarity could be made with the Conservative Party in Britain.

Political parties with transparent names such as *socialiste/socialista* or *comunista* or *radical*, may translate semantically very easily but this does not always reflect the cultural connotations of both the source and target languages. In Britain the former contains a negative connotative force reminiscent of Soviet Union style austerity and autocratic government. In fact, in the Western European societies where they exist, they are democratically elected left-wing parties participating in governments; it is true that at present their influence is receding and in the case of the Italian Communist party, '*Il partito comunista*' it has changed its name to '*Partito Democratico della Sinistra*' or 'Democratic party of the Left' to reflect a change in stance and its independence but also to shed the connotations of the past. The name translates formally and functionally into English, but depending on audience a footnote would assist the reader. The name '*radical*' or '*radicale*' reflects a preoccupation with secularism and a desire for non-intervention of the Catholic Church in politics. In England, however, the term '*radica*l' has a connotation of subversive or destabilising activity through social and political reform.The distinguishing feature between British, French, Italian and Spanish politics is that in contemporary Britain, the Catholic Church has had very little effect on politics in the last three hundred years, therefore when translating '*radical*' or '*radicale*' as 'radical', a brief note should be appended stating precisely the area of activity. In Italy it is true that the party has been involved in attempts at questionable social legislation.

Other terms related to politics which are often mistranslated in the British press through an insistence on formal equivalence in translation are terms such as '*Assemblée Nationale*' and '*député*' or '*diputado*'. These are rendered as 'National Assembly' and 'deputy'. Occasionally the French Lower House of parliament is referred to as the 'National Assembly', or 'Chamber of Deputies'. I wonder whether they convey very much meaning to an English reader without a knowledge of French institutions or politics. In my view they are culturally misleading. The term 'deputy' does not firstly spring to mind as a political representative meaning a member of parliament. It is more likely to conjure up images of a second-in-command in a school, or an assistant to someone in authority in some capacity.

The term '*président*' or '*présidente*' is another culturally treacherous term due to its transparency. As such it is little used in British English. The functionally corresponding term would be 'chairman' as in 'chairman of the council' or 'chairman of the board of directors'. The cultural equivalent in English of the use of '*President*' is in the paradigm 'President of the Republic' as a translation of '*Président de la République*' or '*Presidente della Repubblica*'. In Spain the 'Prime Minister' is called the '*Presidente del Gobierno*'. This should not be rendered as President of the Government. The terms '*presidente*' or '*président*' in their native languages have a different connotational but also denotational force. They are used commonly to designate anyone in power or authority as in the cases of '*Président du Conseil Général*' or '*Presidente de la Diputacion Provincial*'. It is such a widely used term in French Italian and Spanish, but culturally inappropriate to render it as 'president' in English except in the instances mentioned.

A further term giving rise to confusion in this field is the Spanish term '*autonomia*'. In recent years since the re-establishment of democratic government in Spain, this term has undergone a semantic shift, from an abstract to a concrete meaning. It has conserved its original concept of independence but also refers to a regional government, as in the phrase '*Estado de las Autonomias*'. The term has become a concrete denotative one. There is no cultural equivalent in England, but to convey the concept in a meaningful functional way, it would be appropriate to translate it as 'autonomous region'. An accompanying adjective '*autonómico*' has also been coined as in '*gobierno autonómico*' which refers specifically to the regional government of one of the 20 regions in Spain. It is worthy of note that '*autonómico*' is far more denotative than '*autónomo*' as a general word which refers to any official body considered independent or self governing.

Terms that are exclusively culture-bound in a historical sense constitute a real challenge to the translator in a quest for comprehensible conveyance of meaning. In Spanish the term '*somatén*' has no cultural equivalent in history. It has both a connotation and denotation. It was used in the late nineteenth and early twentieth century to denote a civil militia movement fighting for its political and social rights against a corrupt governmental authority. It carries with it a connotation of sudden uproar and attack. At the time of the Dictatorship of Primo de Rivera (1923-31) he himself wrote in *La Vanguardia*:

> Somos el somatén de legendaria y honrosa tradición [...] queremos un somatén reserva y hermana del ejército.

'*Somatén*' could be rendered functionally into English as 'people's militia' or 'civil militia' but it would require a footnote to place it in its historical context.

Other social, political and cultural terms which are difficult to transfer across linguistic and cultural boundaries are those relating to the Italian Mafia. The term is connotationally loaded in many languages and has taken on the meaning of an underground criminal association, which may be true. The organisation itself is referred to as '*Cosa Nostra*'- our business - but usually remains in Italian. It has other related terminology which are all culture-bound. '*Cosca*', '*piovra*', and '*omertà*' are all metaphorical terms and carry connotation and denotation. In order to transfer their meaning effectively they need to be translated functionally as there is no equivalent organisation. '*Cosca*' is best rendered by '*clan*'. Literally it refers to the leaves of an artichoke overlapping. By analogy it refers to the mafia families and their close ties. '*Piovra*' literally means 'octopus', referring to the pervasive structure of the Mafia to many fields of criminal activity world-wide. A functional equivalent would be 'tentacular organisation' in order to preserve the metaphor. '*Omertà*' is another culturally exclusive term. It refers to the code of silence or refusal to divulge information to anybody outside the mafia families or clans. 'Conspiracy of silence' is a functional equivalent, and is used for other criminal organisations, including the '*ndrangheta*' and '*camorra*' which can only really be explained in a footnote.

The lexical field of law

Progressing to the field of law and legal terminology, this lexical field is the most culture-bound as all legal systems are exclusive to the culture of the respective society of the country concerned. There are cultural similarities between the legal systems in France Italy and Spain as they share a legal tradition inherited from Roman law and catholicism in a social and political sense which has exerted an influence on institutional developments in those countries. The terminology and nomenclature have a similar greco-latin root in a semantic sense and there are similarities with English law and its institutions but many terms have been subjected to semantic shifts which render the translation of such terms very difficult. There is the added difference in the nature of English law in that it is based on precedent and custom as opposed to a code as in the case of countries with a 'latin' tradition. Some legal terms appear transparent in their form, but because the semantic shift has been so extensive and cultural factors (legal traditions) have intervened original meaning has been so modified that translation of such terms requires a functional-dynamic approach as a formal one would lead to inaccuracy. It must be said that the language of law as a discipline is very denotative and specialised and hence requires special care in order to render the message and intention accurately and to avoid ambiguity.

Let us examine some terms that are semantically equivalent but culturally divergent. In English the term 'magistrate' and 'magistrate's court' has a denotation and a connotation. The similar word exists in French '*magistrat*', Italian '*magistrato*', and Spanish '*magistrado*'. In these three latter cases he terms are synonymousand carry the same cultural weight and are generic terms referring to all levels of judiciary. In England the term magistrateis far more denotative and is the lowest official on the bench in the court hierarchy and is not usually paid as a professional member of the judiciary. Indeed a magistrate is not necessarily legally trained. He or she relies on the knowledge of the clerk of the court for reference or points of law. The corresponding semantic terms in French Italian or Spanish do not have the same meaning. They are all professional highly trained lawyers, have become judges by passing a competitive examination and sit at the bench conducting legal proceedings in court. They do not rely on a clerk of the court. They do not sit at lower level courts or at committal proceedings. The functional equivalent in Britain would be a 'judge' or a 'high court judge' depending on the court and level of jurisdiction. In order to preserve accuracy and the correct connotation, I suggest the following translation of the English term 'magistrate' and 'magistrate's court':

French	*'Juge de paix'*	*'Tribunal de police'*
Italian	*'Giudice di pace'* *'Giudice Conciliatore'/'pretore'*	*'Pretura'*
Spanish	*'Juez de paz'*	*'Juzgado de guardia'* *'Juzgado de Instuccion y de primera instancia'*

Another culture-bound term frequently encountered in legal matters in France Spain or Italy is *'instruction'*, *'instrucción'* or *'istruttoria'*. These terms all belong to a common legal cultural evolution and are both formally and dynamically equivalent. There is no equivalent in England because of a different legal system and culture. In terms of referential meaning a corresponding term to convey the concept would be and indeed is accepted as being 'investigation' or 'judicial examination' supervised by the *'juge d'instruction'*, *'juez de instrucción'* or *'giudice istruttore'* this term is usually rendered functionally by 'examining magistrate' although such a person does not exist in the English legal system. In some respects it may be said that s/he carries out similar duties to that of the Criminal Investigation Department staffed by police detectives. Other terms with a specific and specialised denotative and connotative meanings present in the legal systems of the countries concerned are *'Procureur' (de la République)*, *Procuratore (della Repubblica)* and *Fiscal* (*General del Estado*). Again they are formal and dynamic equivalents in France, Italy and Spain. In England the translation given is a generic *'Prosecutor'* or if he or she is of the highest grade, then *'Prosecutor of the Republic'* or *'General State Prosecutor'*. In a translation a footnote may be required. These terms and many others pose a challenge to the translator who would need to know something of the criminal and civil legal process in the societies concerned to be able to transfer meaning correctly and succinctly. The aforementioned judicial personnel work for the *'Procura'* or the *'Pubblico Ministero'* in Italy; in Spain, the *'Fiscalía'* or *'Ministerio Público'*, and in France the *'Ministère Public'*. They are termed in English for convenience as the 'Public Prosecutor's Department' although I have seen the formal equivalent 'Public Ministry' used to describe the concept. The cultural equivalent in England would be the 'Director of Public Prosecutions' or the 'Crown Prosecution Service'. The principal difference with all nomenclature dealing with the law in France Italy and Spain, and many other 'latin' countries is that the legal system is inquisitorial and not prosecutorial as it is in England.

Regarding other comparisons between the structure of the hierarchy of courts in France, Italy, Spain and England, similarities exist both in powers of the courts concerned and the terms used to designate them except in England where the legal system differs culturally, which reflects terminology used. The criterion is common law as opposed to Roman or codified law enshrined in the Napoleonic Code which forms the basis of the legal sytems in France Italy and Spain. It is true that the names of courts and the levels of jurisdiction they deliver may have formal equivalents both semantically and culturally but in other cases a functional or dynamic equivalent may be necessary to make the meaning clear. The highest court of appeal in France is called *'la Cour de Cassation'*, in Italy *'la Corte di Cassazione'*, in Spain *'el Tribunal Supremo'*. In England the dynamic equivalent would be the 'House of Lords' but to render the meaning in keeping with the source language and culture, this would have to be translated functionally as the 'highest court of appeal'. I would suggest the same strategy for all names of courts although some can be said to be transparent (*Cour d'Appel / Corte d'Appello / Court of Appeal*). Care must be taken when translating terms which may be transparent, which may translate formally very readily but which refer to institutions which no longer exist in the culture of the target language. A good example would be '*la Cour d'Assises*' or '*la Corte d'Assise*' in France and Italy with both countries sharing a similar justice system and and a common linguistic and cultural heritage. In Britain the current term and court known as the Assises ceased to exist in 1971 when the court system was reorganised, this level of jurisdiction passing to the newly created Crown Court.

Other legal nomenclature between languages of a similar cultural and linguistic heritage can be easily translated formally and functionally, although the term is only strictly speaking culture bound in the source language. A similar semantic term with similar connotations allows this process to convey clear meaning. On 2nd November 1998 in an article on the official request for extradition of General Pinochet to Spain, *Le Monde* reported:

> Massés depuis plus de cinq heures devant L'Audience Nationale à Madrid, la plus haute instance pénale du pays [...] une centaine de manifestants [...].

Here, we find a an example of formal equivalence in French of the Spanish term '*Audiencia Nacional*'. It translates semantically because both languages share a common semantic and legal cultural heritage. In Spanish, the term '*Audiencia*' is a concrete denotative term and the French has adapted to this usage. In French, the term '*audience*' is an abstract noun used to denote a court hearing, but is not the name of a specific court or level of jurisdiction. In the article, an explanation is given of the term '*la plus grande instance pénale*' to avoid doubt or ambiguity. In English, a more functional or dynamic equivalent would have to be used to convey the meaning clearly. 'High court' would suffice and a note stating that the competent authority in this case would be the 'House of Lords'. The semantic equivalent of '*audiencia*' - '*audience*' is not used in English in judicial contexts, the nearest equivalent being the term 'court'. The term used in French and Spanish to denote 'the highest criminal court in the country' is '*instance*' or '*instancia*'. It would have to be translated functionally as 'court' or 'authority' as it refers to a specific level of criminal jurisdiction. In other contexts, literally and semantically 'first or second instance' it would refer to 'committal proceedings' or 'appeal'. In the two cases under discussion here, regarding the French and Spanish similarity of semantic form, '*audiencia*' in Spanish has assumed a wider semantic meaning (*signifié*) than '*audience*' in French. In the case of '*instance*' or '*instancia*' the terms are synonymous.

A further legal term peculiar to Spanish is '*la vista*'. There are functional equivalents in other language, it is unique as there is no semantic equivalent in other related languages. Its best functional equivalent is '*hearing*', *audience*' in French or '*udienza*' in Italian. It deceptively looks as if it refers to 'sight' but this is not the case. It is used in contexts such as '*la vista del recurso*' or '*la vista de la providencia*' as 'the hearing of the appeal' or 'the hearing of the ruling/decision' given by the appropriate court. The term '*providencia*' is a polysemous term. In legal contexts it refers to the '*ruling*' or '*decision*' - it has no connotations of 'providence' although its semantic form might give that impression.

In Italy there is a court designated the '*Tribunale Amministrativo Regionale*' (created in 1970). It is culturally exclusive to Italy with powers to hear cases brought to it by individuals or corporate bodies who feel that their rights have been harmed in some way by other state institutions. Such cases in other societies would be heard in appropriate civil proceedings against the offending institution, as there is no specific court in existence to deal with such disputes. However, the term could be effectively translated into English as 'Regional Administrative Court' because semantic equivalent terms exist which convey acceptable cultural connotations in the meaning. It may be necessary to append a note explaining more detail, but the translation is sufficient to convey the *signifié*.

In all cases of legal culture-bound terms, it is sufficient to translate them formally if semantic equivalents exist in the target language and cultural connotation permits, even if the institutional equivalent does not itself exist. The individual terms must convey an acceptable cultural concept in the society concerned. "Look after the words and the meaning will take care of itself !"

The lexical field of health and social welfare

In the lexical field relating to health and social welfare, the terminology used also reflects the cultural heritage of the languages and respective societies. In France, Spain, Italy and Britain the gradual evolution of institutionalised health care and welfare provision for the disadvantaged has been transferred from the established Church (Catholic and Protestant) to governmental bodies. The heritage of this development has left its mark in the connotations inherent in the nomenclature of the vast array of services and assistance available.

A common strand to the 'health services' in the countries and societies concerned in this paper is that of insurance and provision. To take concrete examples, in France the expression first used in the nineteenth century was '*l'Etat-providence*', which would translate formally and functionally as 'the state as provider'. In the same way in Spain the embryonic health service was first designated the '*Instituto Nacional de Previsión*' and included limited health and social security benefits as we know them today. In Italy the '*Istituto Nazionale della Previdenza Sociale*' created in the early twentieth century dispensed social security payments while the '*Istituto Nazionale Malattie*' coordinated health care and hospitalisation. In all the nomenclature of these institutions, we see the common semantic thread of provision or providing a service, '*prévoyance*', '*previsión*' and '*previdenza*'. The term we would use culturally in English is 'social security' as a functional and dynamic equivalent. As life and working conditions advanced such institutions evolved and placed health and social security under one heading which has in fact become a linguistic paradigm.

In France, the term '*Sécurité sociale*' appears to be transparent, translating semantically into English as 'Social Security'. This is misleading in terms of cultural reference as its functional equivalent is the 'Health Service' dispensing health and medical care, which is what '*la Sécurité sociale*' in France does. In Britain 'Social Security' refers to the payment and administration of financial benefits and allowances. The same can be said of '*la Seguridad Social*' in Spain, especially as the recently created '*Instituto Nacional de la Salud*' deals exclusively with health and hospital provision. These terms and many others are all potential hazards for translation,because of their transparency and divergent connotation. The *signifié* is more important than the *signifiant* to correct transfer of institutional texts.

Another term leading to possible confusion is the current usage of the term '*solidarité*' in French in the expressions '*fonds de solidarité*' and '*emploi et solidarité*' which could be rendered as 'financial support fund' and 'employment and social security' although this may be too dynamic. The English semantic meaning of 'solidarity' is inherent, but to use the term 'solidarity' when referring to social security or unemployment benefit would be ludicrous. In

French '*solidarité*' has a denotative meaning whereas this is not the case in English. It remains an abstract term of social and political cooperation and mutual support. In French the concept can relate to financial support or benefit.

At the present time in France, there is social and political preoccupation with the '*Pacte Civil de Solidarité*' which is a movement to recognise personal partnerships and responsibilities. It constitutes a legal agreement or contract between both parties for the raising of children or care for a dependent. This is a culture-bound term as no dynamic equivalent exists elsewhere (yet). It would best be translated as a 'joint responsibility agreement'. I would omit 'civil' as I think this concept is implied and would make the expression too heavy in English. In any case, a footnote would help the reader.

Turning towards health matters, medical doctors in France Italy and Spain often work privately as well as for the respective health services of their countries. To ensure that patients can be consulted as part of the government health care scheme, and not have to pay extra, the term '*conventionné*' (France), '*convenzionato*' (Italy) or '*concertado*' (Spain) is added after the name on a plaque outside the surgery. These culture-bound terms are comparable with each other in a semantic and cultural terms. However in Britain where social developments and legislation have evolved differently, it is assumed that all doctors are 'national health' unless stated clearly that they are private. The above terms would best be rendered as 'agree' or 'approved' to convey the precise functional meaning.

Peculiar to Italy, there is a charitable health and medical care service run by the Catholic Church known as '*Misericordia*'. It is similar to the Red Cross, but does not solely operate as a first-aid post. It has surgeries and dispenses certain prescriptions free of charge. As an institution it is unique; to convey in English its functional meaning, we could call it a 'Charitable Health Unit' with a couplet and a footnote if deemed necessary. The term '*Misericordia*' assumes a special denotative force as a concrete noun, whereas as an abstract noun it embraces a a wider connotative sense of compassion and pity, which is nevertheless included in its function.

Other terms with a similar semantic and cultural form in terms of welfare in France Italy and Spain are '*assistance*', '*assistenza*' and '*asistencia*', respectively. Although semantically they could be translated into English as 'assistance' the term is too vague and abstract. The functional meaning is 'welfare' or 'social care'. The full force is only transferred when a more functional and communicative approach is adopted. A similar comparison in terminology can be made with '*benificencia*' (Spanish) and '*beneficenza*' (Italian).They are both culturally and semantically linked and have both extended an abstract meaning into a concrete one. The functional English equivalent would be 'charitable organisation' which communicates the concept of dispensing medical care, education and financial benefits.

A common cultural link in the subject area of health and social welfare in latin countries is the role played in the past by the Catholic Church and its charitable work. They have all left their mark both culturally and linguistically on present day structures. Many government funded and private health schemes co-exist which have created their own culture-bound terminology with similar connotative values. In Britain, where similar institutions exist the terminology differs due to semantic shifts and the anglo-saxon protestant dominant culture resulting in more prosaic phraseology.

Conclusion

From all the above examples and discussion, when rendering culture-bound institutional terms into another language and culture, the strategy may vary between a formal, functional and dynamic approach in order to convey the meaning clearly. From the instances I have quoted, to which many more could be added, it can be seen that owing to semantic and cultural heritage and history, institutional terms in French, Italian and Spanish overlap and share common characteristics. In English, where cultural phenomena and linguistic features have shifted or evolved in a totally different way, culture has been a determining factor in translation only where semantics permits. The only meaningful strategy to convey the meaning of a foreign culture-bound term is to render it functionally or even dynamically according to Nida's theories. To use a formal equivalent to respect the structure of the source language and culture would be to corrupt the message and natural form of the target language. It would be tantamount to an intrusion, leading to ambiguity, or obscure meaning not intended by the original author; it may result in unconventional grammar or clumsy style - in short translationese. The translation of culture-bound terms will always pose a challenge to the translator who not only acts as intermediary between languages but also between a wide range of cultural manifestations. It is the meaning the – signifié - rather than the signifiant which is paramount in the translation of institutional and non-literary texts in the present day.

References

Le Monde 1998
El País 1998
España '98. 1998. (Review published by) Oficina de información Diplomática.
La Repubblica, November 1998.
Newmark, Peter. 1988. *A Textbook of Translation*. London/New York: Prentice Hall
Newmark, Peter. 1991. *About Translation*. Clevedon: Multilingual Matters 1991.
Nida, Eugene. 1993. *Language, Culture and Translating*. Shanghai: Shanghai Foreign Languages Education.
Nida, Eugene and de Waard, Jan. 1986. *From One Language to Another*, Nashville: Thomas Nelson Publishers.
Collins French Dictionary. 1998. Fifth Edition. New York: Harper Collins.
Collins Spanish Dictionary. 1998. Fifth Edition. New York: Harper Collins.
Collins Italian Dictionary. 1998. Fifth Edition. New York: Harper Collins.
Pacet, Pierre.1991. Les Institutions françaises. Paris: Puf. Que sais-je?
Kimmel, Alain. 1986. *Vous avez dit France?*. Paris: Hachette.
Ross, Christopher. 1997. *Contemporary Spain*. London: Arnold Press
Ginsborg, Paul. *A History of Contemporary Italy*. London: Penguin Books 1990.
Allum, P. A. 1973. *Italy: Republic Without Government*, Birkenhead: Willmer Brothers Ltd.

Glasnost in translation or lost in translation?
A comparison of the translation of opaque and transparent terminology in the translation of legal texts.

Sue Lilley, University of North London

Abstract

The task of translating a legal text or document from one language into another is littered with a series of obstacles and pitfalls of which the translator must be aware if s/he is to provide an accurate translation. Legal translation can be divided into three main categories. These are the translation of documents relating to domestic or municipal law, supranational law (namely an area of law such as European Law which lies between domestic and international law) and international law. The translation of texts concerning national law will require the decoding of terms specific to that particular legal order or system whilst documents pertaining to supranational or international law will involve the transference of terminology which is considerably more transparent. This paper compares and contrasts the translation of culturally specific or opaque terminology with the translation of acultural or transparent terms. In doing this, it will examine the implications for the legal translator and for the status of the legal translation as a document capable of being used as a piece of evidence in its own right. Inevitably, some reference will also be made to the discipline of comparative law since this field and the field of legal translation are, at times, interdisciplinary. Examples will be given from supranational documents and from texts concerning the domestic law of France and Italy.

The translator is generally considered to be a message conveyor and in most instances translation is seen as the process by which a message expressed in a source langage is transferred using linguistic knowledge into a target text which is accessible to native readers of that target language (Houbert 1998). However, in the field of legal translation this process becomes a more difficult task for the translator depending on the kind of legal text to be translated. Texts falling into the domain of international law and supranational law present less of an arduous task than those relating to domestic law. Legal texts may, according to De Leo (1999), present one of the following situations for a translator:

1. the same insitution, governed in the same way;
2. the same insitution, governed differently (albeit only slightly differently);
3. an institution that exists in one legal system but no longer exists in the other;
4. or, an institution that exists in one legal system but does not exist in the other.

Example 1 is a situation which a translator would expect to find in the domains of either supranational law or international law and as a result generally poses quite negligible problems since in this instance the translator would expect to be using relatively transparent or acultural terminology. Examples of texts which fall under this category are those found in the legal reference material by Daniele (1991) and Draetta (1994) concerning issues such as the European legal order and the free movement of people, goods and services within the European Union. Examples 2, 3 and 4 are much more problematic as they pertain to the field of national or domestic law and will most probably present the translator with opaque or culturally specific terminology to decode.

It is on the basis of the above premises that this paper will compare and contrast the aspect of opaque (culturally specific) terms and transparent (acultural) terms found within legal texts. In doing this, the discussion will focus upon the implications of these terms for the translator and for the status of the legal translation as a document capable of being used as a piece of evidence in its own right. The research will examine different text types which are of the same communication level and fall within the same subject field i.e. law but which fall within a different sub-area i.e. national and supranational law. For a more complete discussion, reference will also be made to examples concerning international law although texts of this nature were not translated in previous project modules.

Sarcevic (1997) points out that although translations of legal documents are amongst some of the oldest and most important translations in the world, legal translation has received a relatively small amount of attention and is still a long way from being recognised as an independent discipline. This observation was supported by the relative lack of literature to be found on the translation of opaque terminology in legal texts. Whilst it is to be expected that there is little literature on the translation of transparent terminology given its inherent nature, most literature concerning opaqueness was concentrated more specifically on political terminology.

It is true to say that to a certain extent the same theories concerning culturally specific terms in political texts may be applied to legal terminology however, the former text type is very unlikely to be used as a legal document in its own right and also as a piece of evidence for testimony in court. Therefore, although literature concerning cross-cultural communication and culturally specific terms was widely consulted and provided information which was to a certain extent relevant to this discussion, the majority of works consulted did not address the fact that a legal translation may be used in evidence and may also be a piece of evidence or documentation upon which further legal action may be brought at a later date. That subsequent action often being based on the way in which culturally specific terminology has been translated. The only sources of reference which took this issue into consideration were those written by legal translators, lawyer linguists or comparative lawyers and consequently, they were the most useful to this discussion; a large proportion of the reference material consulted thus being rejected for its unsuitability to the particular nature of legal translation.

The texts used as a reference point for investigating opaqueness and transparency in legal terminology fell into the categories of domestic law and supranational law. (Copies of the texts have not been attached since reference will only be made to single lexical items concerning the issue of terminology). In terms of domestic law, one example used was a general introductory textbook on French law (Terré 1991) and the other was a text on the Italian legal order (Marino & Landolfi 1992). As regards supranational law the two texts translated were from Italian textbooks on European Law of the kind that would be used by law students in Italy to learn about the supranational aspects of EU Law (Daniele 1991 & Draetta 1994). Other examples from the reference sources consulted will also be given were international law is concerned. Examples from these texts have been applied in support of the theories relating to opaque and transparent terminology advocated by the reference sources used.

Culturally specific terms have long since provided obstacles in legal translation and the difficulty was often dealt with by a literal decoding of the terminology. One example of this is the translation of '*la Corte di Cassazione*' (Marino & Landolfi: 1992) and '*la Cour de cassation*' (Terré 1991) as the 'Court of Cassation'. This method of translation has given an incorrect impression that legal translation and in this case the translation of culturally specific terms is merely a process of exchanging words and phrases of the source legal document and thus legal system for corresponding lexical units in the language of the target document and thus the target legal system. (Fluck 1985 in Sarcevic 1997). This process of decoding culturally specific terms may be seen as ineffective if the example of the French '*loi*' and the Italian '*legge*' is analysed. Direct decoding of these two terms into English would produce 'law', however, the terms are by no means identical in meaning. A French law is voted by an institution and a system completely different to the English Houses of Parliament likewise, an Italian law is voted in a different way again and all of these laws or acts would need different majorities in England to those required in France and Italy (De Leo 1999). Thus, if a legal translation including the translation of culturally specific terminology is to be both acceptable and effective, solutions cannot be found simply by matching up seemingly equivalent terms. The problem of opaque terminology and consequent incongruency in comparison to transparency has been the subject of much scrutiny. The selection of suitable equivalents is particularly important when translating culturally specific terms since in terms of the communication process, equivalents proposed by the translator may require the reception of the courts if the target document is to be used in evidence. Sarcevic (1997) draws attention to the fact that in this context, it is the task of the translator to select equivalent terminology that will achieve desired results and may also be responsible for the success or failure of a particular legal action. Thus, the translation of culturally specific terms in contrast to transparent ones may also involve the acceptability of a possible equivalent term and the way in which it is used for legal effect.

The problem of culturally specific terminology in comparison to transparent terminology is further exacerbated by the consideration that the basic unit of translation is not the word but the text. A text takes its meaning from one or more legal systems, legal translation and consequently the translation of opaque terminology in national law, is fundamentally a process of translating or decoding particular legal systems. The example of the French '*tribunaux de commerce*' illustrates this point. This is a court which deals with specifically commercial matters (Terré 1991). It is peculiar to the French system in that it deals only with commerce and its panel of judges is made up of '*juges consulaires*' who are initially elected for two years and then for four years but are not eligible for a year if they have been judging continuously for 14 years. Anyone who is at least 30 years old, registered as a trader for at least five years and is not currently subject to a procedure of '*redressement judiciaire*' (administration of a business under judicial supervision) or of a '*liquidation judiciaire*' (liquidation) is eligible for the functions of '*juge consulaire*' (Dadomo & Farran 1993). There is no such equivalent to this in the English legal system and therefore all the concepts relating to this particular institution would interlink within a source text and influence the translation of the source text into the target text.

The above example also illustrates the fact that each legal system and thus each document relating to national law has its own language and its own system of reference. This means that the translator of culturally specific terminology has to be concerned with the reference and thus the "relationship which holds between an expression and what the expression stands for on particular occasions of its utterance" (Lyons 1974 in Sarcevic 1997). This premise needs to be taken into account when translating opaque terms but not when decoding transparent terminology. Of particular interest to the translator of culturally specific terminology is the fact that the linguistic signs refer not only to particular concepts but also to particular relationships, acts and procedures as can be seen in the example of the '*tribunaux de commerce*'. This issue does not occur to the same extent with transparent legal terminology. The language of law belongs to the group of languages for specific purposes and as a result particularly in the translation of domestic law, difficulty for the translator arises when a term is given a legal meaning that has little or nothing to do with the object referred to by the term in ordinary everyday language (Sarcevic 1997). This, together with the fact that most opaque terminology derives its meaning from a particular legal system, makes the translation of culturally specific terminology much more incongruent than that of supranational or international legal terminology.

There are many subject disciplines whose terminology may be standardised in different languages. An example of this is the work carried out by the International Terminology Working Group which is an informal association of cultural-heritage information professionals who have come together to produce "Guidelines For Forming Language Equivalents: A Model Based on the Art & Architecture Thesaurus" (Baca 1997). In some disciplines, this process is considerably easier because in the majority of instances the same objects exist in each society and thus in each language. Whilst this application may function acceptably in the field of supranational and international law for transparent terminology, it does not apply in the domain of national law. National law is the product of different institutions, history, cultural background and often also socio-economic principles to the extent that each legal system has its own conceptual system and knowledge structure. In addition, within the same language, the same term may stand for different concepts in different legal systems (Arntz 1993 in Sarcevic 1997). Liquidation can apply to five different kinds of 'bankruptcy proceedings' in the United Kingdom and completely different systems or procedures such as that of Chapter 10 within US law. The same applies for the word domicile between UK and US legal systems.

Since all legal systems contain a number of culturally specific terminology with no comparable counterparts in other legal orders or jurisdictions, unlike when dealing with transparent terminology, the translator is left with choices to make as regards the use of 'equivalent' or 'near equivalent' terminology in the target text or legal system. This task is made more arduous since the majority of linguistic terms chosen as equivalents are terms which designate concepts foreign to the target legal system. Bearing in mind that the target text may well be used as evidence itself, the translator is left, when dealing with opaque terminology, to search for equivalents. According to Sarcevic (1997), legal translators cannot be expected to use natural equivalents of the target legal system that are identical to their source terms at the conceptual level and therefore it is perfectly legitimate for the "closest natural equivalent" to be used. This being the equivalent that most accurately conveys the legal meaning of the source term and which brings about the desired results in the target legal system. This being particularly the case if the document is being adduced as evidence.

In the translation of opaque terminology, one method of equivalence which may be employed and which is not needed in the translation of transparent terminology, is that of functional equivalence. An example of this would be the French term '*hypothèque*' (Terré 1991). In the search for an equivalent in English, a functional solution could be the pledging of security for the payment of a debt on land (Sarcevic 1997) but the fact that a functional equivalent has the same function as the source concept does not necessarily mean that it is acceptable for the purpose of translation. However, in order to determine the acceptability of a functional equivalent, a translator should compare the target and source concepts to establish their degree of equivalence since some functional equivalents have been misleading to the point that they have encouraged litigation.

When translating equivalence in documents relating to specific national law, the translator may find the establishment of legal concepts a useful application within the theory of degrees of equivalence. In the translation of legal concepts, the use of monolingual dictionaries as a translation tool may be misleading and so the translator of opaque terminology may rely upon the ideas of intension and extension as advocated by Lyons (1977 in Sarcevic1997). Using this concept the intension of a term includes "the set of essential properties which determines the applicability of the term" and the extension "is the class of the things to which it is correctly applied" (Lyons supra). The result of this application is often that general terms of different legal systems tend to have the same intension but a marked different extension. Again, this result would not appear in the translation of acultural terminology.

In relation to functional equivalents of opaque terminology, the translator of a legal document, particularly if it is to be adduced as evidence, will want to determine its level of acceptability as both a whole text and in terms of the culturally specific terminology which has been decoded. The success or failure of a text, the case and a translator's reputation may depend on the choice of equivalents used. Less risk of this being found in the translation of transparent terminology which has to an extent already anticipated these problems within its supranational or international nature. De Vries (in Sarcevic 1997) issues the warning that a translator must bear in mind the fact that a translation which is satisfactory for information purposes may however, be quite inadequate and even potentially detrimental in adversary proceedings if they are conducted with a particular skill and degree of advocacy. On a similar note Houbert (1998) supports this by contending that "any [...] direct communication text, includes an extra dimension as compared to usual informative texts: this dimension could be referred to as the 'listener-oriented' aspect of a text." This would imply that in the translation of opaque terminology unlike that of transparent terminology, the translation needs "not only a full understanding of the source text" in order to provide an "accurate rendering in the target language," but also "a great deal of creativity coupled with a wide range of communication skills" (Houbert 1998).

According to Sarcevic (1997) when determining how acceptable a functional equivalent is as a translation (a task which does not have to be employed in the translation of transparent terminology), the translator needs to give careful consideration to the structure or classification of the suggested equivalent, the scope of its application and the legal effects of it and its original source term. If correspondence does not occur in relation to the abovementioned aspects, then the consequence may be that the results are other than those intended by the legislature or those party to the original document. These concerns do not appear in the translation of transparent terms.

Closely linked to the concept of functional equivalence of the translation of opaque terminology and its acceptability, is the idea of legal effect. According to Lampe (in Sarcevic 1997), legal concepts automatically imply certain legal effects within a particular legal order and consequently the translator of culturally specific terms within a legal text needs to examine the potential legal effect of the lexical item proposed as a functional equivalent in the target legal document. This consideration is again not part of the agenda when translating transparent terms.

Having examined the obstacles which confront a translator when tackling a legal text containing culturally specific terminology, it is now appropriate to examine some of the solutions which are available to the translator in an attempt to deal with what may seem to be an almost impossible task. Again, where documents pertaining to supranational law and international law recourse to these solutions is not usually necessary.

The translator of opaque terminology may use lexical expansion as a way of accounting for terminological incongruency. This technique can be employed by adding a single word or additionally, to delimit the meaning of the source term in such a way that it corresponds with a narrower functional equivalent. Sarcevic (1997) observes that a lexical expansion does not however, constitute a true natural equivalent since the concepts depicted do not actually exist within the target legal jurisdiction. As a result of the expansion or restriction of functional equivalents, the process of lexical expansion alters concepts in the target legal system which gives them an artificial correspondence with the culturally specific source language terminology.

The other solution that can be employed by the translator in the decoding of opaque terminology and which does not need to be used in the translation of acultural terminology is the use of descriptive paraphrases and definitions. These are also advocated by Newmark (1984 & 1988) in the translation of political terminology and are perhaps the most effective and acceptable method of compensating for terminological incongruency in the translation of opaque terms. This method is particularly relied upon in the translation of multilateral instruments in international law. This method involves spelling out the intended meaning in relatively neutral language that can be understood by lawyers on a global basis and so whilst still remaining in the specialist subdomain of law, does not use opaque terminology which could lead to disastrous mistranslations.

Other solutions for the selection of translation equivalents are more relevant to the translation of acultural or transparent terminology and so this discussion will now consider the issue of transparency. Transparency is found in documents pertaining to supranational and international law. It has been suggested by Akehurst, one of the original translators of the EEC Treaty (in Sarcevic 1997) that the best solution is to use neutral or transparent terms. These terms are usually broader in meaning and are particularly relied upon when intent is for the source term and its equivalent target term to have a meaning independent of a particular legal system. Examples of this are found in the textbooks on EC Law written by Draetta (1994) and Daniele (1991) where the terminology is all 'eurospeak' in nature and translates as direct equivalents from over and above the Italian legal system to over and above the English legal system. Examples such as '*seduta plenaria*' and '*il diritto di stabilimento*' translate directly and transparently into 'plenary session' and 'the right of establishment' all components of each concept corresponding exactly.

Transparent terminology is also found in the form of neologisms (Newmark 1984 & 1988). If translators reject the use of borrowing terminology, recourse may be made to the creation of neologisms. These are often used in supranational law such as EC law and international law such as the Treaties of the United Nations and their creation does not, according to Newmark, "differ significantly from ordinary methods of designation." They should be "grammatically acceptable and semantically motivated and transparent," the result being that the translator does not have to employ the same kind of selection processes involved when translating opaque terminology. The potential risk of litigation based on the translation of these terms being reduced to a negligible level.

Likewise, the risk of litigation based on the translation of opaque terminology and the implications of this for the translator, are reduced when neologisms are created by assigning existing legal terms new meanings. The legal criteria for these is how they will be interpreted and applied in respect of international law and the instrument in which they are to be used. This procedure is particularly common in international law and creates transparency which is beneficial to the translator. New concepts appear in customary law and are codified into conventions at a later date. An example of this is the use of the term continental shelf in the domain of Energy Law. Although there have been some disputes arising from this term ('continental shelf' in English, '*plateau continental*' in French and '*platforma continental*' in Spanish) it has been relatively acceptable as a transparent term (Sarcevic 1997).

The above comparative analysis of opaque and transparent terminology in legal texts and the implications it has for the translator and the target legal text as a legal document has shown that there is a strong relationship between opaqueness and transparency and the way a legal text and its terminology is translated. Transparency will have a strong effect on the way in which a translation is decoded and consequently the level of the text as a medium of communication. A more transparent text is more likely to fall within the subdomain of supranational or international law whilst a more opaque text is likely to pertain to national law. However, it is also evident from the above discussion that literal translation is not often necessary given the other solutions that may be adopted to deal with culturally specific terms. Indeed, literal translation is the least acceptable solution in terms of the legal document as an adducable piece of evidence and the acceptability of the translation in terms of its legal effect. From the text types examined, there seems to be a clear distinction between the two types of text. The text types analysed show little overlap between the text types of national law v. supranational law or international law. However, in the case of national legal texts there is a very high level of culturally specific terminology to be found. Overlap between culturally specific and acultural terms appearing only when within one national legal order reference is made to a supranational or international domain. The reverse being less evident.

The results do however, show themselves to be quite specific to the area of law. There may be a certain slight overlap with the denotative fields of business and politics but only to the extent that these subjects relate to law or where there is the existence of some culturally specific terminology. Where connotative fields such as engineering or medicine are concerned, these problems do not really exist. The fact that a translation may be used within an adversarial process as evidence to be adduced gives legal translation and the translation of opaque terms a specific nature of its own. The creation of a legal document through translation is, unlike in other subjects, the creation of a document upon which further legal action may be brought.

In conclusion, it is in the above respect that the analysis carried out is unlikely to be useful to other disciplines as the comparative analysis has been based upon the existence of a corpus of language within a corpus of language. Likewise, even where transparent terms do exist, even though they are global terms, they are not likely to be used by everyone, only by specialists to whom this transparent terminology is already part of their everyday yet specialist terminology.

However, in the future there may be much greater reliance based upon the use of more transparent terminology as the world is reduced by the advent of more and more advanced technology, litigation across jurisdictions is likely to increase and there will be a greater need for transparency within the world legal order. Although lawyers are weighed down by the burdens of their own legal systems and the process of unifying and standardising the national laws of the EU Member States has experienced considerable resistance as part of the unification process, there is the need to adopt a common nomenclature by harmonising divergent legal concepts and systems. Transparency has been spread by the use of Community glossaries and also by the database EURODICAUTOM. This is expanding at a considerable rate and will further facilitate the translation of legal texts. However, there is still a long way to go before all the legal orders of the EU are completely harmonised and translators do not need to be able to employ suitable strategies for the decoding of culturally specific terms in the translation of legal documentation.

Finally, in terms of further research, although there is not a great deal of literature devoted entirely to the subject of legal translation and comparative law, what there is is very detailed and would appear to cover the current status of the discipline. There may be a need for further research in the form of glossaries or databases of terminology if greater harmonisation of the national laws within the European Union is achieved in the future.

References

Baca, Murtha. 1997. "Making Sense of the Tower of Babel: A Demonstration Project in Multilingual Equivalency Work". *Terminology*, vol 4(1): 105-116. Amsterdam/Philadelphia: John Benjamins Publishing Company.

Baker, Mona. 1990. *In Other Words - A Coursebook on Translation*. London/New York: Routledge.

Boyd White, James. 1990. *Justice as Translation - An Essay in Cultural and Legal Criticism*. London/Chicago: The University of Chicago Press.

Dadomo, C. & Farran, S. 1993. *The French Legal System*. London: Sweet & Maxwell.

Daniele, L. 1991. *Il diritto materiale della comunità economica europea*. Milano: Guiffrè editore.

De Leo, Davide. 1999. *Pitfalls in Legal Translation*, Translation Journal, vol 3 (2), April 1999.http://www.accurapid.com/journal/08legal.htm

Delisle, Jean. 1988. *Translation: An Interpretive Approach*. Ottawa: University of Ottawa Press.

Draetta, Ugo. 1994. *Elementi di diritto comunitario - parte istituzionale*. Milano: Guiffrè editore.

Fairbairn G. & Winch, C. 1996. *Reading, Writing and Reasoning - A Guide for Students*. Buckingham: Open University Press.

Hatim, Basil. 1997. *Communication Across Cultures - Translation Theory and Contrastive Text Linguistics*. Exeter: University of Exeter Press

Hatim, Basil & Mason, Ian. 1990. *Discourse and the Translator*. London/New York: Longman.

Houbert, Frédéric. 1998. *Translation as a Communication Process*, Translation Journal, vol 2 (3), July 1998. http://www.accurapid.com/journal/05theory.htm

Marino, R. & Landolfi, A. 1992. *L'ordinamento giudiziario*. Napoli: Esselibri.

Newmark, Peter. 1984. *Approaches to Translation*. Oxford: Pergammon Press.

Newmark, Peter. 1988. *A Textbook of Translation*. London/New York: Prentice Hall.

Nogueira, Danilo. 1999. *Legal Workshop - Working in Brazil*. Translation Journal, vol 3 (2), April 1999 http://www.accurapid.com/journal/08legal.htm

Sarcevic, Susan. 1997. *New Approach to Legal Translation*. The Hague/London/Boston: Kluwer Law International,

Terré, François. 1991. *Introduction générale au droit*. Paris: Editions Dalloz.

Aims and objectives in Russian. Linguistic problems of East-West Partnerships

Pieta Monks, University of North London

Abstract

How do you discuss a course on public administration and management in Russian when one word – *upravleniye-* is used for both administration and management? How do you check methods of assessement when methods of assessment and examination are so totally different that there are no equivalent words for them? How do you distinguish between policy and politics when the Russian word *politika* is used for both?

Since the fall of the Soviet Union in 1991 there has been a mushrooming of East-West educational partnerships. It is obviously important to be rigourous when validating a foreign course to which you are lending the name of your institution. But what is not always realised when working through an interpreter is the difficulties of cultural equivalence in language and in fact.

Education is in fact one of the most culturally specific of all areas of translation. The system of education is formed by and forms different societies. Education can present some of the most difficult problems of all for translators/interpreters.

This paper looks at linguistic/cultural problem areas in East-West educational discussions and the reasons and sources of the cultural confusions.

Since the collapse of the Soviet Union in 1991 there has been an enormous increase in the number of East-West educational partnerships. Higher education in the former Soviet Union has been forced to reassess and adapt itself in the wake of the enormous changes in the economy, society and politics that have occurred since 1991 and increasingly it looks to the West for help, advice and sponsorship.[1] Many of these fragile young partnerships, however, founder on the rocks of misconception and incomprehension on both sides:

> In many instances, the evidence suggests that between 50% and 75% of joint ventures and mergers fail, without achieving the objectives for which they were formed.
> (John Harper in Katan 1993: 76)

I would like to look at some of the linguistic reasons for these difficulties with specific reference to the CIS.

I will first define the semantic fields of my analysis. I will then look at the cultural context of education in the CIS, looking at its historical background and the socio-economic political factors that affected and affect the development and change of education and the language used to describe it today. I will compare this briefly with the education system in Great Britain. I will then look at some specific educational and administrative terms in English and Russian which present difficulties for translators and interpreters and which arose from a particular partnership. I will finish with what I hope will be useful pointers for those embarking upon cross-cultural inter-lingual relationships.

The semantic field

The semantic field that we are looking at in this paper is that of education and governmental institutions, which can be classified as realia, as defined by Vlakhov and Florin:

> Those words and word conjunctions of a native language which represent the names of objects, concepts and phenomena characteristic of a geographical environment, culture, material

---

[1] For information on the changing state of Soviet Russian education I have relied mainly on my own research for articles on this subject printed regularly in specialist and non-specialist publications like the THES, TES, Guardian etc.

existence or socio-historical features of a people, nation, country, tribe and function thereby as bearers of national, local or historical colour. Precise equivalents of these words do not exist in other languages."
(Howell 1997: 166)

The Russian critic L. Mikulina agrees with the above definition of realia and goes on to define the information loss that occurs when this non-equivalence is ignored in translation.

> The problem of non-equivalence is most evident in those cases when we are dealing with words that designate objects, phenomena, or abstract concepts, which exist and have specific meaning for the speakers of one language; whereas the same words have quite a different meaning, or do not exist at all in the target language of the translation. If the essential non-equivalence of information conveyed by the original and target languages is ignored, the translation will distort the meaning of the text, or simply not make much sense to the reader.
> (Quoted in Howell 1997: 166)

In order then, to understand the background to non-equivalence of educational and administrative terms in Russian and English and the cultural context in which the different educational concepts and their verbal expression developed let us look briefly at the history of the system of education in Russia/the Soviet Union/CIS.

The cultural context. Different systems of education

The English word for education comes from the Latin and means, literally, to lead out. The Russian word *obrazovanie*[1] means formation. *Urok* the Russian word for *lesson* means a time to be served. In Britain we 'attend' or 'follow' a course, in Russian a course is 'listened to'. Already we have a difference in the concept of education. These words, obviously, pre-date the revolution, but many pre-Revolutionary ideas continued and became fixed under the Communist Party leadership.

The 1917 Revolution not only cut the Soviet Union off from Western ideas it also, of course, ushered in its own ideas and ideology, which embraced education as everything else. Initially a lot of these ideas were innovative and exciting, the ideas of Makarenko, Luria and Vygotsky for example, about the importance of the collective in education and the linking of work and education. The advent of Stalinism, however, put the lid on many of these new ideas:

> In essence an entire period in the history of Soviet pedagogy was being cancelled out – the period of its formation when the basic principles of Communist education were worked out, a Soviet system of preschool education and polytechnic schools joining labor and learning [...] when the great mass of bourgeois and petty-bourgeois pedagogical theories was re-evaluated in the light of Marxist theory [...]. When there was a large methodological literature, not only of a didactic nature but also describing the actual experience of Soviet schoolwork in the period 1918-36.

Roy Medvedev goes on to add:

> The hue and cry about 'excesses' signified the curtailment of polytechnic education, a tacit abandonment of the Leninist principle of combining work with study [...]. The 1933-34 curricula in physics, chemistry, biology, mathematics, and geography virtually ignored practical applications in industry and agriculture.
> (Medvedev 504: 1976)

---

[1] I have used the Library of Congress system of transliteration but without the diacritics.

The Soviet system of education became comparatively fixed and rigid, a centralized system where all power, ideas, timetabling emanated from the centre, with no room for individual initiative or innovation. As such, it achieved considerable success, leading the world in physics and sciences, teaching foreign languages to students, who had never left the country with such skill, that their erudition amazed native speakers. For side by side with an inflexible, traditional rote-learning teaching system went class discipline, respect for teachers, involvement of parents in the behavior of the children, after school clubs, and forming of a real feeling of the collective in class where stronger students helped the weaker ones. Nevertheless, in education, in terms of methodology and subject matter the Soviet Union became frozen in its own political and ideological time warp, until its collapse in 1991.

Compare this with the state educational system in this country, where every new government seemed to urge in new ideas, white papers, green papers and laws on education. In Britain we lecturers in higher education seem to be constantly re-training ourselves, to teach in a more 'communicative', 'transparent', 'student centred' way, incorporating modern technology into our lessons, writing out 'lesson plans' with 'aims' and 'objectives', specifying 'learning outcomes' and reflecting this in the 'assessment', giving students course outlines at the beginning of the course, asking for 'feedback' at the end of the course.

The student population is also different. In Britain students leave school later, at eighteen or nineteen, and then often take a year or two off. There are many more mature students. Once there they also spend less time at the university itself - many students only come in one or two days a week for a couple of lectures. The majority also holds down at least a part-time if not a full-time job.

In the former Soviet Union students come straight from school at sixteen. Except for after the last world war, when soldiers re-entered a disrupted education after having joined up, there is no tradition of mature students in higher education. Lacking the access to technology that we have in this country – most lecturers at University do not have office space of their own, let alone easy access to the inter-net, e-mail or a computer – the traditional methods of teaching at University continue. The Lecturer reads his/her lecture and students take notes. The teacher/lecturer is a venerable figure – to be treated with respect and 'listened' to during lecturers. In fact the Russian word for following a course is to 'listen' to it. Students are expected to take notes, turn up on time for lectures five and a half days a week and then go home and do their homework. The method of assessment is normally entirely up to the individual lecturer who has a bewildering - to us - array of various assessment mechanisms at his/her disposal. The State exams at the end are oral, they can be taken <u>three</u> times and the student 'gives' an exam s/he doesn't 'take' it, again, perhaps expressing a more passive, compliant attitude.

Now higher education in the CIS is being forced to change and adapt to new economic and socio-political realities. But new subjects like capitalist economics, public administration and management need not only information and advice from those who have experience in running such courses but new linguistic terms, new concepts. As Nigel Holden says:

> [...] throughout the entire Soviet period the peoples of the USSR had relatively little exposure to foreign (i.e. Western) influences. This meant [...] that Russian was deprived of lexical resources for the description and apprehension of western phenomena [...].
> (Holden in Somers 1996: 51)

However, precisely at a time when it is necessary to learn new skills, assimilate new concepts, teach in a new way, and teach new subjects, lecturers find themselves with less time than ever before. The traditional respect and prestige enjoyed by teachers and lecturers, together with their life-style, in the former Soviet Union, is under threat. When a lecturer at university earns £6 a month for forty hours teaching it is obvious that they must be supporting themselves from other sources as well. Most lecturers moonlight with at least two other better paid jobs.

Another barrier to East-West partnership is a political one. There are those in the former Soviet Union who think turning to the West is a betrayal of their own culture, beliefs and traditions. They might prefer closer partnership with Russia and countries of the CIS, but, for financial reasons, because of the bankruptcy of the state education systems in those countries have turned to the West for advice, assistance, and partnerships. What in theory is a partnership between equals can become a political humiliation for CIS educationalists. English becomes the language of the new colonisers in this post-Soviet era. The importation of English words to describe new concepts is seen as a cultural invasion heralding often unwelcome economic change and alien lifestyles. Nigel Holden again puts it clearly:

> [...]a high proportion of these imported words are to do with business, management and economics, the lexis of not merely the market economy but of a new way of life and underlying assumptions and attitudes. [...] this language is entering Russia under extraordinary circumstances. *It is to a large extent being thrust on Russia.* This means that western management educators need to be aware that the increasingly documented problems of teaching management subjects to Russians [...] can legitimately be seen as a form of Russian wariness of, even occasionally, resistance to, externally imposed sociolinguistic change.
> (Holden in Somers 1996: 52)

East-West partnerships

I would now like to look at particular linguistic problems that arose from a partnership between Britain and a member of the CIS: we at the University of North London were validating a new MA course in the Ukraine.

The course we were validating had enormous potential for linguistic confusion:

* It was a course that had never run before: the brief was to retrain the civil servants of a newly independent Ukraine to operate in a qualitatively different way from before: i.e. to respond to the public, to take independent decisions, rather than act on orders from above. In other words to act like managers rather than administrators.

* In addition they were taking on duties which had not before been part of their role – like foreign affairs, tax collecting and education. Previously these had been administrated from Moscow.

* Not only was the subject matter of the course new and perhaps lacking the necessary linguistic terms, but the method in which they were expected to teach it was also new – we expected them to teach in a communicative, interactive way with well-defined aims and objectives reflected clearly in the assessment.

* The last potentially confusing item was that neither they nor we were fully aware of the linguistic problems.

This then is the break down of some of the difficulties we faced. I would like to look now, in more detail, at some of the culturally specific educational terms. The most difficult words to translate relate, not surprisingly, to politics and economics, and to new methodology in education in Britain. I will examine the non-equivalence of certain terms, where I shall be l looking for formal and dynamic equivalence as defined by Nida (1974: 199). Dynamic equivalence refers to equivalent effect in the target language. Formal equivalence is closer to a literal, or semantic translation.

Policy/Politics - *Politika*
Like most European languages Russian has only the one word *politika* to translate our policy/politics.

If we look at the Collins English dictionary (1981) definition of policy, we find very positive descriptions :

1. A plan of action pursued by an individual, government, etc.
2. Wisdom or prudence

Whereas the definition of politics is either neutral or pejorative:

1. The practice or the study of the art or science of forming, directing and administrating states and other political units; the art and science of government; political science; (sing. only) the complex or aggregate of relationships of men in society , esp those involving power;(pl. only) political activities or affairs;
   any activity concerned with the acquisition of power, gaining one`s own ends, etc;

2. the policy formulating activities of government as distinguished from the administrative or legal;the civil function of government as distinguished from the military.

Russian has only one word for policy and politics which is *politika* and is defined thus in a monolingual Russian dictionary anterior to 1991 (Ed. Evgeneva 1981):

1. The activity of state power, a party or public group in the sphere of internal state or international relations, defined by the class interests of this power, party or group;
2. events and questions of internal and international public life;
3. the general behavioural characteristics or means of operation of somebody, aimed at achieving a particular goal or relationship;
4. (archaic) participation in revolutionary work in the revolutionary movement.

Thus in a 1998 Russian/Russian dictionary of foreign words (Krysin 1998):

1. As (1) above but without *defined by the class interests of this power, party or group*
2. As (2) above
3. A particular tendency, direction of the state or particular groups.
4. As (3) above.

We see not only the English definitions of policy and politics are not all to be found in the Russian *politika* but that, because of the ideological shift in Russia and the rest of the CIS today, Russian dictionary definitions before and after 1991 also do not coincide. Nowhere in the Russian word *politika* do we find the positive connotations of policy. However the class connotations of *politika* have been lost since 1991 in the dictionaries.

If we take the overall correspondence of these words, policy and politics in English and the word *politika* in Russian we might compare them to two circles that overlap but certainly do not cover each other (Chukovsky 1988: 56).

Academic terms and structures

Traditional CIS undergraduate university courses last five years and are roughly equivalent to our first degree plus an MA. The award Soviet students received was called a *diplom*. After that comes a *Kandidat nauk* (two years upward) which must contain original research and is roughly halfway between an MA and a PhD. Than comes a *Dokturantura* which is a very prestigious award, must be original research and can take anything from three years upwards.

The MA is not a Soviet degree. *Magistr*, the nearest Russian equivalent, has this two relevant translations in a Russian dictionary for foreign words (Krysin 1998):

1. In some countries a second degree after the Baccalaureate (the Baccalaureate here taken to mean an award on finishing university).
2. (hist.) In Russia until 1917 an academic title given to those who had completed a university or a religious academy course and had taken a special exam and defended a dissertation.

On the eastern side there is little familiarity with the shape of a modern MA. Is it a taught award or research? Or a mixture of both? How many modules should it have if it is taught? We in this country normally have no more that eight modules on an MA which lasts one year. Because of the difference in undergraduate modules/courses, it should come as no surprise that forty modules can be packed into a Russian/Ukrainian MA and the length is seen as more flexible.

Many university courses in Britain are now modular. Undergraduate education in the CIS is overwhelmingly still based on whole courses. The term module is not not an academic one in Russian. As with the term MA the meaning may be easy to explain, but it is a foreign concept. *Modiul'* even in the revised 1998 Collins concise Oxford and Krysin's 1998 Russian/Russian dictionary of foreign words is translated as a maths modulus.

Administrative terms

<u>MA in Public Administration</u>

The name of the course we were validating was, in English, an MA in Public Administration. Immediately there is fertile ground if not for misunderstandings then, at least, for misconceptions.

We have discussed the non-familiarity with the Western style MA above.

The word public is translated in several different ways in Russian depending on the particular collocation, none of which contain all the connotations which the word public has for British (as opposed to American) people.

The English (Collins 1981) definitions of public are:

1. relating to, or concerning the people as a whole;
2. open or accessible to all;
3. performed or made openly in view of all;
4. well known, or familiar to people in general;
5. maintained at the expense of, serving or for the use of the community;
6. open, acknowledged or notorious;
7. go public (of a private company): to issue shares for subscription by the public
8. the community or people in general;
9. a part or section of the community grouped because of a common interest, activity, etc.

Which of these definitions do we need for public administration? Interestingly, the Russian translation of public in this context is by a word fitting none of the above descriptions: *derzhavnyi* meaning a) holding supreme power and b) powerful – from the word *derzhava* meaning political power. Thus the title of this course in Russian is "An MA in Administration by the Supreme Power".

Civil servant /Local Government Officer

The Collins (1989) defines the civil service thus:

> The service responsible for the public administration of the government of a country. It excludes the legislative, judicial and military branches. Members of the civil service have no official political allegiance and are not generally affected by changes of government.

Civil is translated as *grazhdanskii.* But civil servant is translated in the Oxford Russian/English (1997) as *gossudarstvenyi sluzhaschii* - which literally means servant of the state.

In pre-revolutionary Russia the Table of Ranks was introduced by Peter the First in the 1722 and lasted until the October Revolution. This placed all state employees in three separate categories: military/naval; civil and royal. These categories were then sub-divided into 14 different ranks, with rank 1 being the highest (*Sovetskii entsiklopedicheskii slovar`* M. 1982). Under this system 1-5 would be the rough equivalent of our civil servant and below that would be various ranks of regional and local government officers. It was a highly centralised autocratic system with power filtering down from the upper ranks.

After 1917 the table of ranks was abolished but the centralised power system remained. A network of local soviets/councils replaced the lower ranks of the Table. Theoretically local soviet officers were democratically elected, but in practice they all belonged to the Communist Party.

After 1991 the Table of ranks was reintroduced into the Ukraine. The term *gosudarstvennyi sluzhashchii* can, then, mean either a rough equivalent of our civil servant or a local government officer.

Administration/Management

The lack of a Russian word for management reflects the reality of the Tsarist and Soviet past when low-ranking civil servants and local Party officials were simply administrators, carrying out instructions passed down from the top and private enterprise officially did not exist in the Russian republic. The Russian word *ypravlenie* Is generally used to translate both administration and management. Recently the English - derived word *menedzhment* and *menedzher* is used but without the fullness of the English meaning. As Nigel Holden says: "[…] the task of management is almost always described in terms of control of production; a view of management that would be seen in the West as narrow, if not somewhat misleading." (Holden in Somers 1996)

Methodological terms

Aims and objectives

The words aims and objectives are generally synonyms and were initially translated by our interpretor by the same word in Russian *tsel`*. This made nonsense of what we were saying in English, as we were distinguishing between the two. The problem here is not one of intrinsic meanings, but of the specific meanings that aims and objectives have acquired in educational terminology in the West. We later produced a glossary of certain words and in this, following the advice of our Russian and Ukrainian colleagues, we translated objectives as *zadachi* – literally 'tasks'/'problems'. However, this is not the correct translation of objectives. A better one would probably be particular aims, i.e. in Russian *obschie tseli* and *spetsificheskie tseli* – learning outcomes and aims.

Learning outcomes

This was translated as *rezul`taty obuchenii* - literally, 'the results of teaching'. This unfortunately maintains the focus on teaching as opposed to learning. A better translation would be *rezul`taty izuchenii* – 'the results of learning/studying'. The difficulty of finding an expressive equivalent of these words in Russian is due to our separate educational development. Our concept of learning outcomes is born of a shift in focus in education from the teacher to the student. This shift has not yet happened in the former Soviet Union. In asking our CIS colleagues to rephrase course descriptions so that learning outcomes reflect what students will be able to 'do' at the end of a module/course, rather than what they should 'know' or 'learn' can be seen as formalism and pedantry if the underlying concepts are not fully understood or accepted.

Assessment

The methods of assessment in Higher Education Establishment in the CIS are many and varied and we had difficulty understanding the various translations:

Kontrol`naia rabota – This could be translated as ongoing and regular assessment in class by a variety of methods, little tests, role play, questionnaires, task solving, essays.

Modul`nyi kontrol` - Exam at the end of the module.

Ekzamen – Usually a state exam, traditionally oral, where the student has to answer three questions on work done during the whole of the course.

But the methods of assessment are very different and usually up to the individual lecturer, so there is not necessarily homogeneity in testing and assessment between modules.

Staff development:

This was initially translated into Russian as expansion of staff, i.e. acquiring more staff. Our idea of staff development had to be clearly explained. The difficulty here is that so many of the staff in higher education in the CIS today, as mentioned earlier, are part-timers and have jobs elsewhere. It is difficult to get full staff meetings and to create a cohesive plan for staff development and, in this time of crisis in education in Russia and the CIS, to find the resources to fund staff development. However, if it had been translated as *povyshenie kvalifikatsii* - improving qualifications - it would have been understood.

Conclusion

This is very much an exploratory paper, written as a result of a personal experience of an east-west validation. A lot more work needs to be done on clarifying our different systems. To do this it is necessary to know first of all where they differ. I hope that I have managed to indicate some of the differences that exist between our respective educational systems and have demonstrated that difficulties in achieving understanding in educational partnerships when working through an interpreter are caused by linguistic non-equivalence formal or dynamic, which themselves are the result of a different concept of education through decades of separate development. Those different concepts in turn reveal different attitudes and values and realities about education as well as teaching methodologies. We both have lecturers/teachers at universities, but over here a lecturer expects access to a computer and e-mail, office space, regular meetings, staff development. In the CIS a lecturer runs from one job to another, often more highly qualified than our lecturers but at a fraction of the salary, with no personal e-mail, no computer access, no office space. That is the economic and cultural difference between the two words and the two worlds.

It is clear that for a cross-cultural intra-lingual partnership to be most effective those involved in negotiating it and in on-going discussions about it on both sides should be briefed on the particular educational culture of the other side. Terminology in discussions should be kept as simple as possible, with both sides aware of the different cultural connotations of different terms. There should also be a glossary of terms to help the interpreter and to save time at meetings. These terms should have explanations beside them where the different connotations of words or terminology are not immediately clear.

The effective interpreter, translator in educational terms must be culturally as well as linguistically fluent. It is our job to brief the interpreters and translators that we work with, to assist them in helping us to cross the East-West cultural barriers that still remain. If we do so, it will be to the mutual benefit of both our educational systems.

References

Baker, Mona. 1990. *In Other Words. London*: Routledge.
Chernykh Pavel.Yakovlevitch. 1994. *Istoriko-etimologicheskii slovar` sovremennogo russkogo iazyka*. Moscow: Russkii Iazyk
Chukovsky, Korney. 1988. *Vysokoe iskusstvo.* Moscow: Sovietskii pisatel`.
Denisova, P.N. and V.V. Morkovkina (eds.). 1983. *Slovar` sochetaemosti slov russkogo iazyka*. Moscow: Russkii iazyk.
Evgen`eva A.P. (ed.) 1983. *Slovar` russkogo iazyka v chetyrex tomax.* Russkii Yazyk.
Hanks, Patrick. 1979. (revised ed.) *Collins Dictionary of the English Language.* New York: Harper Collins
Holden Nigel. 1996. "The reorientation of management language in Russian and Poland in the transition to the market economy: A neglected perspective". In Somers, Harold. *Terminology, LSP and Translation – Studies in Language Engineering in Honour of Juan C. Sager*. Amsterdam/Philadelphia: John Benjamins Publishing Company.
Howell, Yvonne. 1997. "When Physicists are Lyricists". In Grenoble, Leore and Kopper, John. *Essays in the Art and Theory of Translation.* NewYork: Lampeter, Edwin Mellen Press.
Katan, Dennis. 1999. *Translating Cultures*. Manchester: St. Jerome,

Krysin, L.L. 1998. *Tolkovyi Slovar` inoiazychnykh slov.* Moscow: Russkii Iazyk.
Medvedev, Roy. 1976. *Let History Judge.* Nottingham: Spokesman Books.
Makarenko A.S. 1965. *Problems of Soviet School Education.* Moscow: Progress Publishers.
Newmark, Peter. 1988. *A Textbook of Translation.* London/New York: Prentice Hall.
Nida, Eugene and Taber, Charles. 1969. *The Theory and Practice of Translation,* Leiden: United Bible Societies, 1969.
Ozhegov S. I. 1973. *Slovar` russkogo iazyka.* Moscow: Sovietskaia entsiklopedia
Ryazanova-Clarke L. and Wade T. 1999. *The Russian Language Today.* London: Routledge.
Wheeler Larissa, Unbegaun Boris & Falla Paul. (eds.) 1997 (revised ed.).*The Oxford Russian Dictionary.* Oxford: Oxford University Press.

Teaching the translation of Spanish medical discourse

Lola la Torre, University of Portsmouth

Abstract

This paper explores problems related to the teaching of Spanish medical discourse. The focus is on the approach followed for teaching abstracts in a medical journal. The approach involves (I) defining medical discourse and outlining its main features, particularly at the lexical level; (II) cognate recognition exercises; (III) training students to identify salient features of the source text such as genre, purpose, syntactic complexity and lexical difficulties the translator should be aware of; (IV) discussion of strategies to overcome these problems, and finally, (VI) comparing students' translations with a published translation of the abstract.

Introduction

Specialised Translation is a two-semester option in the School of Languages at the University of Portsmouth. This undergraduate course was designed to give advanced students of Spanish an understanding of the issues raised by specialised translation. Training was provided in translating Spanish texts in a range of specialised registers, researching the language for translating them using dictionaries and through parallel texts on the Internet, and consulting professionals.

This paper outlines the approach followed for teaching the translation of Spanish medical discourse into English. The discussion will focus on one of the genres most frequently translated by professional translators: the abstract in medical journals. The aims of the teaching of medical discourse are very pragmatic. The students should develop strategies to overcome problems posed by a specialist medical text. The approach is divided into the following stages: (a) an introduction to the main features of medical discourse; (b) cognate recognition exercises; (c) analysis of source text; (d) translation and discussion of problems faced and strategies to overcome difficulties; (e) comparison of students' translations with a published translation of the abstract.

This paper begins with a discussion of the features of medical discourse which focuses mainly on its terminology and the differences between Spanish and English medical terms. Following this, the importance of cognate recognition strategies is discussed. Finally, some issues relating to the translation of a sample abstract are considered.

The language of medical discourse

Medical discourse belongs to the larger field of scientific and technical translation, i.e., the translation of empirical-descriptive texts written in the context of scientific or technological disciplines. The main feature of medical translation is its terminology, which reflects its highly specialised nature. Although there is a very long tradition of Spanish medical writing and translation, English has become the *lingua franca* for medicine, and Spanish (like many European and Asian languages) somewhat lags behind English as far as the creation of neologisms is concerned. The task of expressing English neologisms in Spanish is sometimes done hurriedly. Translators have three possibilities, either they find adequate Spanish equivalents, borrow from English, or hispanize English terms (Segura 1999).

The vast majority of medical terms derive from Latin and Greek, and this means that Spanish and English share cognate vocabulary. Holmes and Ramos define cognates as "items of vocabulary in two languages which have the same roots and can be recognised as such" (Holmes and Ramos 1995: 88). The two main features of cognates are their orthographic and semantic similarity in both Spanish and English. According to an etymological approach, cognates can be classified into true and false cognates, the latter also known as false friends. True cognates are similar in form and their semantic meanings completely or almost completely overlap in every context (la Torre, 1994). An example is *antibiótico*, 'antibiotic'. False cognates and false friends, on the other hand, are similar in form but their semantic meanings either do not overlap or only partially overlap. Sometimes, either the Spanish or the English word has an additional meaning. Almost any science has such lexical hindrances and medicine is rich in these. For example, the cognate *prospecto*, means 'patient information leaflet', as well as 'prospectus'. Another example is *sanidad*, which means 'health or public health service'. Its cognate, sanity, means 'mental soundness' in Spanish. These examples are striking, especially for the translator, but they are part of a more general phenomenon when we try to pair any lexical items in two different languages.

Cognates. Main features

A trainee translator may assume that translating cognates from Spanish into English should not pose any problems (after all, they look similar), but a brief look at the question will provide an introduction to what are often complex problems.

Latin and Greek roots

While Latin components usually refer to a specific part of our body, Greek ones indicate that the part of the body is being studied or that there is something wrong with it (Albin, 1999). For example, the Spanish anatomical term for the ovary is *ovario*, from the Latin '*ovarium*', and the branch of medicine concerned with the functions and diseases of the female reproductive system is *ginecología*, 'gynaecology'. The Latin root '*mamm/o*' is found in terms which describe the anatomy of the breast, for example, *glándula mamaria*, 'mammary gland', and the Greek root '*mast/o*' is found whenever pathology is encountered as in mastitis (inflammation of the mammary gland in the breast).

Suffixes and prefixes

The ability to recognise the component parts of medical terms is essential because they provide us with the information we need to work out the meaning of each part. Thus, the suffix *-itis* means inflammation, *-graphy* indicates a technique of producing images. Prefixes can indicate, among other things, location (*pre-*, *supra-*), as in predorsal (situated behind the spinal cord), excess (*hiper-*), as in *hipermétrope* (short-sighted), deficiency (*hipo-*), as in *hipoalérgico* (hypo-allergenic, i.e unlikely to cause an allergic reaction) or opposition (*anti-*), for example, *antidepresivo* (antidepressant). Unlike English, all Spanish prefixes (with the exception of *ex*) are attached without hyphens to the words they modify. Thus, in Spanish pre-eclampsia and post-partum would be *preeclampsia* and *postparto*.

Changes in spelling and word order

Many Latin and Greek components are left in their classical form but are written with Spanish spelling. Greek *y* changes into *i,* for example *cystitis* changes into 'cistitis', symptom, '*síntoma*'; *u-* changes into *o-*, as in uterus, '*útero*'; the consonant *h* preceding a group of vowels is omitted, as in diarrhoea, '*diarrea*' and haemorrhage, '*hemorragia*'.

In Spanish, modifiers follow the noun as in *virus del papiloma humano*, 'human papillomavirus'. Sometimes the components can appear in reverse order as in *patofisiológico,* 'physiopathologic'.

Plain English

One of the differences between medical Spanish and English is that, whereas there is a tendency to use Latin and Greek roots in Spanish, many of those terms need to be simplified and written in plain English. Very many good examples can be found in patient information leaflets. For example, the Spanish *somnolencia*, is translated as 'drowsiness' and not 'somnolence'. *Analgésico* could be rendered as 'analgesic', but 'pain killer' or 'pain reliever' is preferred. Likewise, we have *citología* which is 'cervical or pap smear', *cardiopatías*, 'heart disease', or *molestias gástricas*, 'stomach upset'. There are cases when we find examples of a Latin term used in English which have to be simplified in plain Spanish as in cervix, '*cuello del útero*' (neck of the womb), but these are exceptions rather than the rule.

Change from Latin into Greek or vice versa
Since Latin is the language for naming parts of the body, we would expect any Latin term found in English to be unchanged in Spanish, however, we should not make any assumptions. One example of terms which change drastically is the *Latin 'medula oblongata'* which in Spanish changes into Greek: *bulbo raquídeo* (Albin 1999).

Microorganisms and illnesses
Microorganisms are italicised, while illnesses are not. Only the first letter of the first term of an organism is used, and the modifier is written in lowercase. For example *'Helicobacter pylori'* is written *H. pylori*. Some of the very common organisms, have a Spanish version or are the same, as in *Helicobacter pylori*.

To sum up, as these examples show, translators should never make assumptions based on their intuition regarding lexical meanings. Bilingual medical dictionaries can help up to a point. Hence, the need for constant reading and searching for terminology through parallel texts (Segura 1999).

Grammatical and semantic features
Generally speaking, Spanish medical texts lack syntactic complexity. Passive *se* and impersonal *se* sentences preponderate, as in *se estudiaron con carácter prospectivo 101 pacientes,* "101 patients were prospectively studied". The meaning of a sentence is always precise and repetition of words is used to reinforce clarity.

Clarity, concision and correctness, the three main features or stylistic aims of technical writing (Herman, 1993), also apply to medical translation. First, clarity requires that the information be presented clearly, avoiding complex sentences. Second, concision means that the information be comprehensive. Finally, correctness implies that each word convey the exact meaning. Hence, the translator should attempt to produce a clear, concise and accurate translation.

The importance of cognate recognition strategies
The importance of cognate recognition in medical translation is crucial. Although cognate vocabulary is important, there has been relatively little systematic investigation of how we learn and teach these lexical items (Holmes and Ramos 1995). The existence of cognates means that, in principle, an English student of Spanish should recognise the majority of words of Latin and Greek origin when reading a medical type of text. However, as we have seen in section 1, handling Latin and Greek cognates is not an easy task. First, there is the problem of knowledge of the subject and background assumptions not shared by the non-specialist. Second, there are lexical problems arising from the specialised use of the technical terms. In this respect, the most striking feature is that of terms which at first sight have an ordinary use, familiar to the translator, but which in the target text has a completely different use. Medicine is very rich in false friends, and translators must be aware of them. For

example, in Spanish '*estar constipado*' means 'to have a cold' and not 'to be constipated'. Mistaken assumptions on such points can lead to disastrous consequences.

As the above examples show, there is a clear need to help students adopt effective cognate recognition strategies.

The main aims in using cognate recognition exercises are:

1. To equip students with training strategies. As students develop experience they will become better guessers (Holmes and Ramos 1995: 90)
2. To help students to become more efficient translators.

Cognate recognition exercises

One of the possible pre-translation tasks before the translation of an abstract in a medical journal involves asking students, in pairs or small groups, to look at a list of cognates (true and false cognates). The next step involves completing cognate recognition exercises to encourage students to reflect on Latin and Greek terms. The instructions of the task are as follows:

Pre-translation task

Look at the following list of Latin and Greek words.

a) Identify the different components of each word and explain their meaning
b) Find a translation for each technical term
c) Can you think of any other Spanish medical term with the same pattern?

1. *Hipertensión*
2. *Hipoglucemia*
3. *Hemofilia*
4. *Arritmia*
5. *Gastroenteritis*
6. *Ginecología*
7. *Estomatología*
8. *Endocrinología*
9. *Biopsia*
10. *Dermatólogo*
11. *Podólogo*
12. *Arterioesclerosis*
13. *Prenatal*
14. *Constipado*

In the list above we find examples of cognates which may pose problems to the translator. Students are warned that they should not make assumptions on the basis of the form, but they should always check with the dictionary, and when the dictionary is unhelpful, they should look them up in parallel texts. Handling cognates can be a minefield.

A close analysis of the list of cognates reveals the following:

1. All of the cognates above are true cognates, with the exception of *constipado*, which is a false cognate and means 'to have a cold'.

2. *Gastroenteritis* derived from *gastros-* (stomach) + *enter-* (intestine) + *-itis* (inflammation) means inflammation of the stomach and the intestines. This is the only true cognate on the list which completely overlaps in form and meaning with its English equivalent.
3. *Podólogo,* which is formed from the Greek *podo* (foot) and *logo* (specialist) is often translated as 'chiropodist' (*chiro-* 'hand' + *pod-* 'foot'), although "*podiatrist*' (*pod-* + *iatros* 'physician') is also used.
4. A good example of terms that change drastically from Greek to Latin is *estomatología*, derived from the Greek *estomato-*, 'mouth', and *-logia*, which changes into the Latin derived term 'dentistry'.
5. Although the equivalent of *hipertensión,* derived from the Greek root *tension* and the prefix *hiper-*, could be easily rendered as 'hypertension' in English, the simplified 'high blood pressure' is usually preferred.
6. A good example of a cognate that changes the prefix to a different one is *prenatal*, which changes into *antenatal*.
7. There are slight changes in the spelling when translating from Spanish into English. For example, *arterioesclerosis* changes into 'arteriosclerosis', where the intervocalic e- in *esclerosis* must be omitted. The Greek component *-logia* changes into '-logy'. Thus, *ginecología* and *endocrinología* become 'gynaecology', and 'endocrinology'. *Biopsia* (bio + psia) changes into 'biopsy'. The vowel *-i* changes into *-y*, as in *hipertensión*, *hipoglucemia* and *arritmia,* which change into hypertension', 'hypoglycaemia' and 'arrhythmia'. Finally, *f-* changes into ph-, as in *hemofilia*, which changes into 'haemophilia'.

Another task could involve asking students to skim through the source text. This technique builds up a content or schema which then helps in the correct identification of further cognates.

Translation of an abstract from a medical journal

Analysis of the source text

This section will focus on the analysis of an abstract of an article (see Appendix A), "*Análisis de defectos congénitos debidos a la ingesta de drogas durante el embarazo*", by María Luisa Martínez Frías, which appeared in *Medicina Clínica***,** a prestigious Spanish medical journal. The journal is available in electronic format on the Internet (see bibliography for web address). An English translation of the abstract is also available. The format of abstracts is usually the following: Objective or Background, Material and Methods, Results and Conclusions.

The importance of the analysis of the main features of the Spanish text before attempting the translation is crucial. The following elements are analysed (Truman and Zaro 1998):

(a) Content Area. By content or subject area I mean the branch of medicine which the text belongs to.
(b) Genre. What kind of text it is, whether a medical course book, a journal article, a newspaper article, etc.
(c) Purpose or function, i.e., a text can be persuasive, informative, argumentative, etc.
(d) Syntactic complexity.
(e) Lexis. Unknown vocabulary can make the understanding of the text difficult.

In addition, the analysis of parallel texts (such as the *British Medical Journal*), with a view to translating texts of the same genre is suggested.

Content area, genre and purpose
The text belongs to the branch of gynaecology and obstetrics. It is a brief text and the main purpose of the text is to present an objective account of research and a description of the experiment carried out. The text meets the three stylistic features of technical writing (Herman 1993), i.e. clarity, concision and correctness. The evidence is presented clearly and objectively, avoiding long, complex sentences. The structure of the text is clear and some key words are repeated throughout.

Syntactic complexity
Impersonal *se* and present tense constructions prevail. The following 'se' constructions are found:

1. *en este trabajo se pretende analizar*: the purpose of this study is to analyse
2. *se realiza un estudio*: a study is carried out
3. *se efectúa un análisis*: an analysis is carried out
4. *se obtienen riesgos importantes*: we observed important risks /important risks are obtained
5. *estas madres son más jóvenes*: these mothers are younger

Lexis
With regard to terminology, the text is full of true and false cognates. We can divide them into different categories according to the following characteristics:
* True cognates. Similar in form and meaning
Análisis, defectos congénitos, ingesta, drogas, drogadicción, médico, sanitario analizar, proporción, tubo neural, atresia de las coanas, atresia del esófago, gastrosquisis, atresia del ano, polidactilia postaxial, gestación, and *preventivas*

* True cognates but a simplified term is used in English : ingestión de vitaminas – intake of vitamins

* False cognates
Preocupación - concern
Futuro hijo - unborn
Consumidoras de drogas – drug abusers
Se pretende – we intend

Comparing target texts
After completion of the translation and the discussion of how students tackled the problems posed by the source text, a published English abstract is provided. (See Appendix B). Students have the chance to compare their solutions with the ones proposed by the translator and are invited to make suggestions on how the abstract could have been improved.

The translation of the abstract contains a number of orthographical, lexical and grammatical errors which could be easily improved. Therefore the quality and accuracy of the translation is assessed before improvements are suggested.

Lexical errors
Within the group of lexical errors, a number of terms have not been rendered accurately. Thus, *el futuro hijo* was translated as 'the embryo and fetus'. A better translation which conveys the original meaning in the source text is 'the unborn'. Other inappropriate or inaccurate renderings were the translation of *la ingestión de alcohol, el tabaco,* as 'maternal

alcohol, maternal smoking', which could be improved by translating 'the alcohol and tobacco intake by pregnant women'.

We also found some mistranslated false friends. For example, *consumidoras de drogas* was poorly translated as 'consumers of illicit drugs' instead of 'drug addicts'.

Some words were not accurately rendered. Thus, *además*, 'furthermore', was mistranslated as 'on the other hand'.

Grammatical errors

Gramatical errors were also found. These are often due to the influence of Spanish syntax. Unlike English, in Spanish (with some exceptions), the definite article *el/la/los/las* is required before a generic noun, especially when the noun is the subject of the verb. For example, *En la mujer* was translated as 'the women'.

Omission of information

Important information was omitted. In the conclusion section we find: *En la mujer, la drogadicción (y sus circunstancias sociosanitarias) durante el embarazo, y posiblemente durante los períodos inmediatamente anteriores àl mismo, aumenta el riesgo para cierto tipo de defectos congénitos.* In the translation we read: "The women who are addicted to illicit drugs during pregnancy, have an increased risk for infants with several congenital defects". This translation is not accurate, since key information (*sus circunstancias sociosanitarias*, "their health and financial background"; *y posiblemente durante los períodos inmediatamente anteriores al mismo,* "and possibly during the pre-conceptual care period") has been left out.

Orthographical errors

Throughout was misspelt as 'trhoughout'.

Conclusion

This paper has set out to provide an overview of the possibilities for the translation of Spanish medical journal abstracts. It has explored ways of increasing cognate recognition on students' part and their awareness of the difficulties posed by this genre. Finally, a discussion of ways of improving a published translation of the abstract helps students to reflect on options and alternatives, hence developing critical-thinking strategies.

References

Albin, Verónica. 1999. Handling Greek and Latin Terms in Spanish Medical Translation, *The Translation Journal*, Vol 3 (3) July 1999. http://www.accurapid.com/journal/

Herman, M. 1993. "Technical Translation Style: Clarity, Concision, Correctness". In Wright, Sue Ellen and Wright Leland D. (eds) *Scientific and Technical Translation*. Amsterdam/Philadelphia: John Benjamins Publishing Company.

Holmes, J. and Guerra-Ramos, R. (1995) "False Friends and Reckless Guessers: Observing Cognate Recognition Strategies". In Huckin, Thomas, Haynes, Margot and Coady, James. *Second Language Reading and Vocabulary Learning*, Norwood, NJ: Ablex.

la Torre, Maria Dolóres. 1994. "On true cognate recognition by English students of Spanish". Unpublished MA dissertation: University of Newcastle.

Martínez Frías, M. L. 1999. "Análisis del riesgo de defectos congénitos debidos a la ingesta de drogas durante el embarazo". *Medicina Clínica* 112: 41-44.

Medicina Clínica: http://www.doyma.es/copiaini/revistas/mc/resume/

Segura, Jack. 1999. "The Spanish Language in Medicine". In *The Translation Journal*, Vol 3 (3) July 1999. http://www.accurapid.com/journal/
Truman, M. and Zaro, J.J. (1998) *Manual de Traducción*, Madrid: SGEL.

APPENDIX A: Source Text

Análisis del riesgo de defectos congénitos debidos a la ingesta de drogas durante el embarazo

Fundamento: La drogadicción es un tema de gran interés médico, sanitario y social. Pero la preocupación es aún mayor si nos referimos a la drogadicción durante el embarazo, ya que sus efectos no sólo actúan sobre la madre, sino sobre el desarrollo del futuro hijo. En este trabajo, se pretende analizar el riesgo de la ingestión de drogas durante el embarazo para distintos tipos de defectos congénitos.

Material y métodos: Se realiza un estudio de las características maternas, así como la evolución temporal de la proporción de madres consumidoras de drogas. Así mismo, se efectúa un análisis de casos y controles, mediante modelos de regresión logística múltiple, con objeto de controlar posibles factores relacionados con la drogadicción y que podrían confundir los resultados del análisis univariado.

Resultados: La proporción de madres consumidoras de drogas está aumentando en el tiempo en España. Además, estas madres son más jóvenes que las no drogadictas y tienen mayor riesgo global para defectos congénitos (*odds ratio* [OR]= 1,84; p=0,007). Al estudiar tipos específicos de defectos, se obtienen riesgos importantes y estadísticamente significativos para defectos del tubo neural, atresia de las coanas, atresia del esófago, gastrosquisis, atresia del ano y polidactilia postaxial, una vez que controlamos los posibles efectos de la edad materna, el nivel de escolaridad, la ingestión de alcohol, el tabaco y la ingestión de vitaminas/minerales durante la gestación.

Conclusiones: En la mujer, la drogadicción (y sus circunstancias socionanitarias) durante el embarazo, y posiblemente durante los períodos inmediatamente anteriores al mismo, aumenta el riesgo para cierto tipo de defectos congénitos. Un buen control médico de las condiciones nutricionales y sanitarias durante la gestación, el tratamiento de la adicción y una buena información a la población son las mejores medidas preventivas.

María Luisa Martínez-Frías. MEDICINA CLINICA, Sábado 23 de Enero de 1999, 112: 41-44.

APPENDIX B: Target text

Analysis of the risk for congenital defects due to illicit drug abuse during pregnancy

Background: Illicit drug abuse is a major area of interest, for clinicians, as well as for public health and social authorities. But one of the major concerns is the illicit drug abuse during the periconceptional period and throughout pregnancy, because of its potential effect on the embryo and fetus. In this study we analyze the possible risk of illicit drug abuse during pregnancy for different selected congenital defects.

Materials and methods: We analyzed the annual evolution of the proportion of mothers who are addicted to illicit drugs, as well as some of their characteristics. We also performed a case-control study using different models of multiple logistic regression analyses, controlling possible confounded factors.

Results: We observed that the proportion of mothers who are addicted to illicit drugs shows an increasing liner trend over time. On the other hand, these mothers are younger that those who are not consumers of illicit drugs, and have an overall risk for congenital defects of 1.84($p = 0.007$). We also studied the different selected types of congenital defects, controlling the potential effect of the following variables: maternal age, maternal cultural level, maternal alcohol, maternal smoking, and vitamins/minerals during pregnancy. In these analyses we obtained statistically significant increased risks for: neural tube defects, choanal atresia, esophageal atresia, gastroschisis, anal atresia, and postaxial polydactyly.

Conclusions: The women who are addicted to illicit drugs during pregnancy, have an increased risk for infants with several congenital defects. The way to prevent these effects should be based on a good information about this aspect to the general population, as well as on a careful medical control of the nutrition of these mothers and their health and social conditions during gestation, and the treatment of their addiction before and during pregnancy.

Med Clin (Barc) 1999, 112: 41-44.

Specialised translation study with view to science and technology terminology

Dora Blagova, New Bulgarian University

Abstract
The present paper deals with the Bulgarian translation equivalents of English Noun + Noun Phrases in science and technology texts. The scope of the data is restricted to NPs because their contextual dependence raises a number of issues associated with translation practices. Another reason is that Bulgarian and English greatly differ with regard to premodification. This leads to employing transformations which usually make the meaning more explicit. With view to finding out the source of the greater explicitness in the translations, the source language structures are compared with the target language structures produced by translators and then with similar structures in Bulgarian texts.
The data is excerpted from a corpus of English - Bulgarian translations. It is systematised according to morphological, syntactic and semantic features. The similarities and differences of the two languages are considered from structural and functional perspective.
The aim of the study is to investigate the transformations employed by translators to render English N+NPs. The resulting taxonomy of the translation equivalents is further used to outline rules for the transformation of English N+ NPs into appropriate Bulgarian structures.

Introduction

Scientific style and terminology

One of the salient features of scientific texts from the point of view of functional style is the frequency of noun phrases. Thus, a great deal of the information to be rendered is compressed in the nominal groups. Sager defines the function of the nominal groups as "building blocks of the sentences" and that of the sentence pattern as "establishing the relationship between the nominal groups" (Sager 1981: 219, 187).

> This is one of the ways in which it might be said that a discourse community owns a genre. (Swales 1990: 46).

Since nominalisation entails implicitation, the referent of the phrase is often difficult to infer. Purely linguistic analysis is not sufficient to arrive at a correct identification of the denoted entity. The inferring of meaning by the participants in the communicative act is also associated with their knowledge about the world. The reference of the expression would be successful if the addresser and the addressee share the same knowledge about the world. A lexical item denotes an object in the extralinguistic reality and it has meaning components, which are based on salient features relevant for the distinguishing of that entity from other entities.

> It is generally the case that obscurity in premodification exists only for the hearer or reader who is unfamiliar with the subject concerned and who is not therefore equipped to tolerate the radical reduction in explicitness that premodification entails. (Quirk, Greenbaum, Leech and Svartvik 1985: 1343)

Knowledge about the world can be divided into general, social (including special) and individual. In special texts, syntactic patterns are often used to classify a concept in the respective field or to identify an entity. In identifying the referent of a terminological phrase one can arrive at the stage of a possible range of entities on the basis of analysis, i.e. a term is an analytic construction in general knowledge. In special knowledge, a term is a lexical unit and if one knows the terminology, they will not have to analyse the construction in order to identify the referent. At the same time, there is a difference in the potentials of languages to render information in a compact form. What is expressed in one word in language A might be expressed in a syntactic phrase in language B. The explicitness-implicitness configuration is different and causes great difficulties in the understanding and translating scientific texts. In addition, technological development in some communities is more advanced than in others, and, naturally, this is reflected in special subject languages. English and Bulgarian substantially differ in the employment of pre-modification. While in English the slot preceding the modified noun can be filled by modifiers derived from various sources, in Bulgarian there are restrictions to the morphological classes of words that can fill this slot. At the same time in English, a word can be adjectivised without adding a morphological marker. In Bulgarian, an adjectival marker is always inserted. The N + N sequence is ungrammatical.

Aim of this study

In a previous study English and Bulgarian were contrasted according to the way they employ participles as pre-modifiers. (Blagova: 1988). In that study a predication analysis was adopted and, as a result, a set of abstract semantic predicates[1] typical for scientific-technical thinking were established, so that they serve as a kind of 'template' to prove the meaningful equivalence of Source Language (SL) and Target Language (TL) phrases. It was also predicted that the same analysis could be used in the study of nominal phrases containing only nouns, because they are a more compressed structure than those containing -ing forms, which yield a more regular meaning based on the syntactic relationships.

The present paper deals with two-component nominals in English and their translation equivalents in Bulgarian excerpted from officially published translations from English into Bulgarian of books on various Science and Technology topics. The analysis is based on the theoretical assumptions stated above. The constructions under analysis are symbolised as follows: N (attribute) + N (headword), or $N_1 + N_2$ for short.

As a result of the analysis, we expect to answer the following questions:

1. Does syntactic regularity help find out the meaning of novel terms?
2. Does the wider context contain clues to the implicit meaning of N + N nominal groups?
3. Does the Bulgarian language exhibit regularities in the selection of translation equivalents depending on deep semantic meaning of SL phrases, i.e. could we say that the possessive relation, for example, between two Ns in English is always expressed by a given preposition in Bulgarian?
4. Could we formalise constraints on the selection of translation equivalents?

Model of Analysis

<u>Theoretical considerations</u>

The model of analysis we have adopted is based on the three meanings of the linguistic sign: structural, semantic and pragmatic, that is its position in the system and its relation with other signs; its relation with the extralinguistic reality and its relation with the participants in the communicative act.

In an attributive construction, the whole NP serves to refer to an entity. The headword denotes a class and the NP picks out members of that class. It is assumed that the attributive construction is a syntactic phenomenon. It does not exist in the lexicon as a separate lexical unit. It exists in the sentence and the way of its realisation depends on the communicative intention of the speaker. Lexicalisation is regarded as a result of an agreement in a given community for a chunk of language to be regularly used to denote a certain entity from the extralinguistic reality. Terms, in their majority, are coined on a syntactic model. The attribute

[1] The set of semantic predicates and their actants were worked out on the basis of the empirical data guided by analyses made in Levi, Judith. 1978. 'The Syntax and Semantics of Complex Nominals'. New York and in Alexieva, Bistra. 1982. 'Implicitness and Explicitness in English and Bulgarian'. (Unpublished PhD thesis) as well as in Bogdanov, V. 1977. 'Semantic and Syntactic organisation of Sentences'. Leningrad.

picks out a feature of the entity which becomes a classificatory feature within the scope of a specific field of knowledge. Terms are remembered and then used as ready units in the process of producing speech. Phrases with descriptive attributes are produced as new units, i.e. they are generated each time they are used.

In our treatment of scientific-technical terms, we have adopted Lyons' approach to compounds since terminological phrases are very much like compounds in general language. The semantic part of a phrase is regarded as consisting of two parts: the first accounting for the regular meaning which is a function of the meanings of the component parts and the second adding the idiosyncratic meaning, if there is one. Thus syntactic and lexical units are represented by the same rule plus the additional meaning. (Lyons 1981)
Example: edge emitter
1. emitter with edges, emitter that has edges;
2. emitter with radiation from the edges;
3. "the radiant output of an edge emitter is emitted from the edges of the diode"(Lacy 1982) - detailed description of the function of this type of emitter.

The regular meaning of the syntactic unit is "a type of emitter with edges"; the terminological meaning is that the radiation of this type of emitters comes from its edges. It is clear that the edges have important function in classifying this type of emitters as a separate class, so on the basis of the regular meaning one can easily find out the terminological meaning if:
1. It is in a context - text in the corresponding special field.
2. The addressee knows this special subject.
If the addressee does not know the special subject, s/he will need the text in 3. above to be able to establish the reference of "edge emitter" correctly.
The entry for a term consisting of two Ns might look like this:
Example: edge emitter

Morphological class of word :	edge - noun (N) emitter - noun (N)
Syntactic construction:	Attribute (N) + Headword (N)
Semantic specification:	
general	special
Edge (classifier), Emitter (thing)	Emitter (agent) has (predicate) edges (object) Edge (agent) emits (predicate) light (object)

In addition to this analysis, a common semantic component is outlined which derives both the English and the Bulgarian phrase following the syntactic and morphological rules of each respective language. It contains predications formulated on the basis of the empirical data. Since the naming function is based on a generalisation of properties, the underlying relational predicates are more abstract and closely associated with the conceptual basis of the respective field of knowledge. Those predications serve as a means of formalising the translator's intuition about the implicit meaning of the SL phrase. Furthermore, the whole text is studied to verify their truth-value and thus prove the equivalence between the SL phrase and the TL phrase.
In the above example the special semantic specification will read as follows:

$PN_{(activity)} = A_{1\ agent\ (emitter)} + P_{do} + A_{2\ patient\ (light)}$

$PN_{(move)} = A_{1\ agent\ (light)} + P_{move} + A_{2\ source\ (edge)}$

The description of the process in "the radiant output of an edge emitter is emitted from the edges of the diode" is atomised into the above predications, which are made explicit in the Bulgarian translation (emitter with radiation from the edges[1]).

<u>Practical steps</u>

Source language – target language pairs of data from the corpus were systematically arranged, rearranged and sorted according to several different parameters, namely:

1. Alphabetically sorted by the first member of the SL phrase (N_1), so that all the possible collocations of the first member could be analysed.
2. Alphabetically sorted by the second member of the SL phrase (N_2), so that all the possible collocations of the second member could be analysed.
3. Sorted by the translation transformation employed - addition, omission, word order changes, regularisation of metaphoric usage
4. Sorted by the morphological equivalents of the components of the TL phrase
5. Sorted by the semantic roles of the components of the phrase based on the presumption that: a) a verbal noun, which is a component of the complex nominal, is a deep semantic predicate combining with its arguments in an attributive relation in the surface structure; b) two nouns forming a complex nominal are often related in deep structure by a predicate. The following meanings are expressed:

* Classificatory properties - type
* Descriptive properties - shape, size, parts
* Characteristics - ability, capability of doing sth, measure
* Activity - function
* Change of properties or state
* Cause and Effect

This was done with view to analysing translator's intuition so that consistent rules be written for the employment of translation equivalents based on dependencies on semantic meaning, morphological and syntactic parameters. The predication analysis is based on the information in the text and is used to establish the underlying predicates and their actants, which can further help in developing the SL phrase in a more explicit manner.

Finally, the translation equivalents were classified according to the morphological class of the Bulgarian word that is lexically equivalent to the N-modifier. Within each class, the differences are accounted for by means of transformations such as addition, omission, and rearrangement of the components of the phrase as well as the semantic roles of the members of the phrase.

Results Outline

The analysis yielded the following results:

<u>Morphological classes of words used</u>

The morphological classes of words employed to translate N_1 are adjective, noun and present participle, while N_2 is always rendered by a noun.

Adjectives

---

[1] This is a back-translation from the Bulgarian .

The meanings that are rendered through adjectives as translation equivalents of N_1 are as follows: N_1 causes N_2; N_2 use for N_1; N_1 is property of N_2; N_1 classifies N_2 as a type; N_2 is at $N_{1\,(place)}$; N_2 is in $N_{1\,(place)}$.

Nouns

The meanings that are rendered through nouns as translation equivalents of N_1 are as follows: N_1 is/happens at(location, time) N_2; N_2 is property of N_1; N_1 is a hyponym of N_2; N_2 acts on N_1; N_2 is manner of N_1; N_2 names change of N_1; N_2 is used for N_1; N_2 is about N_1; N_2 is in N1; N_2 contains N1; N1 is medium/instrument of the action done by N_2; N_2 while in the process of N_1

The most frequently used preposition in translating $N_1 + N_2$ is a preposition in Bulgarian, which is equivalent of the English preposition "of".

Present participles

Present participles are usually used to explicitate a deep semantic predicate with N_1 and N_2 explicitating its actants. This is done on the basis of inferences the translator has made about the process based on clues in the context.

Examples:

gate pulse - "[…] an appropriate gate pulse is applied to the gate terminal, at which time it rapidly switches to the conducting state"(Gardner,1976).

The Bulgarian present participle in the translation of "gate pulse" expresses the result of the "application of the gate pulse", namely "conduct".

target area – The translation is based on the translator's inference that the target area is the area where the signals are received, so the Bulgarian equivalent of "receiving" is used instead of "target".

For "decoder circuit" and " storage disk" the translator has chosen to explicitate the function of N_2 through attributive participles instead of the nouns "decoder" and "storage".

Studies of the structure and properties of Bulgarian terminology show that the two-component terms are mainly of the type Adj.+ N and N + prep. + N. The most frequent preposition is the preposition equivalent to the English preposition 'of'. The frequency of usage of this preposition for transforming premodification into postmodification leads to its desemantisation, turning it into a relational element between two nouns. As there never is a 1:1 relation between SL and TL the fact that the Bulgarian and the English preposition 'of' play the same function is not sufficient to make the translation process easier and simpler for the following reasons:

* the phrase has to be made more explicit in Bulgarian, as post-modification usually is more explicit,
* there are also other prepositions used both in English and Bulgarian,
* differences in the selection of lexical equivalents for the SL nouns,
* differences in transitivity/intransitivity,
* the underlying semantic structure determines the selection of the translation equivalent.

The transformation of premodification to postmodification also entails the necessity of making decisions about the usage of articles and plural markers. The languages exhibit differences with regard to the theme-rheme organisation of the text, which also leads to different choices.

<u>Transformations</u>

Rearrangement
Rearrangement is observed with nouns, but not with adjectives and participles. This is so because when two nouns are used as translation equivalents premodification (in the SL) is transformed to postmodification (in the TL).

SL: $N_1 + N_2 \Rightarrow$ TL: N_2 + prep. + N_1
SL: $N_1 + N_2 \Rightarrow$ TL: Adj. + N_2
SL: $N_1 + N_2 \Rightarrow$ TL: $V_{participle} + N_2$

Addition and Omission
SL: $N_1 + N_2 \Rightarrow$ TL: N_2 + Prep. + N_1
SL: $N_1 + N_2 \Rightarrow$ TL: N_1
SL: $N_1 + N_2 \Rightarrow$ TL: N_2

Addition is observed more often than omission. This is due to the fact that a preposition is added when a noun is used for N_1 as well as to a characteristic feature of Bulgarian translations to be more explicit than the source text. Another reason is that in Bulgarian terms are lacking for some new technological developments, or the existing ones are not popular (not yet accepted in the respective professional community).
Besides prepositions, there are other instances of addition, most often due to explicitation of the underlying predicate.
Examples:

life tests	⇒	tests for testing lifetime[1]
character data	⇒	information comprised of symbols[2]
path specification	⇒	specification of the path for access[3]

Omission is usually observed when one N is a hyponym of the other N (e.g. display screen) or to avoid repetition as well as because of the thematic development of nominal groups which is different in English (premodification is used when the information is given and postmodification when it is new) and Bulgarian (nouns cannot be used as premodifiers, so the attribute is sometimes omitted).

Translation equivalent constraints
There are constraints on the selection of translation equivalents for a given N+N sequence. The same phrase can be rendered in different ways, but N_1 is either translated by an adjective or a noun, N_2 is always translated by a noun. Deep semantic relations revealed by the wider context or special knowledge prevent the free 'adjective' interchangeability with noun translations of N_1.
Examples:
For "driver section" one can find out from the wider contexts that X has a section and that this section functions as a driver. This meaning is explicitated in the Bulgarian translation by employing an adjective for $N_{1(driver)}$.
For "collector current" the choice is again an adjective and not a preposition because the meaning is "current in the collector".

[1] This is a back-translation from the Bulgarian.
[2] This is a back-translation from the Bulgarian.
[3] This is a back-translation from the Bulgarian.

4. Rules can be worded like this:

N_2 is always translated by a noun.

N_1 can be translated by an adjective, present participle or a noun with the following constraints:

If N_1 is translated by an adjective or participle, premodification is preserved.

If N_1 is translated by a noun, premodification is transformed to post-modification with the addition of a preposition between the nouns.

If N_1 names the agent and N_2 names the abstract predicate change, the translation equivalent is N_2 + na + N_1

If the property is named by N_2, the choice should be 'na'; if the property is named by N_1, the choice should be an adjective.

5. There are variations:
The consideration for selection is most probably due to the thematic development of the sentence.
Example:

input signal ⇒ $N_{1\ adj.}$ + $N_{2\ noun}$)
$N_{2\ noun}$ + prep. for location + N_{1noun}

Conclusion

In conclusion, we can say that syntactic regularity is helpful, but without the clues in the wider context and consultations with professionals in the respective scientific field the task is rather too difficult. On the other hand, with novel terms which have not yet been introduced in the target language the translator needs linguistic knowledge to find out the regular meaning and then, with the help of a specialist, to coin a proper term in Bulgarian. Bulgarian translation equivalents exhibit regularities depending on deep semantic structure, which make it possible to outline rules and constraints. Another consistency that was found out was that most of the nominal phrases in the corpus exhibit meanings which make it possible to put them into two different groups: one comprising phrases in which either N_1 or N_2 stands for the deep semantic predicate (e.g. recombination area) and another, comprising phrases in which the deep semantic predicate expresses the semantic relation between the two nouns (e.g. data file). The rules that have been outlined as a result of this study will be helpful not only to translators but to ESP teachers to develop teaching materials. The outlined constraints will allow to say that the most frequent translation equivalent of a given SL string is default if the requirements stated in the constraints are met. We hope this would be useful for the elaboration of an algorithm for machine translation of those terms based on decision-making involving analysis of the whole text.

References

Blagova, Dora. 1988. "Noun Phrases containing Attributive –ing forms in English and their Translation Equivalents in Bulgarian". Unpublished MA thesis, Sofia University.

Lyons, John.1981. *Semantics.* Vol.1, 2. Cambridge: Cambridge University Press.

Quirk, Randolph, Leech, Geoffrey and Svartvik, Jan. 1985. *A Comprehensive Grammar of the English Language*. London: Longman

Swales, John. 1990. *Genre Analysis: English in Academic and Research Settings*. Cambridge: Cambridge University Press

Sager, Juan. 1980. *English Special Languages. Principles and Practice in Science and Technology*. Wiesbaden: Brandsetter.

Books from which data was excerpted

Martin, James. 1982. *Application Development without Programmers*. London/New York: Prentice Hall.
Norton, Peter. 1989. Norton's DOS Guide, BRADY.
Gardner, Hershal.1976. *Handbook of Solid State Troubleshooting*. Reston, Virginia: Reston Publishing Company.
Lacy, Edward. 1982. *Fiber Optics*. London/New York: Prentice Hall.
Crouse, W. 1977. *Automotive Emission Control*. New York: McGraw-Hall Book Company.

A grey Area of translation
On the treatment of human and place names across languages

Kang Zhihong, University of Guangzhou

Abstract

The present paper attempts to obtain a clear picture of what happens when people and places are to be known or referred to in a language other than the one which has first provided them with due appellations.
It is argued in this paper that the traditional concept of translatability based on text-to-text correspondence is applicable only to a rather limited extent to the cross-language treatment of human and place names due to the fact that instead of semantically translating or phonetically transcribing a given SL name, the translator can deliberately rename the bearer of an SL name at the expense of either the semantic description or pronunciation of the SL name. The central issue of the cross-language treatment of names, therefore, is not how names should be translated or transferred in a conventional sense, but rather how effectively the bearer of an SL name can be referred to in the TL context. In this respect the role played by the original translator is crucial. More often than not, the translator's decision is final and even obvious morphological errors he commits are tolerable and the otherwise wrongly produced TL names will eventually become conventionalised through usage. Despite the latitude the translator enjoys in treating the names, he nevertheless has to work within certain cultural and esthetical confines of the TL context. The nature of human and place names is such that in the process of cross-language treatment of names, not only is confusion caused, but attempts at standardisation are made possible as well.[1]

Secondary importance of translatability

If we adhere to one of the very tradtional theories which sees translation as essentially a process of rendering the semantic content conveyed in the SL into the TL, it would seem natural for us to say that only when the meaning of a particular SL name is available can this name be said to be translatable. At a first sight, the idea of having names translated semantically would seem appealing and it would appear logical to base translatability on whether or not the meaning of an SL name can be determined before it is transferred into the TL. As most names do have meaning at least from an etymological point of view, it would follow that most names are translatable semantically. In translation practice, many place names are in fact translated for meaning and most human names, although perhaps not so frequently translated for meaning, would be ultimately translatable in this sense provided that the translator took the pains to trace, even though exhaustively, to the etymological origins of the names in question.

However, if most names are theoretically capable of being translated for their meanings, they are not easily so in translation practice, or simply they are not always in need, or worthy, of semantic translation. Semantic translation is vulnerable and is far from omnipotent for an overall solution to the transfer of names across languages. Most human names, for instance, are not translated for meaning into a TL even though the surface lexical meanings of many such names are easily accountable. English names like 'Smith', 'North' and 'Fisher', French names like 'Dubois', 'Beaufils' and 'Deschamps', etc., all contain surface lexical meanings plain enough to be interpreted semantically. Nevertheless, they have all made their way into Chinese by means of phonetic transcription, resulting in the complete loss of their surface lexical meanings in the newly reconstructed TL names. Also, it would not appear wise and suitable, for instance, to have the name 'John' translated for meaning from its Hebrew origin into English as 'God has been gracious' (Lyons 1977), nor would it appear necessary to have the place name 'Beijing' rendered into English as 'Northern Capital'.

---

[1] Let us note that since this paper was written, the Place Name Committee of Guangzhou has invited the author to work as an advisor on the issue of cross-language treatment of place names.

Even though some SL names have been translated semantically and their TL counterparts can effectively become established as names in the TL usage, these SL names are not translatable in the sense that common nouns are. In fact, the relationship which holds between an SL name and its TL counterpart is essentially that which holds between a lender and a borrower whereas such a relationship is never true of an SL common noun and its TL counterpart. For instance, for the English common noun 'place' to be translated into Chinese, semantic translation would be the only logical way and normally only the semantically equivalent Chinese words like '*di fang*' would be the right match. The African state of Ivory Coast, on the other hand, has so far had two official Chinese versions from the original French '*Côte d'Ivoire*': the meaning-based '*xiang ya hai an*' which was the only standard translation until the mid-80s, and the phonetic transcription '*ke te di wa*' which gradually replaced '*xiang ya hai an*' as the standard Chinese version of '*Côte d'Ivoire*' in recent years. Since what 'place' and '*di fang*' designate in their respective contexts of use turns out to be the indefinite things of a same category observable by speakers of both languages, 'place' and '*di fang*' are tightly bound together semantically and are mutually substitutable in interlingual translation. Neither can be simply transcribed phonetically to stand for the other in any serious translation. The semantic equivalence between '*Côte d'Ivoire*' and x*iang ya hai an*', however, is vulnerable and literally expendable not only because '*Côte d'Ivoire*' was eventually transcribed phonetically into Chinese to refer to what '*Côte d'Ivoire*' refers to in French, but also because what 'x*iang ya hai an*' designates in Chinese is not readily observable by any Chinese-speaking communities prior to the interlingual treatment of the name '*Côte d'Ivoire*'. While it is legitimate for us to say that 'x*iang ya hai an*' is a loan translation from '*Côte d'Ivoire*', however, it would be totally groundless to regard '*di fang*' as a borrowed word from 'place' or vice versa.

From the two Chinese versions of '*Côte d'Ivoire*', it can be seen that the loss of the surface lexical meaning of the SL name does not cause any serious damage to the ultimate function expected of the transferred name, viz., the function of referring to its bearer within the TL environment. The fact that the supposedly meaningful 'x*iang ya hai an*' should give way to the semantically insignificant phonetic transcription '*ke te di wa*' to refer to the very same Ivory Coast in Chinese clearly points to the vulnerability of semantic translation and the weakness of the semantic binding force in relating the SL name to its TL counterpart. Obviously, as long as the ultimate reference function is fulfilled, there is no question of semantic translation being superior to phonetic transcription.

Given the vulnerability of semantic translation and the plausibility of phonetic transcription, a rather embarrassing question awaits for answer: what does phonetic transcription suggest as regards the translatability of names? Although by no means a second best solution, phonetic transcription can tell TL speakers virtually nothing meaningful about the SL name but the mere phonetic resemblance. Indeed, as long as human and geographical names are concerned, phonetic transcription does not differ from semantic translation in any important ways. Both semantic correspondence and accuracy in phonetic transcription, though strongly recommended by some, are in fact secondary to effectiveness in referring to given persons or places in the TL context. For instance, Mr Chris Patten, the last British governor of Hongkong, is known to the Chinese communities in both Hongkong and the Mainland as '*Peng Dingkang*' (although pronounced somewhat differently in Mandarin and Cantonese). The first character '*Peng*' is one of the 100 best known Chinese surnames and the two other ideographic characters forming the 'given name' '*Dingkang*' literally mean 'prosperity secured'. Despite the newly acquired surface lexical meaning conveyed in the three Chinese characters, however, the Chinese version of the English name 'Chris Patten' virtually reveals nothing about the original English name semantically or phonetically. Suppose that an ethnic Chinese also bears the very name '*Peng Dingkang*', which might well be the case, it would be interesting to find out how this person would eventually be known in English. Of the many possible alternative names, 'Chris Patten' would almost certainly not stand a better chance of being selected to assign to him.

From the above, it can be seen that when a given human being or a geographical place is to be known or referred to for the first time in a TL context, there are at least 3 possibilities, viz., semantic translation as evidenced in '*Côte d'Ivoire*' being put into Chinese as '*xiang ya hai an*', phonetic transcription like '*ke te di wa*' being used to satnd for *'Côte d'Ivoire'* and the translator's deliberate act of renaming the bearer of an SL name as shown in Mr Chris Patten's being known to the Chinese as '*Peng Dingkang*'. From the fact that an SL name is potentially capable of undergoing different modes of interlingual transfer, the follwoing implications can be drawn:

* The descriptive meaning attached to a name is virtually expendable if it is to be transferred from an SL into a TL;
* Translatability on a name-to-name basis is of secondary importance vis-a-vis the ultimate function expected of the transferred TL name, viz., that of effectively referring to a given human being or a geographical place in the TL context;
* Terminological problems arise and the term 'translation' defined on a text-to-text basis may prove rather inappropriate for the description of the interlingual transfer of names
* The translator has an important role to play in this process of interlingual transfer.

The role of the translator

In terms of the chronological order in which SL names appear in a TL, an important distinction can be made between first hand treatment, second hand treatment and retranslating. In first hand treatment, the translator deals with SL names which are relatively new in a TL context. First hand treatment is of extreme importance to the TL speakers because it normally dictates how a particular person or place should be known in the TL context and once treated, the newly formed TL name tends to persist in the TL usage and normally no amendments can be made to the TL names even though they may prove inappropriate at either semantic or phonetic level. In second hand treatment, the translator deals with SL names which have long-established institutionalised translation equivalents in the TL. The translator's role is apparently reduced to copying down existing institutionalised names to match their SL counterparts. Thus 'London' is in translation equivalence with '*Londres*' in English-French translation and '*Peng Dingkang*' is now substitutable with 'Chris Patten' in Chinese-English translation. The retranslating of names, whose effectiveness is highly questionable, may still be called for due to various reasons. For instance, out of standardisation concerns, the Wade-Giles System which was used in the past for the phonetic transcription of Chinese human and place names into English has now largely been replaced by the Pinyin system, a Romanised system for the phonetic transcription of Chinese characters.

The role of the translator appears quite unique when he deals with names which have already been transferred from a third language into the one he is working on as an SL. The translator may behave in some interesting ways depending on his knowledge and his principle of translation. This is especially true of many non-English names which have been transferred into Chinese via English. For instance, the French place name '*Bourgogne*' is known in

Chinese as '*bo gen di*', which is clearly a phonetic transcription based on the English 'Burgundy'. More often than not, a Chinese translator working with English as an SL tends to be unaware of the fact that translation equivalence may already exists between a third language and Chinese. For instance, a TV station in the Chinese province of Guangdong once transcribed the French place name '*Bordeaux*' into Chinese as '*bo duo ke si*'. In this case, the translator seems to have based his phonetic transcription entirely on his knowlege of English phonetics and remained ignorant of the long-established translation equivalence between the French '*Bordeaux*' and '*bo er duo*' in Chinese. Unconscious attempts at retranslating which represent a major source of confusion are now on the increase in China due to the world-wide expansion of the use of English as a *lingua franca* among different peoples.

The translator's role can also be perceived through his political sympathies in his interlingual treatment of certain politically controversial names. For instance, what the British call 'the Falkland Islands' is known as '*Malvinas*' in Argentina. In an ordinary map of the world in Mainland China, both '*fu ke lan qun dao*" (Falkland Islands) and '*ma er wei na si qun dao*' the Malvinas Islands) are listed with the former inside brackets whereas in Hongkong's mass media, only the former translation is available.

In both first hand treatement and to some extent, retranslating, the translator can choose between semantic translation, phonetic transcription and deliberate renaming. Perhaps, it is renaming that is the most revealing of the role of the translator and to some extent, of the very nature of human and place names. Whether or not a person or a place should be renamed through interlingual treatment is highly controversial. This is due to two reasons. First, the very exotic flavour of the SL name usually preservable through semantic translation and phonetic transliteration may be lost through renaming. Secondly, names are culturally embedded. Normally, any given human beings and places cannot be known to a foreign culture before they become known in their own culture and are named in their own vernacular language. The most natural way of dealing with the transference of names across languages, therefore, would still be based on the SL name at either semantic or phonetic level.

Clearly, renaming is bearer-based rather than named-based, i.e., the translator may deliberately bypass the SL name and rename its bearer in the TL instead. A real challenge is here posed to the very concept of translation since nothing of the original SL name can be transferred into the TL through renaming. However, what results from renaming are TL names which, in terms of their referential function, can be of equal value as compared with semantically translated or phonetically transcribed names.

At this point, we can sense the somewhat pervasive influence of the original translator on the interlingual treatment of the SL names. To a large extent, how a person or a place should be referred to in a foreign language appears to depend on the translator. His linguistic ability, his knowledge of the world and even his personal preferences or political bias will all eventually affect the TL versions of the SL names. Basically, the translator derives his power in deliberate renaming particular persons or places across languages from the very nature of human and geographical names, viz., from the fact that anything descriptive attached to the name at a surface morphological level is virtually expendable vis a vis the vital function of referring to a given person or place.

The belief that language is arbitrary is at least true of the naming of human beings, and places. When something is to be known for the first time in a certain language community, it can be assigned, rather arbitrarily, a name when what Austin (1961) called "felicity conditions" are met. Thus, according to Austin: "When I say I name this ship the Queen Elizabeth I do not describe the christening ceremony, I actually perform the ceremony." The naming results in a relatively stable referential link between the assigned name and the bearer of the name and this link will persist in everyday language use as long as the bearer of the name is in need of being referred to. What is true of performative nomination which occurs within one given language may also be true of the cross-language treatment of proper names. Again arbitrariness of language becomes manifest with the original translator's deliberate act of renaming. Here the "felicity conditions for cross-language renaming are met largely thanks to the fact that particular human beings or places who or which are known in their vernacular language virtually remain unknown and nameless in the TL context prior to their treatment because SL names in their original phonetic and semantic forms are not readily applicable in a TL context without suffering any morphological change at either semantic or phonetic level.

Given the cross-cultural "felicity conditions", the act of renaming Mr Chris Patten as '*Peng Dingkang*' in Chinese, for instance, was further made possible because in the course of treating the SL name 'Chris Patten' , the translator was, in the final analysis, able to transcend all superficial elements of the name and come face to face with the referent, viz., the bearer of the name. For Mr Chris Patten to be known to the Chinese and referred to in Chinese, all that matters is not how his English name should be translated or treated, but rather how effectively he as a person can be referred to in a different language that carries a different culture. The key issue here is not the name being translated or treated by any means, but rather Mr Chris Patten the bearer of the SL name 'Chris Patten' being again successfully referred to in another cultural context. As long as '*Peng Dingkang*' assumes the function of referring to the last British governor of Hongkong in Chinese just as 'Chris Patten' does in English, the two names become substitutable wherever there is need for translation. The mechanism by which SL names become known or referable in the TL now appears obvious. Underlying the interchangeability between 'Chris Patten' and its Chinese counterpart '*Peng Dingkang*' in translation is in fact a crucial link between the SL name and its Chinese counterpart - the common referent of 'Chris Patten' in English and '*Peng Dingkang* in Chinese, viz., Mr Patten the person.

The nature of human and place names is such that while attempting to get SL names transferred to the TL, the original translator may actually be working at two different levels. First, he may work at a purely linguistic level or to be more exact, at a surface lexical level. In this case, he appears to either translate the SL name semantically or transcribe it phonetically into the TL. Secondly, he works in such a way that he is brought into direct contact with the bearer of the SL name rather than the name itself. He is now performing a deliberate act of renaming. While semantic translation and phonetic transcription yield borrowed words, in the unusual cases of deliberate renaming, however, the end products can no longer be related back to their SL counterparts semantically or phonetically although they may effectively be linked in real terms thanks to the fact that they both refer to a common person or place in their respective cultural contexts. As one of the strategies involved in the interlingual treament of names, however, the act of renaming can hardly be viewed as an act of translation in its own right.

Cultural and aesthetic constraints

We have argued in the previous section that in the interlingual treatment of names the translator may eventually be brought into direct contact with the bearer of the name rather than with the name itself. Theoretically, this would eventually free the translator from all formal constrains imposed on him by the SL name and endow him with unlimited latitude in treating human and geographical names. Nevertheless, as a process that relates one culture to another, the treatment of human and place names across languages is subject to certain influence from both SL and TL systems as well as the cultural systems embedded by them and the translator has to work within certain cultural confines.

First of all, although, as we have argued, the SL surface lexical meaning and the phonetic symbols of the SL names are theoretically dispensable, it would be unusuallly hard for the translator to deliberately ignore all SL morphological elements altogether. Thus, most translators will still try to focus on the semantic and phonetic surface forms of the names since they are the most noticeable features about the SL names. Moreover, the SL name is after all the very means by which the referent can be accounted for in linguistic terms within an SL context. Also semantic translation and phonetic transcription provide more dependable links between the SL names and their TL counterparts at either semantic or phonetic levels. This will not only facilitate the work of the translator but may also be beneficial to cross-cultural communication and the standardisation on the part of the TL.

On top of the constraints from the SL, SL names also need to confront sociopragmatic realities of the TL context. SL names will have to shape themselves in order to get adapted to the new TL language environment. That Chris Patten should be renamed in Chinese as '*Peng Dingkang*', despite its apparent inappropriateness, appears nevertheless to be on good terms with naming conventions in Chinese. The same is true of many a Hongkong Chinese and Chinese living in an English-speaking country. More often than not, they would bypass their original Chinese given names and adopt Christian names instead. As a result, peculiar translation equivalence is created. For instance, the Financial Secretary of the Hongkong Special Administrative Region has his Chinese full name as '*Tsang Yan-Kuen*' (pronounced in Cantonese), but he is frequently referred to as 'Donald Tsang' in English. Not only is his Chinese given name replaced, the order of his Chinese surname is reversed as well to sound more acceptable to English-speakers. Here we can see that the interlingual treatment of names is sometimes dependent on the degree of acceptance on the part of the TL speakers and the translator may feel the overwhelming pressure from the TL community for adaptation.

Human and place names are sometimes used in cases where reference to given persons or places is subordonate to the expression of certain idea or concept. Names in such cases are embedded in certain culture-specific expressions such as "keep up with the Jones's", "to go Dutch" "All roads lead to Rome", etc. Here the focus of translation is on the message conveyed as a whole in the phrases rather than on a given human or place name. Therefore, names in such phrases may or may not be treated depending on the degree of acceptance on the part of the TL speakers. For instance, 'Rome' in the proverb "All roads lead to Rome" was phonetically transcribed when the whole proberb was translated into Chinese. On the other hand, 'Rome' and 'Romans' in "When in Rome, do as Romans do" were simply not treated at all when the proverb was translated into Chinese as Chinese speakers tend to be more familiar with one of their vernacular expressions which conveys a similar idea.

Also the need for standardisation on the part of the TL may impose certain restrictions on how interlingual treatment of names should be effected. Deliberate renaming at the expense of either the semantic content or the phonetic representations of SL names, although feasible theoretically, is potentially damaging to the standardisation of the TL and cross-cultural communication. For instance, there were literally no limits on how Chris Patten should be referred to in Chinese before Christ Patten was, known to the Chinese people at all and '*Peng Dinkang*' may well be chosen to stand for the last British Governor of Hong Kong in Chinese. However, several disadvantages of this deliberate act of renaming become obvious. First of all, the very Englishness of 'Chris Patten' is nowhere to be traced in the excessively assimilated name '*Peng Dingkang*'. This, in the view of many translation theorists, is in contradiction with what some regard as one of the most important purposes of translation, viz., to have the very exotic flavour best preserved in the TL. Besides, due to the lack of morphological link whatsoever between the SL and TL, a second hand translator or a foreign language learner would find it difficult and awkward to stick to the translation equivalence thus established or to memorise the apparently unrelated translation equivalents. In fact, the more translation names like '*Peng Dingkang*' gain ground in the TL usage, the more difficult cross-cultural communication will be. Obviously there exists a practical problem between the theoretically unlimited latitude of the translator in renaming and the need for standardisation on the part of the TL. Interestingly enough, it is this very latitude of the translator in renaming that makes attempts to standardise the interlingual treatment of place and human names possible. The interlingual treatment of names can be more or less standardised through prescriptive rules. In fact, the China Place Names Committee worked out 13 articles on the transfer of place names from other languages into Chinese and rules for phonetic transcription involving several major translation directions, viz., English-Chinese, French-Chinese, German-Chinese, Spanish-Chinese, Arab-Chinese and Russian-Chinese.

How SL names should be treated depends on a number of cross-cultural factors and aesthetics may eventually brought into play in this particular area of translation. This can be illustrated in the transfer of names from major European languages into Chinese. For instance, the English name 'Mary' is traditionally assigned to females. The feminine characteristics of 'Mary' is somewhat reconstructed in Chinese by means of two characters '*ma*' and '*li*', both signalling feminine gender in Chinese. Aesthetic considerations are perhaps more imperative in the transfer of foreign names into Chinese because of the ideographic nature of the Chinese written language. Even though characters used for purely phonetic transcription purposes are supposed to be meaningless, extra connotations may still prop up. For example, the African state of Togo is known in Chinese as '*duo ge*' and the two characters can be easily interpreted as 'many brothers'. In fact, quite a few Chinese word puzzles have been coined for people to guess what countries they point to. Thus, 'no lack of brothers' suggests '*duo ge*' (Togo), 'Red, orange, yellow, green, black, blue and purple' indicates 'y*i se lie*' (phonetic transcription from 'Israel' involving three characters that give rise to an extra meaning 'a spectrum of colours'). More often than not, in English-Chinese or Chinese-English translation, the name 'Britain' is usually matched with '*ying guo*' the literal meaning of which is 'the country of heroes' or 'heroic country' in Chinese. Surprisingly, 'y*ing guo*' was originally the shortened form of 'y*ing ji li*' which was a phonetic transcription from 'English'. Obviously, there is no morphological link between 'Britain' and '*ying guo*. Despite the fact that 'Britain' does have '*bu lie dian*' as its standard translation equivalent, this latter one is rarely used in Chinese if not altogether abandoned. The reason is that the characters forming '*bu lie dian*' in their literal sense may sound awkward. While the character '*bu*' suggests 'no' or anything negative, '*lie*' can either mean 'list', 'every', 'row' or 'rank'. Worst of all, the character '*dian*' is usually understood as 'collapse' in Chinese. Here we can see how cautious the original translator ought to be in choosing the right Chinese character for certain phonetic transcription purposes.

Conclusion

One of the difficulties in writing this paper has been to find an appropriate term to describe the process by which human beings and places become known to speakers of a TL. The term 'translation' proves rather inadequate because the conventional sense assigned to it gives the unfortunate impression that what happens during all this process does never transcend the lexical level and thus on a name-to-name basis, translatability would seem to be the only concern for the translator. However, as is argued, it is to a rather limited extent that the concept of text-based translation can be applied to the cross-language treatment of human and place names. By the side of the ultimate need for effectiveness in referring to given persons or places in the TL context, translatability in its conventional sense eventually pales into insignificance. The cross-language treatment of names can in fact be either SL name-based or bearer-based, depending to a large extent on the initiative of the original translator. In the former case, morphological elements of the SL name, viz., its surface lexical meaning or pronunciation are made use of in an attempt to recreate a new set of name-referent relationship in the TL. For this reason, semantic translation and transliteration are in essence acts of borrowing since they result in TL names which are based on their SL counterparts morphologically at either semantic or phonetic level. When the translator is dealing with the bearer of a given SL name rather than the SL name itself, however, he is deliberately performing the act of renaming a person or a place, which of course does not seem to be a typical case of translation in its traditional sense although this may create translation equivalence that later translators will have to follow. The key issue in the interlingual treatment of names, therefore, is not how a given SL name should be translated or transferred, but rather how effectively the bearer of a given SL name can again be referred to in the TL context.

As has already been shown above, how an SL name should appear in a TL context depends to a large extent on the original translator. His linguistic knowledge, his knowledge of the world and even his personal preferences may have some impact on the eventual translation versions. Theoretically the translator enjoys unlimited latitude in treating SL names because in the final analysis, it is possible for him to bypass all the superficial elements of the SL, viz., its semantic description and phonetic form, and come face to face with the bearer of the name in an attempt to rename the person or place in question, leading to translation equivalence between two sets of names which can be mutually unrelated semantically or phonetically. Once an SL name is treated or its bearer renamed, however, translation equivalence will eventually become stablised between the two sets of names despite the apparent lack of semantic correspondence or phonetic resemblance between them.

The translator, despite his theoretically unlimited latitude in treating names, has nevertheless to work within certain cultural and aesthetic confines. The nature of human and place names is such that in the process of cross-language treatment of names, not only are confusions and inconsistencies caused, but attempts at standardisation are made possible as well.

References

Austin, John. L. 1962 *How to do things with words*. Oxford: Clarendon Press.

Lyons, John. 1977 *Semantics, Vol. I.* Cambridge: Cambridge University Press.

1977 China Place Names Committee.

1987 *A Handbook on the Translation of Foreign Place Names*. Beijing: Commercial Press.

Translating the suffix -eme in linguistics terminology from English into Arabic

Jamal Giaber, University of Edinburgh

Abstract

The suffix -eme is not an original lexical item in the English lexicon as it has been extracted from the linguistic technical term 'phoneme' and morphologically employed as a suffix by modern linguists to form nouns denoting 'units of structure'. On the analogy of phoneme, a number of technical terms have been coined and used by different linguists to designate theoretical units of structure related to the different levels of linguistic analysis such as 'lexeme', 'morpheme', 'glosseme', 'sememe', 'grapheme', 'tagmeme', 'toneme', etc. In addition to being used as nouns denoting units of structure, the majority of the -eme derivatives serve as bases for further suffixation to create other morphologically and semantically related terms to fulfil syntactic and semantic functions in the treatment of linguistic analysis. The concept of 'unit of linguistic structure' as such is not available in traditional Arabic linguistics, but the general concept of 'unit' is available in Arabic. It is expressed lexically by the word *wah̲dah* rather than morphologically. Through lexical combination, *wah̲dah* is employed to create genitive compounds to denote different types of unit. In transferring the modern linguistic concepts expressed in English by the -eme derivatives, Arab terminographers and linguists give different translation equivalents, reflecting diversity in interpreting some of the original terms, and variation in the use of translation techniques. A survey of the translation equivalents given by Arab terminographers to the -eme terms in English reveals that a number of factors seem to have determined their translations. These factors include (a) differences between Western linguists in using some -eme terms, (b) the lack of one-word equivalents in Arabic to express the concepts denoted by -eme derivatives in English, (c) the employment of different translation techniques, (d) the lack of consistency, (e) the difficulty to combine denotative precision and formal concision simultaneously, and (f) the psychological influence of the formal characteristics of the English terms, which is manifest in the use of direct borrowing and hybrid creation when translation is possible. In this paper, the technical use of the suffix -eme in linguistics terminology in English and the problems it generates in translating linguistic terms from English into Arabic will be thoroughly discussed in the light of the structural differences between Arabic and English on the one hand, and the requirements of terminological translation on the other.

Arabic and English are two morphologically different languages. Each has got its own morphological system with special word-formation devices. In forming words, English relies heavily on affixation, while Arabic relies on the manipulation of morphological patterns (*al-s̲iyagh al-s̲arfiyyah*). In translating terminology from English into Arabic, translators usually encounter problems related to how English suffixes and prefixes, as word-formation devices, are rendered into Arabic. These problems include the lack of a single morphological device in Arabic to render a concept expressed by an affix in English and the difficulty to achieve concision and consistency. This paper explores these problems in respect of translating the suffix -eme in linguistics terminology from English into Arabic. In discussing these problems, the following methodology is adopted: (1) identification of the origin and general use of the suffix -eme in English; (2) identification of the technical use of this suffix in linguistics terminology; (3) exploration of the word-formation patterns used in forming the -eme derivatives in linguistics terminology in English; (4) exploration of the ways in which Arabic normally expresses the concept of 'unit of structure'; (5) discussion of the translation techniques used by five Arab terminographers in rendering the linguistic technical terms formed by the suffix -eme and the translation equivalents offered; (6) identification or suggestion of the translation technique(s) that achieve(s) denotative precision, morphological concision, and terminological consistency and relatedness; and (7) verification of the selected translation technique(s) and Arabic linguistic devices by suggesting suitable Arabic equivalents for all -eme terms discussed in this paper.

The suffix -eme is not an original lexical item in the English lexicon as it has been extracted from the linguistic technical term 'phoneme' and morphologically employed as a suffix by modern linguists to form nouns denoting "units of structure" (New Shorter Oxford English Dictionary). The term 'phoneme' itself is also new in English as it was borrowed from French by the late nineteenth century, when it was technically used in linguistics to denote "a unit of sound in a language that cannot be analysed into further units and can distinguish one word from another" (*Ibid.*). On the analogy of phoneme, a number of technical terms have been coined and used by different linguists, developing similar or different theories in different places, to designate theoretical units of structure related to the different levels of linguistic analysis such as 'lexeme', 'morpheme', 'moneme', 'glosseme', 'sememe', 'grapheme', 'tagmeme', 'plereme', 'ceneme', 'toneme', 'chroneme', 'syntagmeme', etc. In non-verbal communication, -eme has also been put to use to create terms such as 'kineme', which denotes "a meaningful unit of body movement or gesture" (New Shorter Oxford English Dictionary). However, "of the many units created in recent decades, most are restricted to specific theories and works, and have little current use" (McArthur1992: 348) such as Bloomfield's 'glosseme', 'phememe', 'taxeme', 'tagmeme' and 'episememe', Hjelmslev's 'glosseme', 'ceneme', 'prosodeme', and 'plereme', and Pike's 'tagmeme', 'syntagmeme' and 'behavioureme'. The most established and widely used are 'phoneme', 'lexeme', 'morpheme', 'toneme', 'chroneme', and 'grapheme'. Following the establishment of these terms, which reflects the establishment of the basic linguistic notions they stand for, the suffix -eme has become very much less productive than it used to be during the earlier decades of modern linguistics. Of the recent idiosyncratic coinages in -eme is 'listeme' used by some linguists to refer to "the items listed in the lexicon" (Katamba 1993: 295).

Morphologically, the derivatives formed by the suffix -eme can be divided into five types:

1. Full word + -eme: behavioureme, classeme, grapheme, kineme, phememe, syntagmeme, syntaxeme, toneme, soneme

2. Contracted word + -eme: prosodeme (prosod (ic) + -eme
lexeme = lex (icon) + -eme
proxeme = prox (emity) or prox (emics) + -eme
narreme = narr (ation) or narr (ative) + -eme

3. Combining form + -eme: moneme, chroneme, glosseme.

4. Greek root + -eme: ceneme or keneme = *kenos* (empty) -eme
morpheme = *morph* (form) -eme
plereme = *pleres* (full) -eme
semanteme = *semanticos* (significant) -eme
sememe = *sema* (sign or mark) -eme
tagmeme = *tagma* (some thing arranged) -eme
taxeme = *taxis* (arrangement) -eme
(cf. New Shorter Oxford English Dictionary).

5. Blending: stroneme = stress + phoneme

Semantically, the derivatives of the first two types are more transparent than those of the third and fourth types, because in the first two types, -eme is appended to words already used with specific meanings in linguistics, while instances of the third and fourth types are either formed on combining forms of Greek origin, as in type three, or on borrowed Greek roots as in type four. In other words, the determinants in the syntagmas of the first two types are more or less semantically specific and well established, while the determinants in the syntagmas of the third and fourth types, especially the fourth, are semantically less specific and, therefore, they are subject to idiosyncratic interpretation. This morpho-etymological background might be one of the reasons why some of the terms from the third and fourth types were used differently by different linguists during the past decades such as 'glosseme' and 'tagmeme' as used by Bloomfield and as used in glossematics and tagmemics[1], 'morpheme' as used by Martinet and as used by American structuralists, and 'plereme' as used in componential analysis and in glossematics[2].

In addition to being used as nouns denoting units of structure, the majority of the -eme derivatives, as well as the original term 'phoneme', serve as bases for further suffixation to create other morphologically and semantically related terms to fulfil syntactic and semantic functions as can be seen from the following list:

ceneme:	cenemic, cenemics
plereme:	pleramatic, plerematics
toneme:	tonemic, tonemically
tagmeme:	tagmemic, tagmemics, tagmemist
sememe:	sememic, sememically
morpheme:	morphemic, morphemics, morphemically
grapheme:	graphemic, graphemics, graphemically
phoneme:	phonemic, phonemics, phonemist, phonemicise, phonemicisation

Formal and conceptual relationships exhibited by these terms have to be taken into consideration when translating the -eme derivatives into Arabic in order to preserve the conceptual structures they represent.

Manifestations of the theoretical entities denoted by the -eme terms can semantically be divided into concrete and abstract groups as follows:

1. Concrete group:

keneme or ceneme	in glossematic phonology, a minimal unit in the phonological system of a language, corresponding approximately to the phoneme in other systems
prosodeme	a distinctive prosodic feature such as stress and intonation
toneme	a tone or set of tones functioning as a distinctive phoneme in a language

---

[1] Bloomfield defines 'glosseme' as the smallest meaningful unit of linguistic signalling (Bloofield, 1933: 264) and 'tagmeme' as the smallest unit of grammatical form (*Ibid*.: 166). In Glossematics, 'glosseme' is a 'cover term for minimal linguistic units of *langue* [...] which on the expression plane consist of phonological features (kenemes) and on the content plane of semantic features (pleremes)' (Bussmann, 1996: 191). In Tagmemics, 'tagmeme' is 'the correlate of a grammatical function and the class of items which can perform it' (New Shorter Oxford English Dictionary).

[2] In componential analysis, 'plereme' is "the minimal unit, a semantic feature", e.g. [human] and in glossematics it is "the minimal unit of meaningful expression" (Asher 1994 X: 5157).

akueme	a minimal distinctive characteristic in the tone of voice of an individual speaker, such as timbre, rhythm, loudness, etc.
phoneme	a unit of sound in a language that cannot be analysed into smaller liner units and can distinguish one word from another
kineme	a meaningful unit of body movement or gesture made in non-verbal communication
morpheme	the smallest morphological unit of language that cannot be analysed into smaller units
lexeme	a lexical unit in the vocabulary of a language
grapheme	the minimal contrastive unit in the writing system of a language
moneme	for Martinet, the smallest unit of language consisting of content and phonetic form that cannot be broken down further into smaller meaningful units
chroneme	a distinctive unit of length in a speech sound
syntagmeme	in tagmemics, a unit in a grammatical hierarchy viewed as a sequence of the tagmemes it consists of
phememe	for Bloomfield, the smallest and meaningless unit of linguistic signalling
glosseme	1. for Bloomfield, the smallest meaning-bearing unit in a language structure 2. in glossematics, cover term for minimal linguistic units of *langue*, which on the expression plane consist of phonological features (kenemes), and on the content plane of semantic features (pleremes)
plereme	in glossematics, the minimal unit of meaningful expression
behavioureme	in tagmemics, the distinctive unit of any behaviour such as the sentence, which is regarded as the verbal behavioureme
chereme	the minimal contrastive unit in a sign language
stroneme	a unit of phonological stress, regarded as a kind of phoneme, i.e. stress phoneme
proxeme	a distinctive unit of distance, etc. between speakers
narreme	a unit in the literary analysis of narrations
soneme	an apparent phonemic unit in a dead language recorded only in writing

2. Abstract group:

taxeme	a single minimal feature of grammatical arrangement
tagmeme	1. for Bloomfield, the smallest meaningful unit of grammatical form 2. in tagmemeics, the correlate of a grammatical function and the class of items which can perform it
syntaxeme	a unit of syntactic analysis, especially one which cannot be further analysed into components
sememe	the unit of meaning carried by a morpheme
semanteme	a unit of linguistic meaning understood as segmental rather than componential item
classeme	a distinctive semantic feature shared by lexical items belonging to different semantic fields, such as animate/inanimate; adult/child.

plereme	in componential analysis, the minimal unit of meaningful expression
grameme	an older term for tagmeme

The concrete manifestations are physical entities such as a sound, tone, gesture, letter, simple lexical item, or a string of lexical items, while the abstract manifestations are either grammatical or semantic relationships or features. In each case, a single entity is denoted by each of the above listed items.

Following this analytical view of the origin, linguistic nature and technical employment of this suffix in English, let us see how Arabic normally expresses the concept of 'unit of structure'. In Arabic, the concept of 'unit' is normally expressed lexically by the word *wah̲dah*, which is equivalent to the English word 'unit'. Through lexical combination, *wah̲dah* is employed to create genitive constructions to denote different types of unit such as *wah̲dah naqdiyyah* (monetary unit), *wah̲dah ʻadadiyyah* (numerical unit), *wah̲dah tarkiibiyyah* (construction unit), *wah̲dah qiyaasiyyah* (measurement unit), etc.

In transferring the modern linguistic concepts expressed in English by the -eme derivatives, Arab terminographers and linguists give different translation equivalents, reflecting diversity in interpreting some of the original terms and variation in the use of translation technique. A quick survey of the translation equivalents given by Arab terminographers (cf. Table) reveals that a number of factors seem to have determined the translations given to the English terms ending in -eme. These factors include (a) differences between linguists in using some terms such as 'glosseme' and 'morpheme', (b) the difficulty to identify the precise meanings of some terms due mainly to their intricate technical use and/or morpho-etymological background such as 'tagmeme', 'glosseme', 'taxeme', (c) the lack of one-word equivalents in Arabic to express the above English concepts, (d) the employment of different translation techniques (to be elaborated on later), (e) the lack of consistency, (f) the difficulty to combine denotative precision and formal concision simultaneously and (g) the psychological influence of the formal characteristics of the English terms, which is manifest in the use of direct borrowings when translation is possible and in the unjustifiable resort to hybrid terms such as *s̲arfiim* for 'morpheme, *h̲arkiim* for 'kineme', *s̲awtiim* for 'phoneme' and *h̲arfiim* for 'grapheme' (al-Khulii 1982). As can be seen from the following comparison between the translation equivalents given by five Arab terminographers, different translation techniques have been used by the same or different terminographer producing formally and semantically different translation equivalents. The translation techniques include transference (or direct borrowing), free translation, literal translation, paraphrasing, hybrid creation, employment of the Arabic suffix *-iyyah* and the dropping of the suffix -eme:

SL Terms	**al-Khuulii 1982**	**Bakalla et al 1983**	**ALECSO 1989**	**al-B'albakii 1990**	**Mubaarak 1995**
Akueme	-	-	-	*akwiim*	-
Behaviour-eme	-	-	-	-	-
Ceneme	-	-	*Siniim*	*siniim*	-
Chereme	-	-	-	*imaa'ah*	-
Chroneme	*kruniim* + *funiim*	*al-kruniim*	*Maddah* + *kruniim*	*kruniim*	*wah̲dah kammiyyah*

	kammii				
Classeme	-	-	-	*sinf dilaalii*	*majmuu'at al-wahdaat al-dilaaliyyah*
Glosseme	*ghluusiim + murfiim*	*al-ghluusiim*	*Kluusiim*	*ghluusiim*	*'asghar shakl lughawii*
Grameme	-	-	*Wahdah nahwiyyah*	*qaalab*	*'asghar wahdah sarfiyyah + qaalab*
Grapheme	*ghraafiim + harf mujarrad + harfiim*	*al-graafiim*	*harf khattii*	*ghraafiim*	*harf mujarrad + 'asghar wahdah khattiyyah*
Keneme	-	-	-	*kalimah waziifiyyah*	-
Kineme	*kiniim + harakah mujarradah + harkiim*	-	*Wahdat al-'ishaarah al-jasadiyyah + wahdah 'imaa'iyyah + al-harakah*	*kayniim*	*harakah mujarradah*
Lexeme	*liksiim + mufradah mujarradah*	*al-mufradah*	*Mufradah mutamakkinah*	*liksiim*	*mufradah mujarradah*
Moneme	*murfiim*	*al-muniim*	*'unsur daall + muniim*	*muniim*	*wahdah lughawiyyah sughraa*
Morpheme	*murfiim + murfiimiyyah + sarfiyyah + sarfiim*	*al-murfiim*	*'unsur daall + daallah nahwiyyah*	*murfiim*	*wahdah sarfiyyah mujarradah*
Narreme	-	-	-	-	-
Phoneme	*funiim + fuuniimiyyah + sawtiim + sawt mujarrad*	*al-funiim*	*Wahdah sawtiyyah + harf sawtii*	*funiim*	*wahdah sawtiyyah + harf*
Plereme	*mukawwin dilaalii + mushtarak dilaalii*	-	*Mushtarak dilaalii + bliriim*	*bliriim*	*mukawwin dilaalii + mushtarak dilaalii*

Prosodeme	*funiim fawqit̲'ii*	*al-wah̲dah al-s̲awtiyyah al-tat̲riiziyyah*	*Wah̲dah nabriyyah*	*wah̲dah tat̲riiziyyah*	*wah̲dah s̲awtiyyah fawqit̲'iyyah*
Proxeme	-	-	-	-	-
Semanteme	*simantiim + wah̲dat al-dilaalah*	*al-simantiim*	*Daall al-maahiyyah + daalla 'ifraadiyyah + ma'naa al-mufradah*	*simantiim*	*wah̲dah dilaaliyyah*
Sememe	*simiim + al-wah̲dah al-mujarradah li-ddilaalah*	*al-simiim*	*Wah̲dah dilaaliyyah + ma'naa murakkab*	*simiim*	*madluul + wadah mujarradah li-ddilaalah*
Soneme	-	-	-	-	-
Stroneme	-	-	-	-	-
Syntagmeme	-	-	*Wah̲dah binaa'iyyah*	*naz̲m qaalibii*	-
Syntaxeme	-	-	-	-	-
Tagmeme	*qaalab*	*al-tagmiim*	*Takmiim*	*qaalab*	*qaalab + mithaal*
Taxeme	*taksiim + simah nah̲wiyyah*	*al-malmah̲ al-naz̲mii*	*Wah̲dah tarkiibiyyah*	*ma'lam nah̲wii*	*simah nah̲wiyyah*
Toneme	*tuniim + funiim naghamii*	*al-wah̲dah al-naghamiyyah*	*Wah̲dah naghamiyyah*	*mangham*	*wah̲dah naghamiyyah*

Let us now consider the adequacy of the above translation equivalents. Direct borrowing is normally the translator's final resort when all other translation techniques fail unless the SL term enjoys an uncompromisable international status or is an eponym. This is because direct borrowings are opaque and create breaks in the morphological and conceptual associations between the related terms of the same conceptual system. Consider, for example, the translation equivalents given by al-B'albakii (1990) to the set of terms used in Glossematics: glosseme (*ghlusiim*), ceneme (*siniim*), plereme (*bliriim*), prosodeme (*wah̲dah tat̲riiziyyah*) and morpheme (*murfiim*). Taking into consideration the semantic function of the suffix -eme, only the Arabic equivalent given to 'prosodeme', *wah̲dah tat̲riiziyyah*, is semantically transparent in Arabic. The direct borrowings given to 'glosseme', 'ceneme', 'plereme' and 'morpheme' formally have no relationship with the Arabic equivalent given to 'prosodeme', therefore, conceptually they are not indicative of any association with *wah̲dah tat̲riiziyyah*. In this case, conceptual association can only be maintained through the presupposed knowledge of the intensions of these English terms. In addition to opacity and lack of conceptual transparency, and taking into consideration the structural diversity between Arabic and English, direct borrowings from English are not always easily accommodated by the Arabic morphological and phonological systems and, therefore, may not be accepted by the users of Arabic, especially when alternative Arabic terms are proposed by other translators or terminographers. The terms *mus̲arrif, 'ajamah* and *s̲iitah* coined by Ali (1993) for 'morpheme', 'lexeme' and 'phoneme' respectively, for example, are expected to be more acceptable than the direct borrowings *murfiim*, *liksiim* and *funiim*. The reason for this is that *musarrif* is derived from the same lexical morpheme (*s-r-f*) from which the Arabic linguistic term *al-sarf* (morphology) is derived (Ali 1993: 11). Meanwhile, *musarrif* is functionally transparent because its underlying pattern, *MUFA''IL*, denotes the active participle, that is to say, the agent which causes change in the form of the word, and extensionally this is what the 'morpheme' actually does. The term *'ajamah* in Arabic means 'a kernel' of a date or raisin ('Aniis et al. 1987: *al-'ujaam/al-'ajam*) and is metaphorically employed to designate the concept denoted in English by 'lexeme' because lexemes of any language are the kernels of its lexicon. Morphologically, *'ajamah* also maintains formal and derivational relationships with the conceptually related terms of *mu'jam* (lexicon) and *mu'jamii* (lexical) (Ali 1993: 11). The term *siitah* is also conceptually indicative because its underlying pattern *FI'LAH* either denotes the manner of doing what is expressed by the verb, i.e. the noun of kind (lit. *'ism al-hay'ah* or *al-naw'*) (Wright 1859/I: 123) or a small piece of any thing (*Ibid*.: 175). It is also derived from the same lexical morpheme (*s-w-t*) from which *sawt* (phone) and *saa'it* (vowel) are derived.

Paraphrasal equivalents such as *wahdat al-'ishaarah al-jasadiyyah* for 'kineme' (ALECSO 1989), *'asghar wahdah sarfiyyah* for 'morpheme', *'asghar wahdah kitaabiyyah* for 'grapheme', *wahdah lughawiyyah sughraa* for 'moneme', *'asghar shakl lughawii* for 'glosseme' and *majmu'at al-wahdaat al-dilaaliyyah* for 'classeme' (Mubaarak 1995) are lengthy expressions as they contain somehow redundant elements such as *al-jasadiyyah*, *'asghar* and *sughraa* respectively. Consequently, with time, these paraphrasal equivalents either get shortened or replaced because they do not comply with the terminological need for concision and speedy communication. Another disadvantage related to these paraphrasal equivalents is that they are not easily amenable to further derivation and, therefore, derivative concepts can only be represented through compounding such as *'ilm wahdaat al-'ishaarah al-jasadiyyah* for 'kinemics'!

Hybrid equivalents such as *harfiim* for 'grapheme', *sarfiim* for 'morpheme' and *sawtiim* for 'phoneme' are based on the direct borrowing of the suffix -eme, which is employed in Arabic to produce similar terms to those formed by the same suffix in English. This method of term creation does not normally pass the test of time due to the basic fact that it is not one of the natural methods of word-formation in Arabic. Borrowing derivational suffixes can succeed only when the two languages involved have similar word-formation devices such as affixation in English and French. Naturally acceptable formations can only be produced through natural methods of word-formation because languages are just like animates, their bodies do not easily accept alien parts.

Translation equivalents created through free translation such as *sinf dilaalii* for 'classeme' (al-B'albakii 1990), *qaalab* for 'tagmeme' (al-Khuulii 1982 and al-B'albakii 1990) and *harf* for 'phoneme' (Mubaarak 1995) are denotatively imprecise because they neither correspond intensionally nor extensionally to their supposedly related English terms. In English 'classeme', for example, is used to describe "the relatively abstract semantic features shared by lexical items belonging to different semantic fields, e.g. animate/inanimate, adult/child" (Crystal, 1997: 62). In other words, 'classeme' refers to any single semantic feature that makes difference in determining the class of an entity, while *sinf dilaalii* refers to the class itself not to the feature that distinguishes it. If 'classeme' is translated as *musannif*, for example, the translation will be plausible because through its underlying pattern, *MUFA''IL*, *musannif* denotes the agent (in this case the semantic feature) that classifies or distinguishes a class of entities from another. *Qaalab* is given as a translation equivalent to both 'tagmeme' and 'episememe' (al-Khuulii 1982, ALECSO 1989 and al-B'albakii 1990), while, according to Bloomfield (1933: 166), a tagmeme is the smallest meaningful unit of grammar, i.e. a unit of grammatical form, and 'episememe' is the grammatical meaning of a tagmeme. Finally, to translate 'phoneme' as *harf* is conceptually misleading because the former denotes 'a distinctive unit of phonological structure' while the latter denotes 'a graphic representation of a human speech sound'.

Employment of the Arabic suffix *-iyyah* to produce terms such as *surfiyyah*, given by al-Khuulii (1982) to 'morpheme', is also suggested by Fehrii (1983: 142), who considers the Arabic suffix *-iyyah* as equivalent to the English suffix -eme and can produce equivalent terms such as *sarfiyyah*, for 'morpheme', *sawtiyyah* for 'phoneme' and *mu'jamiyyah* for 'lexeme'. These proposed Arabic equivalents are denotatively inaccurate because in Arabic they either denote the feminine form of the adjective or a state or condition. In the case of denoting the feminine form of the adjective, *-iyyah* consists of two suffixes: the adjective forming *yaa' al-nisbah* (relative *yaa'*), which is derivational, and the feminine terminal *taa'*, which is inflectional. In this case, the proposed Arabic equivalents can have negatives such as *ghayr sarfiyyah, ghayr sawtiyyah* and *ghayr mu'jamiyyah*. In the case of denoting a state or condition, *-iyyah* will be that of *al-masdar al-sinaa'ii* and, therefore, the terms will refer to the state or condition of being *sarfii* (morphological), *sawtii* (phonological or phonetic) and *mu'jamii* (lexical), which corresponds to the denotative function of the English suffixes of -ity and -ness.

The translation equivalents created through literal translation such as *al-wahdah al-sarfiyyah* for 'morpheme', *al-wahdah al-naghamiyyah* for 'toneme' (Bakalla et al. 1983), *wahdah sawtiyyah* for 'phoneme', *wahdah dilaaliyyah* for 'semanteme' (Mubaarak 1995), *wahdah nabriyyah* for 'prosodeme', *wahdah tarkiibiyyah* for 'taxeme' and *wahdah 'iymaa'iyyah* for 'kineme' (ALECSO, 1989) are semantically precise though formally not very concise. These translation equivalents are based on the fact that since each of the translated English terms consists of two linguistic elements: the base and the suffix -eme, and because -eme has a lexical not functional denotation, i.e. unit, and because Arabic does not have an equivalent suffix, then -eme is translated by an equivalent lexical item, i.e. *wahdah*. Although employment of the term *wahdah* through literal translation is semantically very adequate, formally it is problematic. More will be said on this point later.

Finally, the translation equivalents which do not take the suffix -eme into consideration such as *iymaa'ah* for 'chroneme', *qaalab* for 'grameme (al-B'albakii 1990), *maddah* for 'chroneme' (ALECSO 1989) and *mithaal* for 'tagmeme' (Mubaarak 1995) are semantically inaccurate because the concepts they refer to do not include the semantic component referred to by the suffix -eme in the English terms, i.e. 'unit of'.

Based on the above critical review, none of the above quoted Arab terminographers has given consistent translation equivalents, neither semantically nor formally. But is the case as hopeless as it seems to be? The answer is definitely 'no'. The literal translation technique can be employed consistently to produce semantically and formally consistent Arabic translation equivalents for all the English terms formed by the suffix -eme. This technique consists in the employment of the Arabic term *wahdah* to render the -eme derivatives consistently as follows:

ceneme	*wahdah sawtiyyah*
prosodeme	*wahdah nabriyyah*

toneme	*wahdah naghamiyyah*
akueme	*wahadah tanghiimiyyah*
morpheme	*wahdah sarfiyyah*
lexeme	*wahdah mu'jamiyyah*
kineme	*wahdah 'iymaa'iyyah* (in body language)
chereme	*wahdah 'iyshaariyyah* (in sign language)
grapheme	*wahdah khattiyyah*
moneme	*wahdah sarfiyyah*
narreme	*wahdah qasasiyyah*
chroneme	*wahdah maddiyyah*
syntagmeme	*wahdah nasqiyyah*
phememe	*wahdah lughawiyyah*
plereme	*wahdah dilaaliyyah* (in componential analysis)
	wahdah ta'biiriyyah(in glossemstics)
phoneme	*wahdah sawtiyyah*
proxeme	*wahdah taqaarubiyyah*
behavioureme	*wahdah sluukiyyah*
glosseme	*wahdah 'alaamiyyah* (Bloomfield)
	wahdah nazmiyyah (Hjlmslev)
taxeme	*wahdah nahwiyyah*
tagmeme	*wahdah shakliyyah/binaa'iyyah* (Bloomfield)
	wahdah qaalabiyyah (tagmemics)
syntaxeme	*wahdah tarkiibiyyah*
classeme	*wahdah tasniifiyyah*
sememe	*wahdah dilaaliyyah (mu'jamiyyah)*
semanteme	*wahdah dilaaliyyah*
soneme	*wahdah siyaatiyyah*
stroneme	*wahdah nabriyyah*
grameme	*wahdah shakliyyah/binaa'iyyah*

As already indicated these intensional (or literal) translation equivalents, though semantically and formally consistent, lack the property of concision exhibited by their English counterparts. In other words, the linguistic concepts expressed in English by one-word terms are expressed in Arabic by two-word equivalents. This disadvantage has problematic implications for the translation of English terms derived from some -eme derivatives such as: morphemic, morphemics; graphemic, graphemics; phonemic, phonemics, phonemist, phonemicize, phonemicization; kinemics, etc. However, structural diversity between English and Arabic entails the acceptance of diversity in the method of expression allowed by each of the two languages. Accordingly, the above mentioned terms derived from some -eme derivatives are rendered into Arabic through the employment of suitable morphological or lexical devices as follows:

morphemic analysis	*tahliil al-wahdaat al-sarfiyyah*
	al-tahliil hasab al-wahdaat al-sarfiyyah
morphemics	*'ilm al-wahdaat al-sarfiyyah*
	diraasat al-wahdaat al-sarfiyyah
	al-sarfiyaat
graphemics	*'ilm al-wahdaat al-khattiyyah*
	al-khattiyaat
phonemist	*'aalim al-wahdaat al-sawtiyyah*

kinemics — *'ilm al-wahdaat al-'imaa'iyyah*
diraasat al-wahdaat al-'imaa'iyyah
al-'imaa'iyaat

The term 'phonemicisation' does exhibit a real challenge to the translator in respect of concision in Arabic. The problem here is related to the translation of the English suffix -isation, which forms nouns of action from verbs in -ise or by analogy where no verb exists (New Shorter Oxford English Dictionary). In linguistics, 'phonemicisation' has two meanings: (a) the process or result of classifying, analysing or describing in terms of phonemes, and (b) the process or result of changing from allophonic to phonemic status (*Ibid.*). In Arabic, three equivalents are needed for sense (a):

al-tasniif hasab al-wahdaat al-sawtiyyah
al-tahliil 'ilaa wahdaat sawtiyyah
al-wasf hasab al-wahdaat al-sawtiyyah

and two equivalents for sense (b), according to whether the underlying verb is used transitively or intranstively:

al-tahawiil 'ilaa wahdaat sawtiyyah
al-tahawwul 'ilaa wahdaat sawtiyyah

Thus, terminologically, the literal translation of 'phonemicisation' has two implications: semantic variation and formal length. In translating linguistic material, the problem of variation in meaning can be solved contextually, but in terminological work and terminography all variant senses have to be represented. Formal length, or lack of concision, represents a real terminological problem because the Arabic equivalents have turned out to be long strings of words.

A relatively, but not absolutely, practical alternative is the employment of some morphological patterns in translating -eme derivative to produce extensional translation equivalents that denote individuality and represent, more or less, the actual functions or nature of the entities referred to by the English terms formed by the suffix -eme. On the analogy of the translation equivalent *musarrif* given by Ali (1993) to 'morpheme', the pattern *MUFA''ILAH*, which denotes the feminine form of the active participle, can be employed to translate some -eme terms as follows:

moneme	*musarrifah* (that which changes word forms)
chroneme	*musawwitah* (that which changes the length of a speech sound)
classeme	*musannifah* (that which decides or changes the class of an entity)
syntaxeme	*murakkibah* (that which constructs a structure)
tagmeme	*mushakkilah* or *muqawlibah* (that which forms or moulds)

Other patterns can relatively be utilised to translate some of the English terms ending in -eme as follows:

FU'AYLAH :	(denoting the feminine form of the diminutive)
toneme	*nughaymah* (a small single tone compared with a bigger one)
kineme	*uyaymah* (a small single gesture compared with a bigger gesture)
syntagmeme	*nusayqah* (a small single syntagm compared with a bigger syntagm)

TAF'IILAH: (denoting the process or result of a single action)
prosodeme *tanbiirah* (the process or result of a single act of stressing or pitch raising)
FAA'ILAH: (denoting the feminine form of the active participle)
plermeme *daallah* (that which signifies)
FI'LAH: (denoting a small piece or portion of any thing)
phoneme *s̲iitah* (a single portion of sound)
ceneme *s̲iitah* (a single portion of sound)
MAF'UUL: (denoting the passive participle)
semanteme *madluul* (*'aam*)
sememe *madluul* (*mu'jamii*)

The term 'lexeme', as already pointed out, is translated metaphorically by Ali (1993) as *'ajamah* whose underlying pattern is *FA'ALAH*, the denotation of which includes 'individuality'. It is worth mentioning here that the above suggested extensional Arabic equivalents do not denote the concept of 'unit of structure', but extensionally denote the functions or nature of the entities denoted by the -eme derivatives. Formally, these Arabic equivalents are concise, with the exception of those given to 'semanteme' and 'sememe', and, therefore, amenable to further derivation. Morphologically and semantically related terms derived from the above extensionally translated -eme forms can also be concisely translated into Arabic as follows:

phonemic	*s̲iitii*
phonemics	*al-s̲iitiyaat/'ilm al-s̲iitaat*
phonemicisation	*al-tas̲yiit/al-tas̲ayyut*
morphemic	*mus̲arrifii*
morphemics	*mus̲arrifiyaat/'ilm al-mus̲arrifaat*

Finally, the above extensional equivalents are formally more concise, but denotatively less precise than their literal translation counterparts.

References

Ali, Muh̲ammad. 1993. *Wasf al-Lughah al-'Arabiyyah Dilaaliyyan*. Tripoli: Jaami'at al-Faatih̲.
'Aniis, Ibraahiim, et al. 1987. *al-Mu'jam al-Wasiit̲*. 2nd. ed. Beirut: 'Amwaaj li al-T̲ibaa'ah wa al-Nashr.
ALECSO (Arab League Educational Cultural and Scientific Organization). 1989. *Unified Dictionary of Linguistic Terms (English-Arabic-French)*. Tunis: ALECSO.
Asher, R. E. (ed.). 1994. *The Encyclopedia of Language and Linguistics*. Oxford/New York. Seoul and Tokyo: Pergamon Press.
Al-B'albakii, Muniir. 1967. *al-Mawrid: Qaamuus 'Inkliizii-'Arabii*. 23rd ed. 1989. Beirut: Daar al-'Ilm li al-Malaayiin.
Al-B'albakii, Ramzii. 1990. *Dictionary of Linguistic Terms (English-Arabic)*. Beirut: Daar al-'Ilm li al-Malaayiin.
Bakalla, Muh̲ammad, et al (1983). *A Dictionary of Modern Linguistic Terms (English-Arabic)*. Beirut: Librairie du Liban.
Bloomfield, Leonard. 1933. *Language*. New York: Henery Holt and Company.
Bussmann, Haumod. 1996. *Routledge Dictionary of Language and Linguistics*.

trans. and ed. Gregory Trayth and Kerstin Kazzazi. London and New York: Routledge.

Crystal, David. 1997. *A Dictionary of Linguistics and Phonetics*. Oxford: Blackwell.

Fehrii, 'Abdu al-Qaadir al-Faasii. (1983). "al-Mus̲talah̲ al-Lisaanii". *al-Lisaan al 'Arabii*, vol. 23 (pp. 139-147). Rabat: Maktab Tansiiq al-Ta'riib.

Katamba, Francis. 1993. *Morphology*. London: Machmillan.

Al-Khuulii, Muh̲ammad. 1982. *A Dictionary of Theoretical Linguistics (English- Arabic)*. Beirut: Librairie du Liban.

McArthur, T. 1992. *The Oxford Companion to the English Language*. London, New York, Sydny and Toronto: BCA.

Mubaarak, Mubaarak. 1995. *Mu'jam al-Mus̲talah̲aat al-'Alsuniyyah (French- English-Arabic)*. Beirut: Daar al-Fikr al-Lubnaanii.

The New Shorter Oxford English Dictionary. ed. Lesley Brown. 1993. Oxford: Clarendon Press.

Wright, W. 1859. *A Grammar of the Arabic Language*, vol. 1. trans. Smith, W.R. and de Goeje, M. J. 3rd. ed. 1967. Cambridge: Cambridge University Press.

Issues relating
To
Literal
And
film translation

Translating French philosophy into English: Benjamin Constant as a case-study

Dennis O'Keeffe, University of North London

Abstract

Constant is typical of eighteenth and early nineteenth century writing in a number of ways which touch on the special joys of translating work from this period. The oddity is that it is easier to translate a late eighteenth early nineteenth century writer like Constant into good modern English than is the case with many French moderns, not just the complexifiers (or innovating and original grapplers with truth, according to taste) such as Foucault and Derrida, but even modern French liberals such as Alain Finkielkraut.

What are the features of the intellectual world of France and Britain today that make mutual intelligibility less now than of old, and the translator's task therefore more difficult? There is a thesis here waiting to be articulated with which I do not yet feel fully equipped to deal. Indeed, it may defeat me definitively. It is not clear what all the elements in the problem are but some can be spelled out. First intelligibility is hampered by the abandonment of some ground rules and the adoption of others. The ground rule for Constant (and Montesquieu etc) is the same as that for Burke. Given that many human problems are complex, we should nevertheless try to express them in language of the maximum simplicity. The difficulty hitting the reader should always arise from the intrinsic difficulty of the subject-matter and never from the intervening difficulty of the author's language.

The ground rule in Marx as in Foucault or Talcot Parsons, by contrast, is that intellectual solemnity must be achieved by forcing the reader through an obstacle course. If it it easy to read it is not very serious. So we are faced with a problem of *scientism.*This has been a major French problem - Althusser etc. - and the adulating Americans and British have followed suit.

The second influence has been the rise of a kind of privatisation. Obscurantism has permitted a process of intellectual insider-trading to arise, where people are writing for each other, for a smallish clique of insiders, rather than to the world at large.

The defeat of clarity

Constant is typical of eighteenth and early ninete"enth century writing in a number of ways which touch on the special joys of translating work from this period. It was a time when French and English writers identifiable as broadly influenced by the Enlightenment formed part of a more obvious international unity than one could easily identify today.

There are, admittedly, improvements which can be made to Constant's terminology in the light of subsequent advances in social science and political theory. Some of the vocabulary needs to be opened up. When he is referring to what in English is called 'power', Constant uses "pouvoir", "puissance" and "autorité" more or less coterminously. We can find the same thing in English writing of the same period. But in the late nineteenth and early twentieth centuries Max Weber persuaded us in considerable degree to subdivide, to identify nuances in certain concepts. Power is still a matrical concept but civilisation has to tame power and the modified version - the kind of power civilisation requires - is called 'authority'. Constant uses the various cognates of power more or less coterminously and in this sense he is a pre-modern. It is true that in the modern world 'power' has been rendered analytically vacuous by overemployment - neo-Marxian writings and those of Foucault spring to mind in this regard - which is only to say that intellectual progress is subject to retrogressions and periodic amnesia. Weberian subtleties are the best we have arrived at yet and it is perfectly legitimate to suggest that Constant would benefit from them, retrospectively.

All this, however, is small criticism of a writer who is marvellously luminous in a way which makes us regret what happened to some French writing, and, mostly in imitation, also to some British and American writing, in the twentieth century. There is certainly an *intellectual* gulf between France and Britain today greater than their social or economic differences, and one wider than in Constant's day between their styles of writing. This suggests that there are international variations and inconsistencies within the broad homogenisation embodied in global trends. The world is moving towards a kind of international homogeneity in economic terms, and towards convergence in *certain* cultural terms, but within this overall process there are countertrends. Do I have a small thesis for the reader here, one that I have constructed especially from reading Constant? Yes, namely that in the area of speculative/philosophical writing there is probably less intelligibility between the French and the English now than there was almost two centuries ago. Lots of influential French writers have deliberately sought to be obscure. The British and American writers who do this are mainly under French tutelage.

It has of course be admitted that the adverb 'probably' makes my thesis fairly timid. I would also add, first, that French friends have told me that it in France people no longer read Althusser, or Foucault or even Derrida very much, whereas there is an Anglophone minority obsessed with these writers. I still suspect strongly that the oxymoronic flames of obscurity burn brightly in French philosophy and social theorising.

Secondly I would draw attention to the continuing presence of Marxism in French economics departments. Just in itself this must be a powerful source of language obfuscation, one which British and American students of economics are mercifully spared.

Clarity and innocence

In eighteenth century France and Britain alike there was a love of clarity. Constant is as lucid as Johnson or Burke, for example. This limpidity was conveyed, however hard this may be for us to imagine, through very long and elaborate passages, with many subordinate clauses. These, despite their complexity, involved none of the deliberate obfuscation characterising say - to talk in terms of my own field of sociology of education - the work of Pierre Bourdieu in France or Basil Bernstein in Britain. These writers are masters of baroque obscurity. Constant is as baroque in his flowing rhetoric as Burke, in both cases without the fundamental lucidity being impaired. They are never obscure. Within the artful elipsis and subtle, ironic and rhetorical nuances, there is a profound clarity.

What has changed such as to impair this fundamental lucidity? I think we are faced with a fundamental loss of innocence, one to which language has responded, one it has subsequently compounded. It is innocence which clarifies the world and cynicism which obscures it. Intellectual innocence and innocent language handle the baffling complexities of existence better than does the hermeneutics of suspicion, as Paul Ricoeur called the habit of distrusting the world. Take a truly complex question, such as what makes a free society and what sustains it? Read through Constant's *Principes de politique* and you will find the problem laid out with stunning intellectual brilliance and clarity. I am not saying Constant's version is definitive - though within its limitations it is very persuasive - but it is marvellously clear. The rule of law, modest but inalienable individual rights, limited government, religious and intellectual freedom, minimal taxation. These are the conditions of political freedom. Modern masters of directness like Hayek and Aron and Friedman could not have put the case better.

On the other hand, sift the vast Sartrean corpus on this subject and find one direct, unambiguous and clearly articulated proposition on the question as to what civilisation is, if you can. The only clarity in Sartre is his hatred of the 'bourgeois order'. Similarly one of the few clear statements in Althusser's celebrated, long and obscure essay on ideology is to the effect that the distinction between the private and the public is 'a bourgeois distinction'. Even here he cannot just say that the private must be abolished. He has to stand at a pompous remove from such appalling clarity.

The problem of innocence in Constant

It may seem odd to say so of a writer like Constant with his huge erudition and his worldliness; but there is an innocence about this man which is noticeable to the modern translator. I do not mean by innocence any naiveté. On the contrary Constant has a devastating eye for cant or hypocrisy. Constant can dig out from a complex social reality a persuasive account of what it really is, of what is really happening.

What I am referring to is Constant's apparent belief that the truth is normally discernible to the intelligent gaze. There is little or no obfuscation in his writing. He says what he means, or certainly he does when he gets to conclusions. Above all his mind and work are not marked by the suspiciousness which now forms much of our world. For Constant everything is what it is and not some other thing. The notion that beneath the apparent surface reality of things there is a sinister hidden order, an idea which some nineteenth century Germans - Marx, Nietzsche - and in the first half of the twentieth century, Freud, and since the Second World War lots of Frenchmen, have promulgated, is far from Constant's mind. This particular conceit has partly ruined modern sociology and psychology it seems to me and also destroyed or compromised literary criticism.

In both countries in Constant's day there was an assumption that educated people having a knowledge of formal philosophy rather than being themselves academic philosophers, had things of interest to say to their readers. This tendency was true of France and England throughout most of the eighteenth and nineteeenth centuries and unites Constant, Voltaire, Burke and Smith and many more. In both countries, moreover, given that the modern social scientific mania for 'evidence' had not yet surfaced, there was no predjudice against engaging in *a priori* anecdotal, history-tinged social reflection.

Now, this kind of writing can fail. At other times, it is astonishingly on cue. In his *Principes de politique*, for example, Constant returns again and again to themes of perennial relevance: the disasters which follow from excessive government intervention, and especially the horrors which attend the abandonment of the rule of law. Many twentieth century writers, drawing on the inspiration of Marx in the mid-nineteenth century, have either denied outright the relevance and centrality of law or have proposed social explanations of the human condition which preclude recourse to law as a remedy. This tendency is apparent in Britain and France, though the inspiration is French more than British. Many political commentators in both our countries have believed in what Constant would have seen as overgovernment. Constant is quite clear that too much government, and too much faith in government, are themselves part of the problem. This is why we so regret the constrictions of his vocabulary. We could interpret his drift as the view that governments have too much power, and that such power should be diminished in volume and elevated in weight, by a shift from crude power to authority as the telos of human governance.

Even writers broadly in the same tradition as Constant tend today to write more obscurely than he did. The oddity is that it is easier to translate Constant into good English than it is to translate some modern writers who are very much in agreement with him intellectually. Alain Finkielkraut is roughly comparable to Constant. Both men are liberal sceptics with their feet in a love of France and her traditions. A little more than a decade ago I translated Finkielkraut's *La Défaite de la Pensée* and I can assure readers that page for page it was a much harder task than translating Constant.

One modern difficulty: guru worship

In eighteenth and early nineteenth century France and England there was little of the guru worship which has characterised some speculative writing today. Some writers, Voltaire, Rousseau, Smith and Burke, had immense prestige in their very different ways. But they were not gurus. Nowadays there is a most odious cult of guruship. It is sad to relate that certain Frenchmen have been much in evidence here: Sartre, Poulantzas, Althusser and Foucault, to name only some of them. One might cite Terry Eagleton in the British case and Stanley Fish in the American.

The French flu

In the earlier period there was a mutual respect between the writers in France and Britain. Nor was there a relationship of intellectual dependency discernible. Burke is as admiring of French civilisation as Constant is of British. Today English and American writers in the humanities tend either to dismiss or to worship their French peers. The early nineteenth century was not thus. There was no equivalent of what Arthur Koestler called the 'French 'flu' - the tendency for some modern writers in the English language to lay themselves open to any nonsense provided only that it was originally written in French. Constant himself has no leaning to any such folly. He is an Anglophile, but no supine admirer of anyone.

On returning to my small thesis

Why, if there is intellectual globalisation occurring, is there also fragmentation and lack of intellectual community, as between France and Britain? What are the features of the intellectual world of France and Britain today that make mutual intelligibility less now than of old, and the translator's task therefore more difficult?

There is a thesis here waiting to be articulated with which I do not yet feel fully equipped to deal. Indeed, it may defeat me definitively. It is not clear what all the elements in the problem are; but some can be spelled out. First intelligibility is hampered by the abandonment of some ground rules and the adoption of others. The ground rule for Constant (and Montesquieu etc.) is the same as that for Burke. Given that many human problems are complex, we should nevertheless try to express them in language of the maximum clarity. Ornate style is permitted; but it must not get in the way. The difficulty hitting the reader should always arise mainly from the intrinsic difficulty of the subject-matter and never from the intervening difficulty of the author's language.

The ground rule in Marx, as in many modern British and American sociologists, is that intellectual solemnity must be achieved by forcing the reader through an obstacle course. If something is easy to read it cannot be serious. This is the problem some writers call *scientism* - the rendering of something in a more difficult form by the use of obfuscating terms. This has been a major French problem - Althusser etc. - and the adulating Americans and British have followed suit. In the Anglophone case - I do not feel competent to pronounce on the French one - the whole problem is made worse by the collapse of grammatical accuracy and syntactical control. It is not obvious whence our help will come, if it ever does. Orwell has received great recognition, for reasons close to the arguments of this essay, since his death. My guess is that if history finally plays fair with them, Aron will last better than Sartre. It is not too much to guess that if the battle for clarity and innocence is ever won again, Constant might reappear in the guise of a *grand maître* from whose direct words we all have much to learn.

Shifting meanings: Translating Grimms' fairy tales as children's literature

Karen Seago, University of North London

Abstract

The Grimms'fairy tales were initially conceived as a collection of scholarly source material demonstrating the existence of a German national literature and thus contributing to the construction of a German nation state. It was in their reception and the course of roughly fifty years of continuous editing that they acquired their status of children's reading. Nevertheless, the German texts never entirely lost the traces of their scholarly origin. It is, however, in their translation into English that the texts were entirely received as children's literature and this paper will examine the shifts due to genre conventions and enforced by didactic demands.

The first volume of the Brothers Grimm collection of German traditional tales was published in 1812 as *Kinder- und Hausmärchen* (Children and Household Tales), a second volume was produced in 1815. Claimed to be the best-known work of German literature, the *Kinder- und Hausmärchen* had seven editions of the two-volume collection (*Große* Ausgabe) and ten editions of the selected tales (*Kleine* Ausgabe) during the lifetime of the brothers (Sutton 1996: 1). Translated variously as *German Popular Tales*, *Children's and Household Tales* or *Home Stories*, the collection is best known in English as *Grimms' Fairy Tales*. This title foregrounds the role of the brothers and the status of the tales as authored or children's stories in a way which Jacob and Wilhelm would not have entirely agreed with.[1]

The Grimms understood themselves as collectors and guardians of traditional folk stories which they perceived to be under threat of extinction. As such, the *Kinder- und Hausmärchen* were conceived as a collection of source material with an extensive scholarly apparatus giving information on mediators, sources, regional variants etc. The brothers defined the *Märchen* as the poetry of the people, seeing folktales as diluted remnants of myths and Wilhelm compared them in a famous quotation to half-remembered "coloured glass pieces, scattered fragments of the once whole diamond of divinely inspired poetry" (Grimm in Rölleke (ed.) 1982. Vol. 3: 409 [421]). Both Wilhelm and Jacob had noted the close affinity between *Märchen* and Nordic myth, carefully demonstrating their similarities in world view and in detailed comparisons of narrative motifs. Their mythic origin meant, as the brothers argued, that the *Märchen* were also remnants of ancient religion and tribal customs. As proof of a once existing German epic literature, they were evidence of the existence of a German cultural heritage. All this was instrumental in the formation of a German identity (Kamenetsky 1992: 55-59 and Michaelis-Jena 1970: 50-51).

The importance of this claim needs to be seen in its historical context. In the same year that the brothers started collecting old German material in 1806, Napoleon was at the summit of his career and German territory was occupied. Turning towards the German language and evidence of its history and cultural validity allowed for a self-identification which resisted the occupying force. Collecting tales which were evidence of a uniquely German literature had a clear political function and the *Kinder- und Hausmärchen* were a consciously conceived contribution to the resistance against Napoleonic occupation (Grimm "*Selbstbiographie*" in Hinrichs 1881 vol. 1: 3-25 (12) and Seitz 1984: 43). But the need to assert a German identity went beyond this and also played an important role in the struggle to create a German nation state. Even before the establishment of French rule in artificially created kingdoms, Germany did not exist as a political entity but consisted of over 300 principalities. Each of these states

[1] The German term *Märchen* refers to a much wider type of traditional material, while 'fairy tales' are closely linked to the authored *contes des fées*, popular at the end of the seventeenth century at the French court and widely translated into English in the eighteenth century.

was fully independent, with a unique dialect, its own customs and regional identity. After Napoleon's defeat in 1814, occupied territories were mostly reconstituted as their previous principalities, and Germany returned to its political fragmentation.

The efforts for unification - an idea to which the Grimms were deeply committed - were based on a perception that the only commonality was a shared language and a shared cultural heritage. Despite regional variation and pride, German as a national language provided a bond across dialects and customs in its opposition to the French or Latin still widely used in aristocratic and academic circles. The hope was that the cultural community could develop into a political nation, and here again the *Märchen* provided proof for the existence of this allegedly shared culture. In the introduction to the second volume of the *KHM* in 1815, Wilhelm declared:

> in these tales we find much original German myth, which had been believed lost.
> (Grimm. "*Vorrede zum zweiten Band*" in Hinrichs 1881 vol.1: 328-332 (330))

Constructed as historical evidence of the origins of a German community, the *Märchen* prove the possibility of a German nation in the present. Even more importantly, the tales transcend the fragmentation of contemporary Germany because there are no local references. According to Wilhelm, the *Märchen* are removed from the actual world and their essence expresses something uniquely German.

The authentication of the folktales as myth and their validation as cultural inheritance requires, as the Grimms argued, that their textual status must be respected and that they should be recorded, contrary to existing practice at the time, without editorial interference (Grimm *Ibid.*: 320-328 (327)). However, the actual publishing history of the *Kinder- und Hausmärchen* quite clearly shows that substantial editing did take place. Between 1812 and 1857 there were seventeen editions of the *Complete Tales* and the *Selected Tales*; these were continuously revised and changed, both in terms of language as well as content and the Grimms quite consciously gave the tales a particular shape. While much of the editing took place as part of a continuous work-in-progress - as the brothers received new stories, these were included or used to revise existing material, editorial input changed over the years partly in response to contemporary critical response. The romantic poet Clemens Brentano, for example, sharply condemned the *Kinder- und Hausmärchen* for aesthetic reasons. He categorically disapproved of the Grimms' refusal to modify the language and composition of the tales, arguing that their professed loyalty to tradition had resulted in "careless, soiled, ragged" language and "boring" tales.[1]

Perhaps more serious was the criticism that the language and subject matter of the *Kinder - und Hausmärchen* were morally inappropriate. Critics objected to the cruelty of many tales, in particular if it was committed in the family and against family members. Offence was taken at the depiction of the devil, and situations which had sexual overtones (Rölleke "*Nachwort*" 1982: 590-617 (573)). The language was criticised as vulgar by educators precisely because the Grimms had refused to adapt the simple vernacular of the tales to conform to the norms of educated and cultured German. Wilhelm responded and introduced morally motivated changes. In the introduction to the second edition in 1819 he reassures readers:

> "We have carefully excised any expression not suitable for children."

[1] Letter to Achim von Arnim in 1813, quoted in Hildebrandt 1985: 106.

(Grimm "Vorrede" 1819 vol.1: V-XX (VIII))

Editorial changes have been documented extensively and the folklore scholar Heinz Rölleke identifies as the main trends an increasing use of diminutives together with a toning down of extreme motifs, an interpretation of family roles which conforms to bourgeois values and an increasingly Christian outlook. Instances of interfamily violence and of incest are edited out, as is pre-marital sex and pregnancy (Röllecke "*Nachwort*" and "*Zur Biographie der Grimmschen Märchen versehen*" 1989: 521-582, Tatar 1992, Bottigheimer 1987, and Schoo1963: 90-99). Thus there is a move away from the original purist approach to accommodate the needs of the children's literature market. Nevertheless, many aspects which critics had objected to and which were features typical of oral material were retained: treatment of profane matter, crude language and jokes, or a less pronounced sensitivity to hints of sexuality and erotic desire, the representation of violence, cruelty, base instincts and intense emotion, the mythic detachment, ambiguous characters and a validation of values in contradiction of didactic considerations (laziness, dirtiness, disrespect of authority, etc.). Wilhelm had defended this by using one of the central tenets of Romantic literary theory: the celebration of nature and its inherent innocence. His argument was that as the offending language and content resulted from loyalty to tradition, it followed that these features were entirely natural. Any perceived corruption in the material was in the eye of the civilised beholder (Grimm "*Vorrede zum zweiten Band*" 1881: 331). Thus some of the authority and integrity of the traditional texts was protected even though the *Kinder- und Hausmärchen* were appropriated as children's texts and the collection retained a substantial number of distinctly non-didactic features.

This was not the case when the tales were translated into English, where they were received entirely as children's literature. The *Kinder- und Hausmärchen* are inserted into an existing tradition of moral and didactic tales within which and against which they posit themselves and many of the features which Wilhelm had retained cause problems for the translators (Butts in Hunt (ed.) 1995: 77-101). In addition, the fairy tale genre had to contend with a very negative reputation in England in contrast to Germany where the romantic poets had elevated it into one of the highest art forms (Darton 1982: 99). The history of children's reading (especially in England) is characterised by the split into acceptable texts - those aimed at instruction - and unacceptable texts - those read for entertainment. The fairy tale was historically perceived as unacceptable children's reading due to its entertaining and imaginative aspects and objected to on rational, moral and religious grounds; a key objection was that its non-factual and non-spiritual nature exposes children to moral and intellectual corruption. The *Kinder - und Hausmärchen* were instrumental in overcoming the fairy tale's negative inflection because the scholarly function allowed the texts to be received within the tradition of reading for instruction (Kotzin 1972: 8-10 and Briggs in Denecke (ed.) 1963: 511-524 (514-515)). But it meant that English translators had to adapt the texts not only to the conventions of children's literature but also had to negotiate the negative reputation of the genre.

Thus the didactic and morally charged context of English reception determines the translation choices and all but one of the nineteenth century translations examined show consistent shifts on the microstructural level and on the macrostructural level.[1] These result in at times

[1] I examined ten nineteenth century translations of *Sleeping Beauty* in detailed textual analyses. 'Transculturations: Making *Sleeping Beauty*; The Translation of a Grimm *Märchen* into an English Fairy Tale in the Nineteenth Century' (Seago 1998). My findings with regard to one particular story are borne out by *the Sin-Complex*, Martin Sutton's similar study into nineteenth-century translations of the

substantial changes in motivation, characterisation, and narrative logic often with explicit additions on the German source texts. Translation and editing choices are strongly influenced by the ideals disseminated in children's literature of the time and many of the strategies and conventions employed in the translations are determined by a defensiveness caused by the continued debate over the fairy tale throughout the nineteenth century.

Areas which remain sensitive throughout the century are 1) the treatment of profane matters, 2) the relationship between the real and the imagination and children's capacity to differentiate between them, and 3) quite strongly enunciated moral sensitivities. In addition, the socialising function of the texts also influences representations of femininity and masculinity. The attributes, behaviour, actions and motivations of male and female characters in the story are didactically adapted to become role models conforming to prescriptive notions of gender roles.

1. Concern over the profanity of some of the material in the German collection is expressed by the majority of the translations and explicitly addressed in their prefaces. Stories about divine characters are either not translated at all or reference to God and the devil has been omitted where it occurs, or the offensive passages have been altered. Taylor famously translated the 'devil' as a 'giant', other generalising choices are the very descriptive 'evil spirit' or 'diabolical agency'. A consistently used strategy is to transpose Christian references to classical or Nordic myth. This translates the devil as 'Pluto' and his grandmother as 'Hecate', while God becomes 'Jupiter', the archangel is 'Mercury' and heaven is 'Olympus' while 'hell' has been translated as the 'Scandinavian hell' or even a cave (Sutton 1996: 35 and Seago 1998: 311).

Sensitivities exist not only where explicit irreverence is shown to religious topics or characters, but also with regard to more general narrative motifs which could be interpreted as blasphemy. So, for example, when the dead Snow White is re-awakened at the end of the story, this could be seen as resurrection which should only be performed by God or his Son. Consequently, some translations ensure with additional comments that the girl is not in fact dead, or edit out passages which describe the wonder that her body does not decay, allowing by this omission the interpretation that she is not really dead (Sutton 1996: 46). Similarly, in *Sleeping Beauty*, several translations add to the description of the princess falling lifeless to the ground when she pricks her finger on the spindle, that she is not dead but only appears so (Seago 1998: 215 & 282). How sensitive this aspect is becomes apparent when one considers that the added comment is actually not necessary because the curse at the beginning of the story states quite explicitly that the princess will fall asleep (and not die).

2. The suspect status of fairy tales as imaginative texts: There are two main strategies in which translations negotiate the negative inflection of the fairy tale. The first is by establishing the usefulness of fairy stories by claiming allegiance with established traditions of endorsed texts of children's literature. This includes giving fairy tale collections titles which explicitly link them to the approved genre of the moral and didactic tale. Examples are *The Fairy Token* (1840) which quite consciously trades on James Janeway's influential Puritan *Token for Children*, a conduct book for religious children still widely read in the nineteenth century, or Edgar Taylor's revised 1839 translation *German Popular Stories and Fairy Tales As Told by Gammer Grethel* which links to Joseph Ritson's *Gammer Gurton's*

Kinder - und Hausmärchen which deals with the same translations but investigates a different story in each collection.

Garland. Alternatively, features are introduced which cast the text in the tradition of instructive reading matter. Several translations, for example, expand the descriptions of the sleeping castle in Sleeping Beauty by adding specifications in a way which is typical of instructional reading matter designed to teach the child about language and the world. So, we have 'the dogs in the yard', 'the cook in the kitchen', 'the king by the throne' etc. or a mediating narratorial voice explains narratorial gaps and reassures the reader about the predictability of the world (Seago 1998: 277 & 242-243).

The second strategy is by engaging directly with the question of reality and the imagination. Such translations introduce a shift in the management of fictive reality and its relationship to the reality of the narrator's/reader's world. In the traditional tale, magical events and those which could happen in reality are described in the same way, existing side by side without any clear boundaries between the possible and the impossible. In the translations, clearly demarcated domains for the real and the supernatural are set up. An 1855 translation of *Sleeping Beauty*, for example, introduces markers into the story to warn the reader/listener when this line is crossed. When the magically transformed thorn-hedge moves apart for the prince, this is presented as a subjective impression and a similar grammatical shift qualifies the magical effect of the prince's kiss: "As if awakened by this, Rosaline opened her eyes." (*Ibid*.: 247)[1]

A more subtle marker is the way the story-telling process is emphasised, calling attention to the fact that there are stories within the story and consequently highlighting that the text the child is hearing or reading is fictional as well. One translation conspicuously raises the question whether the tale of the sleeping princess which "was reported through all lands" is fact or fiction by changing the reason why the princes come to the castle hidden by the hedge. In the German text, the aim of the princes is a typical fairy tale task of overcoming an obstacle in order to rescue the princess. In the English text, the princes are instead motivated by a wish to verify the truth of the story they have heard: "and from time to time kings' sons would arrive for the purpose of discovering for themselves if the history of the sleeping Rosaline were true". (*Ibid*.: 248)

Such strategies ensure that the supernatural is separated and textually marked as non-real while the belief in the narrator's reality is linked to those scenarios which are non-magical. At the same time, the translations introduce dramatic tension and narrative devices which draw the reader into the story inviting identification and participation by directly addressing the reader or setting up comparable experiences which can occur in real life. Thus in an 1872 translation, grammatical shifts in pronoun and tense mean that the prince has been hearing the story of the sleeping princess all his life and was told about it by his own grandfather (*Ibid*.: 273-274). The same text also draws on established literary tropes such as the adventure story by shifting the attributes of the prince and his preparation for entering the castle so that it mirrors descriptions of expeditions in boys' stories popular at the time (*Ibid*.: 281-282).

3. Moral objections cover a very wide area. Instances of overt sexuality, references to conception, birth and even death are omitted or paraphrased. In fact, most aspects relating to the body, its fluids, or even mention of body parts are censored in some way. When Sleeping Beauty pricks her finger on the spindle, or when Snow White coughs up the poisoned apple from her throat, this is omitted. (Seago 1998: 261 and Sutton 1996:47-48) (Interestingly, though, not all translations have a problem with the disenchanting kiss in *Sleeping Beauty*

---

[1] Seago, p. 247

and quite a few texts eroticise the sleeping girl.) All bodily functions or scatological matters are highly problematic. When not absolutely essential to the narrative any such references are omitted; if they are a central motif, they are paraphrased which often leads to narrative inconsistency. Sensitivities around the body's natural processes goes so far that the 'pisspot' in which a couple live in one story has only been translated in the twentieth century, and even here with stylistic shift (as chamber pot) and in the nineteenth century is rendered as 'hut', 'hovel', 'ditch'. 'lowly chamber'. Even a 'heap of dung' appears to be too offensive and is translated as a 'pile of hay or straw' while bird-droppings become 'falling leaves' or 'hail' (Sutton 1996: 219-222). References to 'dirt', to 'lice' or 'fleas', or to personal grooming are omitted or paraphrased (*Ibid.*: 229-230). In the story of *Sleeping Beauty* the associative meanings of 'crab' with 'crab lice', or, sexual disease' are apparently so strong that the queen hears the prophecy of her pregnancy from a fish instead (Taylor 1823, Taylor 1839). There is a great reluctance in the translations to deal with intense emotion or base instincts: great joy, rage, envy, revenge, pride or vanity are all tempered or even omitted (*Ibid.*: 27-29) and great care is taken to show authority figures in non-compromising situations: so for example, all translations (except Hunt) exonerate the king in *Sleeping Beauty* from any carelessness in looking after his child and the blame is shifted either onto servants or his actions are presented in the passive or in an impersonal, abstract manner so that he cannot be identified as the agent. The sanctity of the family is protected to such a degree that even negative figures such as the evil stepmother in *Snow White* are not referred to as 'stepmother' but only as 'queen', obscuring her (actually very loose) familial relationship with the girl (*Ibid.*: 29, 35-36).

4. The construction of appropriate gender roles evolves very much around a disambiguation in characterisation. This introduces flat characters who are either good or bad and through this clear dichotomy of good and evil, unambiguous values and behavioural norms are promoted and I will demonstrate this using the story of *Sleeping Beauty* as an example.
The polarisation of good and bad is particularly clear-cut in the way the translations have developed an unambiguous opposition between the twelve fairies and the thirteenth one. This is achieved by stressing the benevolent character of the well-wishing fairies whose nature is shown to be womanly and attuned to children by adding explicit descriptions of how good and nurturing they are. Every single translation with the exception of Hunt introduces adjectives such as 'good' (Paull), 'benevolent' (Gillies), 'friendly' (Taylor 1839). In two translations in the 1850s, the wise women are described as 'good and kind to children' (Davis, 1855) and as 'kind and affectionate to children' (Wehnert 1853) where the source text foregrounds their mythic power and suggests that the king's invitation is motivated by a desire to propitiate them (*damit sie dem Kind hold und gewogen wären* - so that they were disposed favourably to the child *Kinder- und Hausmärchen* 1850). In contrast, the thirteenth fairy slowly evolves into a witch-like figure whose unjustified rage and revenge are entirely unmotivated so that the curse is the result of her evil nature. All translations, except for Hunt, add modifiers which explicitly identify her as bad: she is 'evil' (Wehnert, Gillies), 'spiteful (Gillies, Paull) and 'wicked' (Paull). Such a characterisation substantially affects the narrative motivation, shifting the story's meaning away from a contemplation of human destiny (the fact that everybody has to die) to a text with clear social implications. In the source text, the thirteenth fairy and her pronouncement of the princess's death retain their links to the third goddess of fate who cuts the thread of life, while in the translations her curse is no longer presented as an inevitable part of life, but comes about because of the witch's evil nature. Where the source text to some extent justifies her reaction and gives her motivation as 'revenge' for her exclusion, in the English texts, the contextualisation of her behaviour is omitted and instead her high emotions are exaggerated: she is 'greatly incensed' (Gillies), in a

'tremendous passion' (Wehnert), 'burning to revenge herself' (Crane). Furthermore, her behaviour is presented as entirely unjustified because the majority of the translations also introduces shifts in the motivation for her exclusion which exonerate the king (see above) and shift responsibility to herself. Because she threatens the human community for no apparent reason, her actions are presented not only as evil but also as without purpose. Since the translations also introduce negative consequences in explicit actions undertaken by the queen and the princess, female activity evolves in the English translations into a signifier of femininity which is clearly negatively inflected. This is particularly stressed with respect to the princess for whom the witch operates as a negative foil and a warning. It is also evident that in passages dealing with the princess, the use of the active and the passive in the translations is distributed in clear patterns which associate activity with narrative disapprobation while the passive is used in a much more pronounced way to promote narrative episodes which are rewarded. So, for example, the translations favour active constructions with the princess as the agent in the passages leading up to the fulfilment of the curse. Her curiosity and active involvement in finding the spindle and her express intention to touch it are stressed thus implicating her and making her at least partially responsible for the disaster. The underlying model of success and rejection in the narrative construction in the translations can be linked to dogmatic ideals of femininity and this again introduces a shift in narrative motivation towards a prescriptive socialising impetus instead of the more descriptive German tale.

While the promotion of normative gender roles focuses on the paradigm of activity-passivity as a benchmark for acceptable and unacceptable female behaviour in the translations, the model of manliness centres on rationality and unimpeachability. This means that the majority of translations enforce a representation of the male figures in the story which shows them to be faultless even if the German text is ambiguous. This is primarily developed around the figure of the king, but is also associated with the prince, especially in later translations where the focus shifts onto a more elaborate characterisation. Behavioural attributes are chosen which match those of contemporary conduct manuals (Nelson 1989: 525-550). Patience, planning, authority and rational decision-making are qualities which are added to the description of the prince and are also used for the king instead of the emotionality and impetuousness of the source text. For example, where the German king loses control of his faculties in his joy over his daughter's birth, the translations are insistent in a portrayal which expresses his delight in a more tempered manner stressing his self-restraint. Male control is an issue which is central in all translations both in terms of self-control, as in the example above where the king is not overwhelmed by his emotions, but also control over others. The king's authority over his family, his servants and his subjects, is stressed in at times elaborate additions when he, for example, enforces the destruction of the spindles, or ensures that servants obey orders. (Davis, Paull)

My final observation links back to the German *Märchen*'s postulated origin as myth. The mythic world-view was one of the defining features of the *Märchen's* authenticity and according to the Grimms, it was evident in the representation of nature as a sentient being. Wilhelm had identified as the distinguishing mark of their texts that they made no difference between the various manifestations of nature, be they human, animal, plant or even the elements. Throughout his editing, Wilhelm had retained, and even strengthened, this integrative world-view, evident in passages where natural features such as the branches of the hedge of thorns, the fire on the hearth, or the wind in the trees outside the castle are described in terms which ascribe to them the same faculties of will and intent as is normally only accorded human beings. It is this humility which conceives of humanity in the same terms as the natural world that presents a problem in the English translations. Instead they present a more traditionally Christian world-view where nature is separate from and subservient to mankind, and, according to Genesis, only created to serve man's needs. This view is implicit in all translations and manifests itself on two levels. Firstly, nature is returned to its non-sentient status, manifesting neither independent will nor intent, and secondly, man is elevated and his perspective becomes the central focus through which the world is interpreted. From the moment the prince enters the story, events are linked to him and relayed through his perception, making his subjectivity the general view. While the prince's passage through the hedge of thorns is only one instance of this androcentric organisation, it serves as a particularly useful example because it demonstrates the double movement of devaluation (of nature) and elevation (of man/kind). In the example, mobility and choice are passed from the hedge to the prince and nature serves as a backdrop to man's activity rather than as an equal participant in the events. In the passage below, the source text in the left column is the second edition of the *Kinder- und Hausmärchen*, the middle column is a literal translation by me, and the right column is a translation of 1855. The shifts in perception have been italicised:

Grimm (1819)	Literal	Gillies (1855)
Und als er sich der Dornenhecke näherte, *waren es* lauter große, schöne Blumen, *die thaten sich von selbst aus einander*, daß er unbeschädigt hindurch ging.	And as he approached the hedge of thorns *they were* all beautiful flowers, *which came apart of their own* so that he passed through unharmed.	And when the prince came to the spot which the old man had described, instead of a dreadful and impenetrable thicket, *he beheld* nothing but the most beautiful flowers and shrubs through *which he made his way* with great ease.

The assertion of the male as the definition of human experience and his place in nature in a position of mastery is particularly evident in a late translation by Mrs. Paull which develops an explicit framework of a biblically based male superiority. In contrast to the source text where the princess's name is generic, in this text it is the prince who names her just as Adam named Eve. Biblical analogies were a commonly employed trope, particularly so in handbooks on 'the etiquette of flowers', a popular convention where lovers conveyed their emotions through a complicated symbolic alphabet of flowers. In order to authenticate the purity and innocence of this language of the flowers, these handbooks draw on Genesis and often identify Eve as a flower herself. Since the prince names the princess 'May Blossom', nature and woman are conflated in a similar move by Paull, who inserts her translation into an established framework of Biblical reference and association.

Textual analysis of the ten nineteenth century translations of *Sleeping Beauty* has revealed that the cultural, historical and ideological context can be traced to specific meanings in individual texts and close examination has demonstrated how minor shifts in lexis and syntax accumulate and cohere to express particular patterns which can be related to specific concerns. Thus, larger cultural patterns and changes can be traced through the translations in the course of the nineteenth century and this historicity is one feature that removes the tales from their folkloric background and inserts them into the framework of children's literature. Other aspects typical of the genre shift are the foregrounding of a narrator who mediates the text's reality to the reader, summarises or expands as deemed necessary for a child's understanding. A change in narrative mode introducing suspense, the at times direct addressing of the readers to pull them into the text, the use of identificatory textual strategies are all features which are alien to folkloric texts (Ben-Amos in Röhrich (ed.) 1991: IX-XII (X

)). Instead, these narratorial strategies have been identified as typical of children's literature and all of them have been introduced into the nineteenth century translations of the *Kinder- und Hausmärchen*, fully inserting the English versions of the Grimms' fairy tales into the genre of children's reading.

References

Bertram, James (ed.). 1861. *The Language of Flowers, An Alphabet of Floral Emblems*. London: Nelson.

Bottigheimer, Ruth. 1987. *Grimms' Bad Girls & Bold Boys: The Moral & Social Vision of the Tales*. New Haven: Yale University Press.

Briggs, Katharine M. 1963. "The Influence of the Brothers Grimm in England". In Denecke, Ludwig (ed.). 1963. *Brüder Grimm Gedenken 1963*, vol. 1. Marburg: Elwert: 511-24.

Butts, Peter. "The Beginnings of Victorianism (*c*.1820-1850)". In Hunt, Peter. 1995. *Children's Literature, An Illustrated History* Hunt. Oxford: Oxford University Press.

Darton, F. J. H., Alderson, Brian (rev.). 1982 (3rd ed.). *Children's Books in England, Five Centuries of Social Life*. Cambridge: Cambridge University Press.

Grimm, Wilhelm. 1819. "Vorrede". In *Kinder- und Hausmärchen, zweite vermehrte und verbesserte Auflage*. 3 vols. Berlin: Reimer.

Grimm, Wilhelm. 1881. "Selbstbiographie". In Hinrichs, Gustav (ed.). *Kleinere Schriften*. 4 vols. Berlin: Dümmlers Verlagsbuchhandlung.

Grimm, Wilhelm. 1881. "Vorrede zum zweiten Band". In Hinrichs, Gustav (ed.). *Kleinere Schriften*. 4 vols. Berlin: Dümmlers Verlagsbuchhandlung.

Grimm, Wilhelm. Rölleke, Heinz (ed.). 1982. *Brüder Grimm Kinder- und Hausmärchen, Ausgabe letzter Hand mit den Originalanmerkungen der Brüder Grimm*. 3 vols. Stuttgart: Reclam.

Hildebrandt, Irma. 1985. *Es waren ihrer fünf, Die Brüder Grimm und ihre Familie* Cologne: Diederichs.

Kamenetsky, Christa. 1992. *The Brothers Grimm and Their Critics: Folktales and the Quest for Meaning*. Athens: Ohio University Press.

Kotzin, Michael. 1972. *Dickens and the Fairy Tale*. Bowling Green: Bowling Green University Popular Press.

Michaelis-Jena, Ruth. 1970. *The Brothers Grimm*. London: Routledge & Kegan.

Nelson, Claudia. 1989. "Sex and the Single Boy: Ideals of Manliness and Sexuality in Victorian Literature for Boys". In *Victorian Studies*, 32: 4 (Summer 1989): 525-550.

Röhrich, Lutz (ed.). Trans. by P. Tokofsky. 1991. *Folklore and Reality*. Bloomington: Indiana University Press.

Rölleke, Heinz. 1989. "Zur Biographie der Grimmschen Märchen". In Rölleke, Heinz (ed.). *Brüder Grimm, Kinder- und Hausmärchen, Nach der zweiten vermehrten und verbesserten Auflage von 1819, textkritisch revidiert und mit einer Biographie der Grimmschen Märchen versehen*. Munich: Diederichs.

Rölleke, Heinz. 1982. "*Nachwort*". In Rölleke, Heinz (ed.). *Brüder Grimm Kinder- und Hausmärchen, Ausgabe letzter Hand mit den Originalanmerkungen der Brüder Grimm*, 3 vols. Stuttgart: Reclam.

Schoof, Wilhelm. 1963. "Zur Geschichte des Grimmschen Märchenstils". In *Der Deutschunterricht*, 15: 2 (June 1963): 90-99.

Seago, Karen. 1998. "Transculturations: the translation of a Grimm *Märchen* into an English fairy talein the nineteenth century." Unpublished doctoral thesis. London: University of London.
Seitz, Gabriele. 1984. *Die Brüder Grimm, Leben, Werk, Zeit*. Munich: Winkler.
Sutton, Martin. 1996. *The Sin-Complex, A critical study of English versions of the Grimms Kinder- und Hausmärchen in the nineteenth century*. Kassel: Brüder Grimm Gesellschaft.
Tatar, Maria. 1992. *Off With Their Heads! Fairy Tales and the Culture of Childhood*. Princeton, N. J.: Princeton University Press.

List of translations referred to:

Taylor, Edgar. 1823. *German Popular Stories*, trans. from the Kinder- und Hausmärchen collected by M.M. Grimm from Oral Tradition. London: Baldwyn.
Taylor, Edgar. 1839. *German Popular Stories and Fairy Tales As Told by Gammer Grethel*. London: Bell.
Gillies. 2nd edn 1855 [182?]. *German Stories: Being tales and traditions chiefly selected from the literature of Germany*. Edinburgh: Fullarton.
Wehnert, Edward. 1853. *Household Stories*, Collected by the Brothers Grimm, Newly trans., with two hundred and forty illustrations. 2 vols. London: Addey.
Davis, Matilda Louisa.1855. *Home Stories*, Collected by the Brothers Grimm. Illustrated by George Thompson. London: Routledge.
Paull, H. H. B. [1872(?)]. *Grimms' Fairy Tales*. A New translation, by Mrs. H.H.B. Paull, Translator of "Hans Andersen's Fairy Tales," and Author of "Lucy West," "Mary Elton," "Pride and Principle," etc. Specially Adapted and Arranged for Young People. With sixteen Original Illustrations by W. J.Weigand. London: Warne.
Hunt, Maragret. 1884. *Grimm's Household Tales*, with the Author's Notes, trans. from the German and ed. by Margaret Hunt, with a Preface by Andrew Lang, M.A. London: Bell.

The value of the semiotic dimension in the subtitling of humour

Jorge Diaz-Cintas, Roehampton Institute, London

Abstract

Due to its culture-bound nature, the translation of humour is certainly one of the most demanding tasks for any translator. Plays on words, puns, double meanings and the like seasoned with cultural references and the linguistic idiosyncrasies of any language can prove to be serious obstacles for the successful transfer not only of the message but also of the effect and impact intended by the original. Add to all this the constraints imposed by the medium when subtitling for the cinema and the task becomes really daunting. It is my intention in this paper to take a look at the limitations under which the translator in this type of specialised field has to work, as well as to foreground the value of the semiotic dimension, of which the written target text is only a component. Examples of the different strategies implemented by subtitlers when transferring into English will be drawn from films in Spanish and French.

Introduction

In his 1959 seminal article, Roman Jakobson proposed his tripartite taxonomy of translation, namely intralingual, interlingual and intersemiotic. Since then, and before, the interlingual type or *translation proper* seems to have been accepted by most scholars as the sole type worth analysing and studying. According to Jakobson (1959: 55) the latter is "an interpretation of verbal signs by means of some other language". Despite the clear attempts by this scholar to put translation firmly in a semiotic framework, the truth is, as successfully argued by Zabalbeascoa (1997), that most studies in the field of translation have concentrated purely on verbal signs and on how to transfer them into another linguistic code thus neglecting other communicative elements that also contribute to the flow of information. Linguistic areas such as morphology, syntax and semantics have been clearly exploited in scholarly exchanges, whereas "matters to do with suprasegmental features, language variation and the combination of verbal and nonverbal elements were either eliminated by definition or swept under the carpet" (*ibid*.: 328). This line of thought has contributed to the marginalisation in academic analysis of translation practices that entail the interaction of several communication channels such as dubbing, subtitling and more generally any instances that fall under the umbrella term of *constrained translation*: songs, opera, comics and the like[1].

It is high time, I believe, to end this state of affairs. Besides the aforementioned bias in favour of the linguistic component and therefore to works made up of words alone, it also seems that some translation practices rather than others have traditionally been deemed to be worth the attention of scholars, notably the translation of literature and poetry. Until very recently, and even still nowadays, most attempts to shape a general theory of translation have drawn exclusively from these two areas, producing statements that are very limited in their scope and unable to accommodate other types of translation such as subtitling, with which I am concerned here.

It is not my intention to give a full account of all the medial constraints that affect the translation of films. Rather, I shall foreground the value of the semiotic dimension when transferring humour in movies, of which the linguistic message is only one component. I will also consider the limitations imposed by the visual and acoustic dimensions which constrain the translator in this specialised field, without neglecting the positive value of this image/sound combination in the translation process.

[1] For a more detailed account on the concept of 'constrained translation' see Díaz Cintas (1998), Mayoral et al. (1988) and Titford (1982).

The language of cinema

The several communicative codes that operate in the film realm can be grouped into two basic categories: codes belonging to the image, and codes belonging to the sound (words, music and noise). Both semiotic parameters, alone and in combination, give rise to a series of limitations that mark the delivery of any audiovisual product[1]. According to Delabastita (1990: 101-102), four types of film signs can be differentiated: “verbal signs transmitted acoustically (dialogue), non-verbal signs transmitted acoustically (noise, music), verbal signs transmitted visually (credits, letters, documents shown on the screen), non-verbal signs transmitted visually”[2]. Although one could argue that the most relevant signs to translation are the verbal ones, the translator cannot neglect the other dimensions of audiovisual communication. If in literary texts the linguistic code is, essentially, the only one used, with the exception of some surrealist experiments in which the iconic distribution of the linguistic material is also highly significant, in the realm of film the verbal code is only one among several.

It is evident that different societies conceptualise humour in very different ways and even find comic impact in disparate if not opposite situations, as Rabadán points out (1991: 167-168) in the pages that she dedicates to the various ways humour is conceptualised in different cultures[3], the transfer of humour between languages (and cultures) is thus complicated and justifies her statement that “it is not surprising that the least translated literary works (assuming that they have been translated) are the humorous ones” (*ibid.*: 168)[4]. If we consider the vast number of comic series and films that are shown, dubbed or subtitled, on both small an large screens in Spain, or the international success that greets Pedro Almodóvar’s or Woody Allen’s comedies, Rabadán's assertion can obviously not be extrapolated to the audiovisual arena. What then are the reasons for the discrepancy between the translation of humorous fiction and audiovisual products? Undoubtedly, the semiotic contribution of the image is invaluable, on many occasions actually taking precedence over the word and facilitating the transfer of humour in filmic formats. Moreover, cultural differences are not as dissimilar as is often believed[5], particularly when the product comes from cultures with which the target audiences are very familiar, such as the USA[6]. Nonetheless, more research is needed in this area before any categorical conclusions can be reached or before offering an answer to the general impression that audiovisual products that (supposedly) have a large humorous component, integrate into the target society without many difficulties, or, at least, more easily than literary works of a comic nature.

---

[1] See Mayoral et al. (1988: 364) for a more detailed analysis of the different degrees of constraint that operate in the various translation practices.

[2] The Polish scholar Tomaszkiewicz (1997: 185) has a similar point of departure, although she considers that information in the film is transmitted by five channels: visual image, printed graphemes and words, dialogue, music, noise and other sound effects.

[3] An idea also subscribed to by Ladmiral (1983: 419) when he claims that from one linguistic community to another people do not laugh about the same things.

[4] The Spanish original reads: “no es de extrañar que las obras literarias menos traducidas (en el supuesto de que lo hayan sido) sean las de carácter humorístico”.

[5] Following this same line of thought, although in his case in the world of interpreting, Viaggio (1996: 181-182) considers that one of the factors that affects the successful transfer of humorous elements resides in the degree of interpenetration that exists between the languages and cultures at play.

[6] The familiarisation with the source culture allows the identification of the referents and the activation of the connotative message in a much quicker and efficient way. It is at this level where one can start talking about cultural imperialism and colonisation. Many youngsters in Spain (although the example could be extended to several other countries) know more about the conquest of the West in the USA or the Vietnam War, than about the Spanish War of Independence or the more recent Civil War.

The attraction and codification of humour

Newmark (1988: 217) finishes the short section that he devotes to the translation of puns by stating that "the translation of puns is of marginal importance and of irresistible interest. Since then, the topic has become much less marginal, given the growing number of publications on this issue that have recently appeared on the market and which emphasises the irresistible attraction that its study has for many translation researchers[1]. In its linguistic configuration, humour is undoubtedly one of the instances of verbal re-creation that fully challenges translators' skills, pushing them to search for imaginative solutions that sometimes need to depart quite substantially from the content of the original in order to achieve a similar effect. This challenge requires the decoding of the source humorous discourse, its transfer to a dissimilar linguistic and cultural context and its reformulation as a new statement that aims to evoke in the target public what Leibold (1989: 109) describes as "an equivalent *pleasurable* and *playful* response". However, as we all know, humour in the movies is not based on words alone.

Until now, many studies on the translation of humour have limited their scope to the analysis of linguistic combinations, thus neglecting the other semiotic dimensions that make up any audiovisual product. As Izard (1999) rightly points out, the recipient of the translated product is different from that of the original one and therefore the expectations of both groups vary. The role of the translators is to try to fulfil the expectations of the target audience and in doing so, they will have to make modifications such as changing some cultural references that may be obscure in the target culture, adding or deleting information, re-creating specific linguistic registers and so forth. The main difference between this negotiation of meaning in a written text and a subtitled film is that in the latter the text has to fit in with images that cannot be altered (unless censorship intervenes). The subtitler is not as free as some other translators since the original image and sound are always present and act as carriers of information.

When we watch a film, "we are faced simultaneously with acoustic, visual and verbal images that provoke a plurisyntactic reading, referring us to different codes, images whose aim is to facilitate an understanding with the least effort possible" (Martínez 1990: 174, in Cómitre Narváez 1997: 91)[2]. In the reception of the original film by the source audience, far from cancelling each other out or entering into conflict, the different codes interact and facilitate the apprehension of the cinematic message. Thus, when subtitling audiovisual products, the translator has the advantage of counting on many non-verbal clues and hints, acoustic as well as visual, that will not need transfer and will help the target audience to supplement the information conveyed in the subtitles and grasp the message. The disadvantage comes when somewhere in the information transfer the smooth symbiosis of codes of the original product is broken off; that is, when the translated product gives rise to a mismatch between elements of the aural dimension and elements of the visual channel that did not exist in the source product.

Before moving on to particular examples drawn from several films, let us try to catalogue our data. On the one hand, Raphaelson-West (1989) proposes a tripartite taxonomy of jokes (linguistic, cultural and universal) but this seems to be functional only in the realm of books since it takes into account neither the value of the visual nor of the acoustic elements. Zabalbeascoa (1996: 251-255), on the other hand, proposes another hypotyposis based essentially on the same concepts, but incorporating the visual dimension and resulting, therefore,

1 An indication of this interest are the two volumes edited by Delabastita (1996 and 1997) in which the main topic of discussion is the translation of humour.

2 The Spanish original reads: "*nos enfrentamos simultáneamente a imágenes acústicas, visuales y verbales que provocan una lectura plurisintáctica y remiten a códigos diferentes en su conjunto [...] están dirigidas a producir una comprensión con el menor esfuerzo posible*".

in a much more appropriate tool to use with audiovisual products. Of the six types of jokes proposed, the first four (international or binational jokes, national-culture-and-institutions jokes, national-sense-of-humour jokes and language-dependent jokes) are based on the linguistic code and operate within its connotations and/or cultural references. Only the last two take into account the visual dimension and are thus the most relevant here: *visual* and *complex* jokes.

All the communicative force of *visual jokes* rest in the image, as it can be with the overacting of some character or the typical situation in which the spectator can see more than some of the actors on screen. A good mime artist can cross international boundaries with humour, as proven by the great success in Spain (and other countries) of British TV series such as *The Benny Hill Show* or, more recently, *Mr. Bean*, in which the linguistic medium is kept to a minimum[1]. The category of *complex jokes* is a kind of safety net that encapsulates jokes that combine two or more of the above mentioned five types. Following Zabalbeascoa's definition, instances which fall into this category are those that combine both visual and linguistic elements. However, another group could be added to this typology to account for jokes based on the other dimension that configurates the film text B noise: understood not only as noise *per se* but also as the suprasegmental and paralinguistic information that comes encoded in the actors' utterances, such as intonation or dialectal/social accent.

Limitations which operate on the subtitling of humour

Applying Zabalbeascoa's priorities and restrictions model for the dubbing of television comedy to the field of subtitling humour in films, the translator (or the patron who commissions the translation) will have to establish a scale of priorities which will underpin the translation process. This hierarchy of priorities will determine whether the translator follows closely the linguistic codification of the original joke, in detriment, perhaps, to the impact of the humour, or whether s/he disregards the linguistic formulation of the source language and strives to find a funny solution that will make the target audience laugh. According to Zabalbeascoa (1997: 332):

> it would seem that there is often a need to strike a balance between a search for comic effect by making the translated jokes as funny as possible, on the one hand, and, on the other, finding solutions that will not put the viewer off because [...] the plot, the structure and the coherence of the text are weakened for the sake of certain witty one-liners.

Authors like Chiaro (1992: 85, in Lung 1998: 99) have “commented on the translator's reluctance to go beyond the text and to replace an untranslatable joke with another one which is completely different from the original, but would be effective and communicative”. This is more likely to be the case with authorial or canonical works, I would argue, at least in Spain. In TV programmes such as *The Prince of Bel Air*, the translator distorts the source referent and brings it as close as possible to the audience's culture, creating communicative situations where belief has to be totally suspended. These tactics operate more frequently in the case of dubbing where the original dialogue track is lost, whereas in the case of subtitling it is a lot more complicated due to the gossip effect of the original dialogue that can been heard at all times. Besides the limitations imposed by these priorities and restrictions, the subtitler faces other difficulties, such as TV series which incorporate 'canned laughter' as a cue for the audience to laugh, or film scenes in which some of the actors laugh because of a funny statement uttered by one of them. In these cases, if the message of the target product is not funny, the viewers will not be able to refrain from asking themselves what it is they are missing. Care also has to be taken when

---

[1] According to Luis Martínez' article, published in *El País semanal* (no. 1085), as *Mr. Bean*, in the series, Rowan Atkinson has only spoken on 38 occasions in the 15 episodes, and almost always uttering simple monosyllables.

dealing with brand names. As Dopheide (1996: 40) states: "uncertainty in legal matters may also be a reason for alterations. Mentioning of persons and brand names (crucial to American humor) may collide with legal provisions [...] More often, the fear of being sued is greater than necessary".

Some jokes may be embedded in strong language, and this is another point of contention. As Toledo (1999: 11) mentions: "to read is a solitary act, and reading is a bet in search of pleasure and, in short, happiness. This is the way the French writer Daniel Pennac expresses himself in his book *Like a Novel*"[1]. However, although reading is always an individual act, reading a book alone is not the same as reading (and watching) a film with a group of people. Some may feel uncomfortable when reading certain expressions in a public place like a cinema whereas this would not be the case if they were reading the same thing in a book and in a private space. It also seems that hearing expletives is not as offensive as reading them, and in the imperative mutation from oral to written in subtitling, Card (1998: 208) comments that the emotive force of the statement is transformed and it can become more intense: "what does not shock the ears can shock the eyes"[2]. Translators may, therefore, activate mechanisms of self-censorship in their attempt to avoid upsetting the target audience, deleting or edulcorating expressions that in the original contributed to the humorous impact of the product but which may be deemed too obscene for the target public. There may well also be instances of clear censorship from the patron who commissions the translation, for example f*** words on the BBC, which can castrate the translator's task *a priori*.

After having considered some of the limitations derived from the product itself, its patronage and its expected audience, I shall now discuss the way in which specific examples of humorous situations in films have been presented to the target audience, focusing only on instances that fall under any of the 3 last categories of the aforementioned taxonomy, that is, visual, sound and complex jokes. The examples are graded from total independence from the linguistic code to the inextricable link between visual image and dialogue. A relationship can thus be established between the translation strategies implemented and the impact achieved in the target product.

Visual jokes

With globalisation and the power exerted by the audiovisual media, it is possible to identify a certain 'universality' of gestures. Thus, the image in itself is sufficient to transmit the (humorous) message and there is no need for the subtitler's mediation. The physical appearance of actors, their performances, their body movements, their gestures... are all part of the kinesic communication that comes encoded in the photography of the original product. Here, the translator is faced with instances of no-translation and full impact in the target audience as, for example, in the case of the great box office success of the British film *Mr Bean* or of any Marx Brothers' film.

Audio jokes

The non-verbal noise or sound can also carry all the humorous force of the scene, as, for instance, in the military symphony of flatulence which Paulino (Andrés Pajares) makes to the delight of the public in *!Ay, Carmela!*. As in the case of visual jokes, the subtitler does not have to intervene in its transfer to the target culture since, except for some rare occasions, there are no obstacles to it producing the same impact as in the original product.

---

[1] The Catalan original reads: "*Llegir és un acte solitari, i la lectura és una aposta a favor del plaer i, en definitiva, de la felicitat. Així s'expressa l'escriptor francés Daniel Pennac en el seu llibre Com una novel.la*".

[2] The French original reads: "*ce qui ne choque pas les oreilles peut choquer les yeux*".

Complex jokes: sound + linguistic codes

In some cases, the director exploits the most basic linguistic instances, such as phonemes, in order to reach the desired humorous impact. An example can be found in the scene of *!Ay, Carmela!* in which the main actress Carmen Maura has a 'conversation' with the Polish brigadier. The communication difficulties between the two characters are solved thanks to exaggerated mime and intonation. Carmela makes the Polish member of the International Brigades name the country she comes from and for which he is fighting in Spanish: España. He fails in his first attempt and can only come up with the phonetic approximation <Ispana>. Carmela insists on good diction, the Pole repeats without success and the humour is born precisely from the apparent inability of the foreigner to pronounce the palatal nasal voiced sound <ñ>, so quintessentially characteristic of the Spanish language. The translation of this phonetic pun in a written text would be rather problematic. Since the same sound does not exist in English, there is no graphic symbol to represent it and the translator would have to find a solution that somehow incorporates the paralinguistic dimension carrying the humorous impact. The subtitler could have opted for the presentation on screen of an approximate phonetic representation. However, in a very wise decision, in my view, the subtitler has resolved to offer no written support in the critical moments of the dialogue exchanges, thus exploiting the semiotic value of the soundtrack, the only informative referent on offer for the target spectator.

Another similar example takes place with the exploitation of the fricative lateral voiced sound <r>. In Spanish, two sounds are represented by this same letter, although one is soft and normally represented in writing by a single <r>, and the other one is stronger and represented by a double <rr>. However, at the beginning of a word and at the beginning of a syllable, when the previous syllable finishes with <b>, <l>, <n> or <s>, the grapheme <r>, although represented by a single <r>, is always strong. This ambivalence in phonetic value of the same grapheme is rather confusing for the foreigner learning Spanish and, as Moliner (1991: 919) points out in her leading dictionary of the Spanish language, the two sounds are so different that "phonetically, they are in fact two different letters, and this should be stressed to foreigners"[1]. The confusion of both sounds is, therefore, a potential source for humour in Spanish and this comic value is confirmed by Moliner (ibid.) when she states that "maintaining the sound *r+ indefinitely to convert it into a strong *rrr...+ is also exploited in order to produce a humorous impact"[2]. This is precisely the sort of play on phonemes exploited by Carlos Saura in his film *!Ay, Carmela!*, in the scene where the variety artist is trying to teach the Pole to say her name properly. In his first attempt, the pupil seems to have problems pronouncing the correct sound since he is overdoing the rolling of the <r>, to the frustration of Carmela and, hence, the humorous impact for the audience, who in this scene identify with Paulino. Here again, a translation for a book would have to resort to an orthographic representation of the paralinguistic joke, but on this occasion an easier solution is on offer than in the previous example. The simple reiteration of the grapheme <r>, with several possible graphic presentations, could be an effective strategy: <Carrrmela>, <Carrr...mela> or <CaRRRmela>, for example. The same strategy could have been implemented by the subtitler of the film, but once more we encounter an instance in which the linguistic mediator has taken the decision to shy away from the final product and relay the humour through the original soundtrack: no translation is needed, although the same impact as in the original is preserved.

---

[1] The Spanish original reads: "en realidad, se trata, fonéticamente, de dos letras diferentes, e interesa subrayarlo así para los extranjeros".

[2] The Spanish original reads: "también se explota para producir efecto cómico [...] el mantenimiento indefinido del sonido *r+ convirtiéndolo en *rrr...+ con sonido fuerte".

Complex jokes: sound + linguistic + visual codes

A prime example of this category can be found in the classic scene from *Jesus of Montreal* where three of the characters are dubbing a pornographic movie into French. The humorous impact arises from the (mis)match of the three different codes. As far as the visual dimension is concerned, the physical appearance of the dubbing actors is certainly a humorous element due to the marked antithesis established between the sexy and erotic nature of what we imagine the dubbing actors are watching on their screen and what we are actually watching on our screen: a chubby and sweaty actor rushed off his feet from one side to the other and a dark-haired actress wearing a ridiculous pair of designer glasses that are decidedly not sexy. The non-verbal audio messages, characteristic of any sexually explicit film, help to create a certain atmosphere which in the soundtrack is complemented by the incorporation of other minimal verbal messages, such as interjections and exclamations. Another paralinguistic factor plays a key part in this example: due to the absence of a second dubbing actor to complete the orgiastic dialogue exchanges, our antihero finds himself in the difficult position of having to produce two different types of voice in order to dub the two male characters in the pornographic film. During the fast and hectic change of voices, he gets confused and uses the same voice for the two characters. His overzealous professionalism forces him to stop the dubbing session to the surprise of his colleagues who consider that the take has been excellent. The attempts to change voices are funny in themselves and the humorous effect is increased by the irony and contrast of such an extremely professional attitude in a working environment of this type. Although stereotyped, the rest of the verbal aural messages, that is to say, the dialogue, are characterised generally by their lack of humour. In a different context, they could easily be read in their erotic sense, but it is precisely their development in this particular audiovisual situation that foregrounds their ludicrous nature and forces a humorous and jocular reading.

The interaction between the different codes that configurate a film operates in favour of the translator. The image and non-verbal audio messages, such as the yelps, moans and the impersonating voices in this example, help to build up the scene and do not need any translation. As for the more linguistically substantial exchanges, thanks to the relative simplicity of their content, the subtitler has decided to carry out a transfer that is faithful to the semantics of the original. The audio verbal messages such as interjections and exclamations, that would appear in their quantitative integrity in any written work of fiction, are, for the most part, eliminated in the subtitles. This is not always the case, however, and one of the pitfalls of subtitling lies precisely in the use and abuse of these elements. Here, the subtitler seems to be aware that their abuse could alienate the viewer and decides to season the subtitles with just a few of them to set the tone of the scene. It is clear, then, that the subtitler has opted to take account of and to exploit all the different channels of communication, giving birth to a target product that, in these scenes, enjoys the same humorous impact as the original.

There are, however, some other instances where the interaction of the different communication codes does not occur in such a felicitous way for translation and can compromise, or considerably reduce, the funny impact of the original. I am referring to those examples in which the humour rests more in how, rather that what, is actually said, be it for the markedness of some dialectal accents, pronunciation defects (stuttering, lisps...) or because of the excessive performance of the actors. The scene in *The Flower of my Secret* in which the mother and the daughter are arguing in the kitchen over trivialities is a prime example. The physical appearance of the mother who is wearing dark glasses inside the house, together with the exasperated and infuriated intonation of both actresses, are supralinguistic elements that do not require translation, although the spectator who is not fluent in the mannerisms of the source language may lose some of the supra and paralinguistic connotations that mark the actresses' performances, especially the mother's. The humour here is to be found not only in the expressions uttered by the mother, a mix of rural wisdom and trendy expressions, of the old and new "Spains" that are amusing in such an old lady, but also in the emphatic and exasperated diction of both female characters. The exchange is stereotypical of two generations of Spanish women who live under the same roof and very close to the personal experiences of many Spanish people, but it may not be the case for people from other countries where family ties are not so close. In such cases, and insofar as the limitations of the medium allow, the subtitler translates all the linguistic elements, hoping that the viewer will retrieve more information from both visual elements and soundtrack. Even in the best cases, the impact of the target product is generally lessened to a certain degree. This gives rise to the situation in which some viewers in the cinema (usually the ones that share the same language as in the film) laugh when the rest (those who do not have that language as their mother tongue) laugh out of synch, or simply do not find anything funny in the scene.

Complex jokes: visual + linguistic codes

So far, we have considered some instances where the final result re-creates, in varying degrees, the same humorous impact as the original. In all cases, the image and the sound are positive elements for subtitlers who know how to exploit to their advantage the different communicative dimensions of the original. In some other cases, however, the humour is completely lost in the target product because of the severe restrictions imposed by the image. The translator encounters a major obstacle whenever the film presents the visual transposition of an idiom, set phrase or cultural denotation that translated literally into the given target language does not retain the same link with the visual dimension. Though some professionals, such as Dopheide (1996: 38), suggest that very often "the only both realistic and elegant solution to this problem is to edit it out", this is a rather drastic measure, which, it seems to me, is difficult to justify and open to criticism. Such a practice is too close to censorship for the translator's comfort and may mean that some crucial diegetic information goes missing with the amputation of the original.

A scene from the Spanish film, *Women on the Verge of a Nervous Breakdown*, offers an example in which image and linguistic content are tightly interwoven. Candela, a young and naive model from the South of Spain who has come to Madrid in search of fame, finds herself involved in a total mess due to men. She shelters in the penthouse of her best friend, Pepa, who is also going through a difficult patch in her love life. Due to a conjunction of circumstances, Candela meets Carlos, the son of Pepa's lover, to whom she relates her difficult situation and her problems with men. Both actors are in the background, behind a cage of rabbits who Candela is about to feed. She asks Carlos if he has ever had any bunnies (*conejos*) and when he answers in the negative, she carries on to say that she has had many and, what is more, she knows a lot about them. She finishes by making reference to how much rabbits love turnips (*nabos*). At first sight, the dialogue seems extremely banal and anodyne. Nonetheless, the sexual innuendo is clearly transparent to any Spaniard. In colloquial Spanish, the word '*conejo*' refers to the female genitalia and the term '*nabo*' alludes to the male sexual organ. This semantic twist means the linguistic exchange is open to a much richer and wittier reading. Unfortunately, due to the presence of the image (the rabbits and the turnips), the subtitler's task is doomed to fail in this particular instance. In a literary text, the translator could resort to an explanatory footnote or the permutation of referents, so that the final outcome retains the *double entendre*, but in film subtitling, the translator has his hands tied by the omnipresence of the original image.

Conclusion

Most published comments on the translation of humour tend to be somewhat negative. Some of the *a priori* obstacles that challenge the transfer of humour in the audiovisual world are summarised by Diot (1985: 259): "loss of the humorous message, weakening of the impact, denaturalisation of the humour, distortion of meaning, and falsification of the humorous relationship"[1]. Nonetheless, neither distortion of meaning nor falsification of the humorous relationship is negative *per se*. If the priority of the translation is to produce humour in a particular scene, those strategies will be necessary where a solely literal translation is doomed to fail. As for the loss of the humorous message, it is evident that there are occasions in which due to the imperatives of culture and media, the subtitler has to eliminate some word play, although we should remember that compensation is a translation strategy that can be implemented and which can help counteract the possible loss. The denaturalisation of humour is another 'sacrifice' that all translations have to pay to their originals since the source material has to go through the catalyst of different cultural referents wrapped in a different language. The inevitability of losses on both denotative as well as connotative levels in some parts of any work (be it a film, novel or poem) is a condition *sine qua non* of any translation attempt, especially when the translator is faced with humorous contexts and some very restrictive limitations pertaining to the medium. To pretend to the contrary is pure illusion which can only lead to an exacerbated and unrealistic critique of any linguistic transfer attempt and will not contribute to the study of translation. Finally, the weakening of the humorous impact is far from being systematic and it must be remembered that the success of any joke depends ultimately on the viewer's subjectivity. I believe we have to be more impartial in our judgements: it is unfair to use the linguistic codification of subtitles as the only parameter to judge the good or bad transfer of humour. The whole product and the interaction of different communication channels must be taken into consideration.

My intention has been to focus mainly on the non-linguistic aspects of translation, yet without neglecting the linguistic component in an attempt, albeit by no means exhaustive, to foreground the importance of the semiotic dimension already hinted at by Jakobson, which is perhaps missed too often in critical analyses of audiovisual translation: "Future attempts to give accounts of translation 'techniques' or solutions might wish to include nonverbal compensatory tactics which to date have not been paid sufficient attention and hence have not been satisfactorily described" (Zabalbeascoa 1997: 341). I hope to have answered to some degree Zabalbeascoa's call and to have offered valuable examples of how image and sound, on their own and in symbiosis with the verbal message, have an essential value not only in the configuration of the film text but also in the transfer of humour which does not rest on the linguistic component alone. It is thus imperative that the subtitler has access to the actual film when translating: this may seem obvious but it is forgotten far too often in the professional world and subtitlers are forced, for one reason or another, to carry out the translation without having had access to the audiovisual product. Needless to say, such practices can only lead to the accumulation of mistakes and misinterpretations, as well as to a deficient exploitation of the information that comes embedded in the visual and sound tracks.

In conclusion, I believe it is wholly unfair to apply only linguistic criteria when analysing the transfer of humour in audiovisual products. Subtitling is a mode of translation that cannot accommodate an overzealous attitude to single words and minute details. So, if as Levý (1967) put it some years ago, translation is a constant decision making process, then, the degree of

---

[1] The French original reads: "*perte de message comique, affaiblissement de l'intensité des effets, dénaturation de l'humour, détournement de sens, et falsification de la relation humoristique*".

excellence of an audiovisual translation has to be measured against what the subtitlers decide to translate as well as what they decide not to translate because they prefer to exploit other semiotic dimensions of the film.

References

Card, Lorin. 1998. "'Je vois ce que vous voulez dire': un essai sur la notion de l'équivalence dans les sous-titres de *37 2 Le matin* et de *Au revoir les enfants*". *Meta* 43(2): 205-219.

Chiaro, D. 1992. *The Language of Jokes: Analysing Verbal Play*. London & New York: Routledge.

Cómitre Narváez, Isabel. 1997. "Algunas consideraciones sobre la traducción del textoaudiovisual. In Santamaría, J. M. et al. (eds). *Trasvases culturales: literatura, cine, traducción 2*. Vitoria: Universidad del País Vasco, Departamento de Filología Inglesa y Alemana: 89-95.

Delabastita, Dirk. 1990. "Translation and the mass media". In Bassnett, Susan & André Lefevere (eds). *Translation, History and Culture*. London: Pinter: 97-109.

Delabastita, Dirk. (ed) 1996. *Wordplay and Translation*. Special issue of *The Translator* 2(2).

Delabastita, Dirk (ed). 1997. *Traductio. Essays on Punning and Translation*. Manchester: St. Jerome Publishing.

Díaz Cintas, Jorge. 1998. "La labor subtituladora en tanto que instancia de traducción subordinada". In Orero, Pilar (ed). *Actes del III Congrés Internacional sobre Traducció*. Barcelona: Universitat Autònoma de Barcelona, Departament de Traducció i d'Interpretació: 83-90.

Diot, Roland. 1985. "Chaos par K.O.: un exemple d'incompatibilité d'humour -le doublage et le sous-titrage des films des Marx Brothers". In Laurion, A. M. (ed) *Humour et traduction*. Special Issue of *Contrastes*. Paris: Centre de Recherche en Linguistique Contrastive: 259-269.

Dopheide, Theodor. 1996. "Just an illusion: a review of practical problems in dubbing American movies". Book of Abstracts of the International Conference Languages and the Media. Berlin.

Izard, Natalia. 1999. "The situational factors in film translation". Manuscript.

Jakobson, Roman. 1959. "On linguistic aspects of translation", in Chesterman, Andrew (ed). 1989. *Readings in Transtation Theory*. Helsinki: Oy Finn Lectura Ab: 53-60.

Ladmiral, Jean-René. 1983. "Sur un cas de rire intraduisible", in Nelde, P. H. (ed) *Theorie, Methoden und Modelle der Kontaktlinguistik*. Bonn: Dümmler: 417-423.

Leibold, Anne. 1989. "The translation of humor; who says it can't be done?". *Meta* 34(1): 109-111.

Levý, Jiri. 1967. "Translation as a decision process", in *To Honor Roman Jakobson*, vol. II. The Hague: Mouton: 1171-1182.

Lung, Rachel. 1998. "On mis-translating sexually suggestive elements in English-Chinese screen subtitling". *Babel* 44(2): 97-109.

Mayoral, Roberto et al. 1988. "Concept of constrained translation. Non-linguistic perspectives of translation". *Meta* 33(3): 356-367.

Moliner, María. 1991. *Diccionario de uso del español*. Madrid: Editorial Gredos S.A.

Newmark, Peter. 1988. *A Textbook of Translation*. New York, London, Toronto, Sydney, Tokyo: Prentice Hall International.

Rabadán, Rosa. 1991. *Equivalencia y traducción. Problemática de la equivalencia translémica inglés-español*. Zamora: Universidad de León.

Raphaelson-West, Debra. 1989. "On the feasibility and strategies of translating humor"" *Meta* 34(1): 128-141.

Titford, Christopher. 1982. "Sub-titling - constrained translation". *Lebende Sprachen* 27(3): 113-116.

Toledo, Alicia. 1999. "Els experts confirmen la fragmentació lingüística". *Nou Dise 68* (Universitat de València), 27th May: 11.
Tomaszkiewicz, Teresa. 1997. "Dialogues de films sous-titrés: code oral ou code écrit?". In Luzzati, D. et al. (eds). *Le dialogique*. Bern, Berlin, Frankfurt/M, New York, Paris, Wien: Peter Lang: 183-194.
Viaggio, Sergio. 1996. "The pitfalls of Metalingual use in simultaneous interpreting". *The Translator* 2(2): 179-198.
Zabalbeascoa, Patrick. 1996. "Translating jokes for dubbed television situation comedies". The Translator 2(2): 235-257.
1997. "Dubbing and the nonverbal dimension of translation". In Poyatos, Fernando(ed) *Nonverbal Communication and Translation. New Perspectives and Challenges in Literature, Interpretation and the Media.* Amsterdam & Philadelphia: John Benjamins Publishing Company: 327-342.

Films cited

Allen, Woody. 1993. *Manhattan Murder Mystery/Misterioso asesinato en Manhattan.* United States.
Arcand, Denys. 1989. *Jésus de Montréal/Jesus of Montreal.* Canada-France.
Almodóvar, Pedro. 1989. *Mujeres al borde de un ataque de nervios/Women on the Verge of a Nervous Breakdown*. Spain.
Saura, Carlos. 1991. *!Ay, Carmela!*. Spain.
Smith, Mel. 1997. *Bean*. United Kingdom.

Achevé d'imprimer en mai 2001
sur les presses de Normandie Roto Impression s.a.
à Lonrai (Orne)
N° d'imprimeur : 011136
Dépôt légal : mai 2001

Imprimé en France